MW01067762

I Am the Immaculate Conception

The Story of Bernadette of Lourdes

Paul F. Caranci

I Am the Immaculate Conception: The Story of Bernadette of Lourdes. Copyright © 2018 Paul Caranci. Produced and printed by Stillwater River Publications. All rights reserved. Written and produced in the United States of America. This book may not be reproduced or sold in any form without the expressed, written permission of the author and publisher.

Visit our website at www.StillwaterPress.com for more information.

First Stillwater River Publications Edition

ISBN-13: 978-1-946-30084-3
ISBN-10: 1-946-30084-5

1 2 3 4 5 6 7 8 9

Written by Paul F. Caranci
Published by Stillwater River Publications, Pawtucket, RI, USA.

Publisher's Cataloging-In-Publication Data
(Prepared by The Donohue Group, Inc.)

Names: Caranci, Paul F., author.
Title: I am the Immaculate Conception : the story of Bernadette of
    Lourdes / Paul F. Caranci.
Description: First Stillwater River Publications edition. | Pawtucket, RI,
    USA : Stillwater River Publications, [2019] | Includes bibliograph-
    ical references.
Identifiers: ISBN 9781946300843 | ISBN 1946300845
Subjects: LCSH: Bernadette, Saint, 1844-1879. | Christian women saints--
    France--Lourdes--Biography. | Mary, Blessed Virgin, Saint--Appari-
    tions and miracles--France--Lourdes. | Immaculate Conception. |
    LCGFT: Biographies.
Classification: LCC BX4700.S65 C37 2019 | DDC 282.092 B--dc23

The views and opinions expressed in this book are solely those of the author and do not necessarily reflect the views and opinions of the publisher.

Dedication

To my best friend, Margie.

Table of Contents

Foreword

By Father Christy David Pathiala, Associate Pastor
St. Mary's Parish, Bismarck, North Dakota

The Gospel of Luke 17: 11-19 presents the story of Jesus and the ten lepers. While going to Jerusalem, Jesus passed through the midst of Samaria and Galilee. As He entered a certain village, ten lepers saw Him from afar. They lifted up their voices and said, "Jesus, Master, have mercy on us." Seeing them, Jesus said, "Go, and show yourselves unto the priests." On their way, they were cleansed. Though ten were healed, only one returned to glorify God with a loud voice, and for that one, Jesus was appreciative. This story teaches us the importance of recognizing the touch of healing from the Lord even in the world today.

The wedding at Cana brings out the initiation of the ministry of Jesus through Mary. *"Ad Jesum per Mariam"*: "To Jesus through Mary" is being revealed to us through this miraculous event. Even to-day, we can experience the mediation of Mother Mary, as the book you are about to read wonderfully unravels the apparitions of our blessed Mother.

I can personally witness to the touch of God through Mother Mary in my life, an event which became the foundational experience for my priesthood. The oldest of two, I was named *"CHRISTY"* because I was born on the day of Corpus Christi. My elder brother, having been born on the feast of St. Faustus, was aptly named Fausty. From those earliest days, my parents were very keen in seeing to the healthy growth of our body, mind and soul. The special prayer *"By Thy Immaculate conception, O Mary, make my body pure and my soul holy,"* which they taught us in our early childhood, helped us a lot in our day-to-day life.

Every stage in life is filled with challenges. The wedding at Cana clearly depicts the aid of Mother Mary to the troubled couple who were running short of wine. She blessed them with her presence and interceded to her son to convert the weakness into strength. Life can be compared to a heartbeat that rises and falls. Every valley has a hill and every problem has a solution.

For me, challenges began at a very early stage of my life when I was strongly affected by a convulsion at the age of four. I was hospitalized in the intensive care unit and was unconscious for more than twelve hours. My body was not responding to any of the medicines. The doctors doubted if I would survive and feared that even if I did, I would either be paralyzed or abnormal! They took fluid from my spine and cultured it. I am sure that it was the prayer of my parents and God's grace that saw me through.

But, challenges from that illness did not subside and subsequently, I would get a high fever if I drank or ate anything cold, or even if I faced a cold breeze. Each time my body temperature would just keep on rising and my parents, on the advice of my doctors, were forced to give me ice baths. As I took these baths my mother taught me to say *"Thank you Jesus! I love you Jesus!"* and I would repeat that prayer many times.

During those days, I was not allowed to have ice cream per the doctor's advice, and my parents' care prevented me from even tasting ice cream during those years. As a child, this was my greatest grief. Out of love and pity my dad used to buy me an ice cream cone without any ice cream in it. This situation continued for a few years when finally, at the age of seven, I was blessed to go to Lourdes, France with my family to pray to Mother Mary.

The main purpose of our visit was to take a bath in the miraculous water of Our Lady of Lourdes. As Catholics, we have a strong belief that Mary, the Mother of Jesus Christ, appeared to St. Bernadette in Lourdes, instructing her to expose a spring of water to which many miracles have been attributed. On June 16, 1989, our family reached Lourdes. In our travels to the miraculous spring we encountered several shops on the side of the road, but one in particular caught my attention: it was a beautifully lit ice cream parlor. I tugged my mother's dress and asked if I could have a cone. It is human tendency to crave what we cannot have, and I just wanted to taste ice cream. My mother told me that if I have faith in Mother Mary, after taking a bath in the holy water at the Grotto of Lourdes, she would buy the ice cream for me.

When we reached Lourdes, we all experienced a heavenly peace and happiness. Those seeking to bathe were directed into one of two queues: one was designated for gents and the other for ladies. That, of course, required that my mother split from the rest of us so as to enter the appropriate queue. Our turn to bathe in the cool miraculous waters of our Lady immediately followed that of a crippled child who was carried into the water by his father.

As we waited for our mother following our bath, a lady came to us with her crippled son. With a smile she asked me, "What is your name" I answered, "My name is Christy." Then, turning to my brother, she asked his name. too. The lady opened her purse and took out some money. She placed a five francs coin in my hand and told me, *"Go and have your ice cream."* She also gave a five francs coin to my brother and then spoke with my father for some time. As she was walking away, she turned to me and said, *"Pray for my son."* Her son was in a wheelchair, challenged both physically and mentally, and was this same boy who had bathed ahead of me.

After some time, my mother came to us, and Dad explained the whole incident to her. We searched for the lady but couldn't find her, prompting my mother to say, *"Even if he dies, we are buying him that ice cream."* It was a simple statement of faith, but a strong one. My mother was so excited to give me that ice cream, the same chocolate flavor that I used to watch my brother eat. My mother handed the two five francs coins to the shopkeeper to pay for four ice creams but was informed by the counter clerk that an ice cream costs fifteen francs and returned the two coins to her. My dad paid for the ice creams as my mother tucked those two coins into her purse. For the first time in two long years, I had the taste of ice cream. I suffered no ill effects from the cold dessert and have not had any from that day onwards. I was completely cured!

To this day, I believe that the lady who appeared to me that June day in 1989 was Mother Mary. The boy, I believe, was Baby

Jesus, who took something I should have had when I was a kid and called me for a purpose. I praise and glorify God and pay reverence to Mother Mary for giving me this foundational experience to my priesthood. My mother has since made two pouches for the two five-franc coins and has kept them safely with her.

On this same trip I was blessed to meet St. Pope John Paul II and St. Mother Teresa in a very unexpected way. During the audience with St. Pope John Paul II, we were placed, by one of the cardinals, on the aisle through which he walked. On seeing us, St. Pope John Paul II blessed us, hugged us, and tried to lift us. It was really a blessed moment that I will cherish forever.

On April 08, 2010, God the Almighty made an everlasting covenant with me and gave me the priesthood of the people. He adorned me with impressive vestments; he dressed me in a robe of glory. *"You have brought me joy, Yahweh, by your deeds at the work of your hands I cry out, 'How great are your works, Yahweh, immensely deep your thoughts'!"* (Psalm 92:4-5).

Duc in Altum [in-depth] are the apt words to describe the contents of this book. This book deals in depth with the history as well as the current message Lourdes has to offer us. It takes us into a journey of a deeper and firmer understanding of the intercession of Our Lady in each of our lives. I sincerely wish and pray that this book be a blessing to our families and the society. Our God will supply all your needs according to His riches in glory by Christ Jesus to live a peaceful, joyful, and blessed life on earth, aiming for heaven. This will be possible when we obey our Mother Mary, who says, *"Do whatever He tells you."*

Preface

Like the story of Jesus as told in the Gospels of Matthew, Mark, Luke, and John, there are variations of the story of Bernadette, as told in many books and other written material documented both at the time of her apparitions as well as in the years that followed. Through voluminous research and painstaking comparison, these accounts have been studied and analyzed. Those elements that could not be verified by independent sources were discounted. Verifiable accounts with minor discrepancies were recounted by consolidating events into a cohesive story told as a day-by-day, hour-by-hour chronicle of the major events. The result is a historically accurate retelling of the story of Bernadette Soubirous, albeit a history that reads more like a novel than a historical account of one of the most intriguing events in human history.

Acknowledgements

Despite the many people who have chronicled the miraculous events that occurred in a small town in southern France over 160 years ago, recounting a story that has been historically greeted with as much skepticism as acceptance is never an easy task. Perhaps because of the controversial nature of the 1858 experiences, several books were written over the ensuing years, some offering varying accounts of the events. Many of the early works were originally penned in French. Most have been translated into English and a smattering of other languages throughout the years. Perhaps one of the most significant of these books was the one written by Henri Lasserre, a renowned French historian and eyewitness to the visions experienced by a fourteen-year-old peasant girl. My thanks to Monsieur Lasserre for his perseverance in recording the historical events and doing so with an unjaundiced eye despite having been beneficiary of the amazing miraculous powers of the occurrences of which he so adeptly wrote in 1870.

My thanks to Margie, Linda, Julien and Pauline, Steve and Dawn, Fr. Pathiala, and all those who had a hand in the production of this work. I would not have been able to complete it without their valuable assistance and support.

As always, I am profoundly grateful to my family for their love, support, and patience.

Above all, I am unabashedly indebted to Jesus and his Blessed Mother, who guide my work with inspiration and love.

A Glossary of Some of the People, Places, and Terms Important to the Story of Lourdes

Abadie, Jeanne – A friend of Toinette Soubirous.

Anastasie, Sister – Teacher at the Hospice School attended by Bernadette.

Aravant-Lagues, Marie - a mill customer who nursed Bernadette for ten months of the infant's life.

Beauhohort, Justin (also spelled Beauhort and Bouhohort) – Two-year old boy ill since birth. Cured after bathing in the spring at Lourdes in July 1858.

Bourriette, Louis – A resident of Lourdes who was cured of blindness after bathing his eyes in water from the miraculous spring.

Cachot – The abandoned prison in which François Soubirous and his family lived.

Calmels, Damien, Sister – Teacher at the Hospice School attended by Bernadette.

Capdevielle, Romain – An attorney who admired Bernadette and published articles in support of her. He was engaged to Maria Dufo.

Casterot, Bernarde – Bernadette's aunt and Godmother. Sister of Louise (Casterot) Soubirous.

Casterot, Basil – Bernadette's aunt. Sister of Louise (Casterot) Soubirous.

Casterot, Justin – Father of Bernarde Casterot and Louise (Casterot) Soubirous, Mill operator.

Clarens, Antoine – Director of the Secondary School in Lourdes.

Cazenave, Dominiquette – The sister of François's employer and a friend of Bernadette.

Cazenave, Jean-Marie – The stagecoach driver, also known as Ganco, who assisted Bernadette to the Grotto for the fifteenth Apparition.

Diocese of Tarbes – The Catholic Diocese that included the area of Lourdes, France.

Dozous, Pierre-Romaine, Doctor – Doctor who treated Louis Bourriette and attested to his being cured of blindness.

Dufo, Marie – Recognized as one of the most beautiful women of Lourdes, engaged to Romain Capdevielle.

Dufo, Monsieur – Prominent attorney, town councilor and President of the Bar.

Dutour, Vital – Imperial Prosecutor

Ere Imperiale – Anti-cleric newspaper with circulation in the district of Lourdes.

Estrade, Emmanuélite – Sister of the tax inspector Jean-Baptiste Estrade.

Estrade, Jean-Baptiste – A tax inspector in the Excise Dept. and witness to the events of Lourdes.

Escoubles Mill – A mill rented by François Soubirous using a legacy left by his mother-in-law following her untimely death.

Fardes, Ursule, Mere - Mother Superior at the Hospice School attended by Bernadette.

Gave River – The river that flows along the banks of the Grotto of Massabielle.

Gesta, Cyprine – Friend of Louise Soubirous.

Grotto – The rock formation in which the Virgin Mary appeared to Bernadette.

Jacomet, Dominique – Police Commissioner of Lourdes.

Journal Des Debats – Large anti-cleric newspaper with circulation in the district of Lourdes.

Laborde mill – A mill rented by Madame Casterot, Louise Soubirous' mother, to allow François the opportunity of operating another mill after failing at his first mill operation venture.

Lacadé, Gerald-August – Mayor of Lourdes

Le Lavedan – Anti-cleric newspaper with circulation in the district of Lourdes.

La Presse – Anti-cleric newspaper with circulation in the district of Lourdes.

Lasserre, Henri – Author and witness to the events at Lourdes

Latour, Monsieur – A Chemist at the Prefecture who tested the Grotto spring water on May 6, 1858 at the request of Prefect Baron Massy.

Laurence, Bertrand Severe, Monseigneur– Bishop of Tarbes and Minister for Ecclesiastical Affairs.

Le Siecle - Large anti-cleric newspaper with circulation in the district of Lourdes.

L'Univers – A pro-religion newspaper with circulation in the district of Lourdes.

Mary Bernard, Sister – The name taken by Bernadette when she joined the Sisters of Nevers.

Massabielle – The dumping ground along the River Gave in which the Grotto is situated.

Massy, Baron – Prefect of the Hautes-Pyrenees which includes Lourdes.

Milhet, Jeanne-Marie – Former servant girl who married her employer. She accompanied Bernadette to the Grotto.

Nicolau, Antoine – A miller at Savy Mill.

Pène, Father – Curate and brother of Jacquette Pène.

Pène, Jacquette – Sister of the Curate.

Peyramale, Dominique, Abbé – Pastor and Cantonal Vicar of the local church (born 1/9/1811 – died 9/8/1877)

Peyret, Antoinette – Friend of, and seamstress for, Madame Milhet.

Pomian, Abbé – Hospice School Chaplain.

Pougat – Magistrate in Lourdes.

Saint Gildard Convent – The convent in Nevers at which Bernadette died at the age of thirty- five.

Sajous, André – François Soubirous' cousin. A stone-cutter who provided a room for the Soubirous family at the "Cachot," an area formerly used as the dungeon of the prison.

Savy Mill – The mill operated by François Soubirous.

Serre, Father – Curate in the parish at Lourdes.

Soubirous, Bernadette – Visionary to whom the Blessed Mother appeared several times. Born January 7, 1844, the first child of François and Louise (Casterot) Soubirous.

Soubirous, François – Bernadette's father, married Louise January 9, 1843.

Soubirous, Jean – Bernadette's younger brother. He died at seven weeks of age.

Soubirous, Louise – Bernadette's mother and Bernarde Casterot's younger sister.

Soubirous, Jean-Marie (I) – Bernadette's younger brother, born in 1848, died in 1851 at the age of almost three.

Soubirous, Jean-Marie (II) – Another son born to François and Louise just after the death of Jean-Marie I and named in his memory.

Soubirous, Toinette – Bernadette's younger sister, born in 1886.

Tardhivail, Antoinette – Accompanied Bernadette to some meetings and agreed to teach her to write.

Vergez, Professor – Member of the faculty of medicine at Montpellier appointed to examine the cures at Lourdes.

Veuillot, Louis – Famous journalist and editor of L'Univers newspaper.

Part I

Introduction
Miracles

Lourdes, France
July 1858

Jean Beauhohorts was a day laborer living in rather squalid conditions with his wife, the former Croisine Ducouts and their son Justin. It was four o'clock in the afternoon and the boy lay motionless in a cradle as his parents wiped tears from their eyes. Though two years old, Justin had never walked. From his birth he "had been wasted by slow fever of a consumptive nature, which nothing had succeeded in reducing."[1] According to the boy's skilled physician, Dr. Peyrus, Justin was quickly approaching his final hours. His heartbroken parents peered into the crib, their eyes red with grief as they looked upon their boy, who "had been reduced by protracted sufferings to a deplorable state of emaciation."[2] Jean tried to remain strong for his wife, who was quickly descending to the depths of despair. He had already arranged for the inevitable by enlisting the help of one of his neighbors, Franconnette Gozos, to prepare the shroud that would be used for little Justin's burial. Struggling to prevent his voice from cracking, Jean offered well-intended, albeit superficial, words of consolation to Croisine.

As he gazed upon his child, Jean noticed that the boy had become still. Not a muscle on his body stirred and Jean could detect no movement in his chest. Choking back tears, Jean announced that their boy was gone. Franconnette encouraged the couple to weep by the fire as she prepared Justin's body in the shroud.

Croisine would hear none of it, however. "He is not dead," she yelled, "and the Holy Virgin of the Grotto is going to effect a cure for me." Jean, knowing his wife was overcome with grief and speaking nonsense to the point of delirium, tried to console her, but she would not listen. Jean and his neighbor, who had just removed the child from his crib and wrapped him in the shroud, tried to reason with her, but she grabbed the child and ran toward the door. "If the boy is not dead," Jean said, "removing him to the cold will surely finish him." Near hysterics, his wife responded as she walked out the door with her lifeless child,

1

"What matters it whether he dies here or at the Grotto! Allow me to implore the mercy of the Mother of God."[3]

It was five o'clock when Croisine arrived at the Grotto of Massabielle. A crowd of several hundred people still lingered from the morning events. She prostrated herself at the entrance and proceeded to walk on her knees toward the miraculous spring. Her eyes were bloodshot and swollen. Tears still rolled down her cheeks as she inched along the path, struggling to carry the lifeless body of her son while still on her knees. Finally, reaching the freshly dug basin that collected the icy water of the spring, she released the naked body of her son from her apron.

People milling about began to murmur among themselves, wondering what the woman intended to do with the child she carried. Shouts of terror could be heard as Croisine made the sign of the cross, first on him and then on herself, and plunged her child neck-deep into the freezing water. "The woman is insane!"[4] one shouted, and people began to press around her from all sides. "Would you kill your child?"[5] another screamed. If Croisine heard, she didn't react. All that mattered was that her child be presented to the Blessed Mother by bathing him in the water of the miraculous spring.

Someone touched her on the shoulder. Without lifting Justin from the icy water, Croisine turned and said, "Let me alone, let me alone. I wish to do all in my power. God and the Blessed Virgin will do the rest."[6] "The child is already dead," someone said, to which another replied that grief had apparently made the woman mad. Croisine was not insane, however, she was exercising boundless confidence in God by addressing herself to her heavenly Mother. It didn't matter that the icy water would ordinarily kill a helpless child in similar circumstances; the mother's faith remained strong.

The multitude watched Croisine, who in a "sublime spectacle of Catholic faith," held her son submerged in the spring water for fifteen minutes before removing his still lifeless body. She then wrapped her son in the apron and departed the Grotto for her return home.

Upon seeing and touching the ice-cold body of his son, Jean cried, "You see now that he is dead?"[7] "No, he is not dead," his wife answered sternly. "The Blessed Virgin will affect his recovery."[8] Croisine then placed her child back in the cradle. Within minutes, the boy began to breathe. The breath was shallow, and his parents had to strain to see and hear, but the boy was breathing. Justin was not dead, rather he was sleeping soundly. There was renewed hope in their home.

For the next twelve hours, Justin's breathing strengthened and became more regular until at daybreak of the second day he awoke. Color had returned to the cheeks of his emaciated body. The child turned his eyes toward his mother and laughed. The boy "sought his mother's breast and drew from it long draughts. Though he had never walked, he [told his mother that he] wished to leave his cradle and walk about the room."[9] Croisine, however, resisted Justin's repeated solicitations, refusing to allow him to walk about in his weakened state. The day turned to another. All the while Justin satisfied his ravenous appetite at his mother's breast.

At daybreak of the third day, Jean and Croisine left the house, leaving Justin sleeping in his cradle. When Croisine returned the cradle was empty. Little Justin was running from one point to another, touching the furniture and moving the chairs. The child who had not walked since his birth was walking. Croisine was frozen at the sight and unable to move as she watched her son shuffle with ease around the room. She trembled and was overcome with a happiness that seemed to deprive her of all her strength. "Be careful not to fall," she told her son as she leaned against the door for support. "But Justin did not fall; his step was firm, and he ran and threw himself into the arms of his mother, who embraced him with tears in her eyes."[10]

Jean returned home some time later with Franconnette Gozos, who had not seen the boy in two days, since wrapping him in the death shroud she had prepared. Neither could believe their eyes at the sight of Justin walking around the room. They all knelt, and Croisine "joined the child's hands to raise them towards heaven; and, all together, they offered thanksgivings to the Mother of Mercies."

Justin was only one of many people that experienced similar supernatural healings owing to the flowing water of this miraculous spring. The story of the fountain, its origins, and its unlikely discovery, originate in a small town lying in the foothills of the Pyrenees Mountains in the south of France. And, they commence with a chance meeting between a fourteen-year-old, ignorant peasant girl, and a mysterious lady at a grotto along the Gave River in a dumping ground called Massabielle.

Part II

Brief History of Lourdes

Though the town of Lourdes has deep roots in history, it was not that well known in the mid-1800s. By all accounts, its geography and strategic location made the town a natural theater of war. It is no wonder then that the most impressive landmark of the small town, the one thing that brought it celebrity and glory, was a fort dating to the Gallic War. It was at that time that Julius Caesar had his Roman builders construct the fortress, which "for seventeen-hundred years remained the strongest, and most hotly disputed, citadel in the province of Bigorre."[11]

After the Roman Empire collapsed, the fort was occupied by the Vandals and subsequently the Alains. The Visigoths destroyed it, but the Saracens rebuilt and occupied it. In the year 733, the Saracens were defeated by Mesclin, but the survivors held the fort and renamed it Mirambel. It was taken during the siege by Charlemagne in 778 and upon his "surrender to the most noble lady who ever existed, ...the Queen of heaven...,"[12] and at the urging of the Bishop of Le Puy, Charlemagne was baptized and took the name of Lorus. From that time, the fort became known as Lordunum or Lordum, which over time became Lourdes.

During the following century, the fort was seized by the Normans and then the Albigensian heretics. In 1218, the Papal Crusaders took the fort until the English took much of the area as part of the Treaty of Bretigny in 1360. However, when England fell upon misfortune, the fortress was lost to others, including the Huguenots.

As the powers of France were consolidated into the Monarchy of France, the value of the castle as a fortress diminished. Louis XV transformed it into a prison and during the French Revolution it held several hundred prisoners. Louis Philippe restored it to a military station, albeit one of little importance, during his reign between 1830 and 1848.

The decline of the town of Lourdes coincided with the demise of its military prominence, prompting Louis Veuillot to write in 1858, that Lourdes was "more passed through than known."[13] Nevertheless, the town remained the key of the Pyrenees in a different way. Lourdes is the place where all roads leading to the warm baths of the Pyrenees mountains intersect. During the summer months therefore, most visitors would stop at Lourdes, staying for a night or two at the Hotel de la Poste. While there, the travelers would visit the fortress, dine, and admire the scenery before resuming their travels.[14]

Narrow streets and alleys were lined with low houses, enough to shelter many of the large families that fashioned its approximately 4,000 inhabitants. In addition to the hotel, the town boasted a government center, a hospital, a prison, a club, a newspaper, and a printing establishment. It was the 10th-century church, however, that created Lourdes' greatest form of diversion, as it served as host to many local fairs held during the summer and autumn months. Along with the presence of tourists, these fairs created some temporary excitement for the poor, but the onset of winter reestablished the town's melancholy caused by its poverty.

Despite the hardships, people were conscientious, deeply religious, and relatively satisfied. Many of the children were sent to various schools, and despite having a relatively educated society, they also possessed a simplicity of rural life. They have been described as warm and affectionate people, "upright in heart, abounding in southern wit, and strictly moral. They are honest, devout, and averse to innovations."[15]

Among the working people of Lourdes there were about 120 notables that included rentiers, physicians, and the like. There was an equal number of tradesmen, mostly catering to small trades. "Shepherds, farmers, millers, and forestry workers, as well as the quarrymen who exploited the marble, stone, and slate found in the mountains,"[16] made up the largest segment of the working population. Women contributed by working the fields or selling timber that was collected in the public forest. In contrast, Lourdes provided little opportunity for employment in the manufacturing industry.

The Early Years

It was sometime during the early part of the 17th century that an English doctor named Boly fell in love and married a local girl from Lourdes. Shortly thereafter, he built a mill uniquely designed with a kitchen and three living rooms, a style that has come to be called the Boly Mill. The apartment was rented to the Casterot family and Justin

Casterot, the head of the family that included his wife, four daughters still in their teens, and an eleven-year-old son, operated the mill and apparently created a lucrative enterprise with which to support his family.

1841 – 1843

By all accounts it was a terrible and most unfortunate wagon accident along the road to Poueyferre that caused the death of Justin Casterot. More than simply unfortunate, Casterot's death created a significant problem for his family as none of his children were capable of operating his mill, threatening to eradicate the family's only source of income. It was decided, therefore, that eighteen-year old Bernarde, the eldest of Casterot's daughters, should be married to someone capable of operating the mill and providing for the family. For this purpose, thirty-five-year-old François Soubirous, an unmarried miller, was considered. Soubirous, however, had a different attraction. He was far more captivated by a blue-eyed blond named Louise, Bernarde's younger sister.

Francois Soubirous, Bernadette's father, struggled with poverty brought about by his own inability to operate the mill to which he had been entrusted following his marriage to Louise.

January 9, 1843

Soubirous was persistent and on January 9, 1843, he and Louise were married. As one might suspect of any bachelor of thirty-five years, François was fairly set in his ways. There was nothing extraordinary about him, being, as he was, of average build with fair skin and blue eyes. He was also considered by many to be far less than ambitious. In fact, most of the time he was idle and without work. Still, his marriage to seventeen-year-old Louise, a very pretty and assiduous girl, provided him a hand up with the opportunity to operate a successful mill business. Neither François nor Louise had a formal education. Neither could read nor write, but the presence of Louise's mother in the house provided a stability to the mill's operation, since she was familiar with the operation, its customers, and the accounts. The entire Casterot family, in fact, continued to live in the mill apartment.

Bernadette's mother Louise Casterot Soubirous married Francois on January 9, 1843, providing him with the opportunity to manage a successful mill operation. His success lasted only until the untimely death of Louise's mother.

1844-1848

The couple was blessed with their first child within a year of their marriage. On Sunday, January 7, 1844, Bernadette Soubirous entered the world crying. She cried a lot, it seems, especially during her baptismal ceremony held just two days later, prompting her embarrassed uncle to say in frustration, "All she does is cry. She'll be a bad one."[17] Father Dean Forgues, the parish priest, presided over the ceremony. Louise's sister Bernarde stood as Bernadette's godmother at the baptism and would become a significant influence in her young life, taking charge of the Soubirous household from Bernadette's birth until 1849. In fact, Aunt Bernarde would later boast of serving as Bernadette's mother for the first several years of her life, though this may have been a manifestation of her frustration at not being chosen for marriage by François as custom of the time would have dictated.

Bernarde wasn't the only person whose intercession would become somewhat of a necessity in those early years. In November 1844, Louise was badly burned by the resin of a falling candle, rendering an injury that made her unable to nurse ten-month-old Bernadette. The baby was taken to the town of Bartrès, located about three miles outside of Lourdes, to the home of Marie Aravant-Lagues, a mill customer who had just suffered the loss of her own newborn. Lagues agreed to nurse Bernadette for the next ten months of the infant's life. Over those months, she had become so attached to the child that when Bernadette was finally returned home, the Soubirouses comforted Marie with a promise to take the child to visit the Lagueses no less than two times each year.

During her absence, Bernadette had missed the birth and death of her baby brother Jean, who died just seven weeks after his 1845 birth. She was home in Lourdes, however, during the birth of two other siblings, sister Toinette, born in 1846, and brother Jean-Marie, born in 1848.

Life in the Soubirous household seemed pretty good as the couple counted among their blessings three children and a successful mill operation that provided all that the young family needed. The mill business, in fact, was booming, but with the expanding family, space was a bit tight and the widowed Madame Casterot, who was so intimately

11

familiar with her deceased husband's mill operation, and her children, was forced to leave the abode. Their departure "marked the beginning of a decline which was never arrested, and which grew rapidly worse."[18]

1850-1851

Around the year 1850, Bernadette began to experience health issues. Stomach problems and a spleen disorder caused many anxious moments as the Soubirouses were no strangers with sickness and death. Bernadette's health issues were not taken lightly by her parents but coincided with the decline of business, making it very difficult for the family to afford adequate care.

The Boly Mill was operated by Justin Casterot until his death. Responsibility for the operation, under the direction of Louise Casterot's mother, was handed to Francois Soubirous, Louise's new husband.

Over the next several years, and despite being handed a thriving mill to operate, success proved an elusive commodity to François, and while his persistence in pursuit of his marriage to Louise may have provided him with opportunity, a lack of responsibility presented him with an even greater challenge. Perhaps it was the anxiety of Bernadette's health issues or the weight of the collapsing business. Maybe it was the combined distraction of the two that made François extravagant in his ways and deserving of his reputation for producing shoddy work. "Customers complained that his contracts were rarely carried out on time, and that his flour was dirty and of poor quality."[19] He struggled to keep the mill operational, but without the guidance, intervention, and knowledge of his mother-in-law, he eventually fell victim to his own bad habits and mismanagement practices. Adding to the family grief, Jean-Marie, the couple's only son, died in 1851, shortly before his third birthday. His death was quickly followed by the birth of another son who François and Louise named Jean-Marie in honor of the memory of the son they lost just a short time earlier.

1854

By 1854, his customers had had enough. Shopkeepers reported that François seldom paid his bills and villagers could frequently find him taking a drink, all of which caused him to lose many accounts. Unable to pay his rent, he was evicted from the mill. Rather quickly, the family, which now included Bernadette's sister Toinette and brother Jean-Marie, was forced to move into the slums. Their descent "from comparative ease to abject poverty and ... destitution" was now complete.

Reasons other than inexperience, poor management, and bad judgement have been identified as contributing to the failure of the Soubirouses' mill enterprise. These explanations include a deteriorating mill infrastructure, the lack of an adequate water supply to power the mill, and the natural decline of clients, all operational and management-type issues that his mother-in-law may have been able to help resolve.

But the causes of the Soubirouses' financial ruin are less consequential than the destitution it brought to the family.

1855 – 1856

The Soubirouses' problems did not subside with the advent of a new year. Despite the joy of the birth of Justin, the couple's second living son, Lourdes was ravaged with an outbreak of cholera, a disease caused by drinking water or eating food contaminated with the cholera bacterium. In an epidemic, the source of the problem is usually a water and/or food supply contaminated with the feces of an infected person, and this was most likely the cause of the outbreak in Lourdes. The sickness struck Bernadette particularly hard, and though lucky enough to recover, the condition exacerbated the asthma that she developed in the early 1850s. Her weakened stomach could no longer tolerate the meal cakes that now constituted the bulk of the family's daily diet. The mashed corn of which *milloc* is made, the staple of the poorest in Lourdes, became almost undigestible for Bernadette. Consequently, François tried to provide her with wheat bread whenever he could, but such luxury was a rarity for the Soubirouses.

François struggled desperately for financial recovery. His mother-in-law did her best to help, and even rented the Laborde mill which François began to operate. Unfortunately, Madame Casterot's untimely death brought an end to that experiment, and the Soubirouses were forced to relocate yet again, this time with the benefit of a small legacy left to them by Madame Casterot. This enabled François to rent the Escoubles mill a few miles east of Lourdes with a renewed vigor for a successful operation. However, "the venture didn't justify the glowing prospects held out by the lessor, and they had to leave the following year, penniless."[20] At their eviction, the couple was "compelled to hand over their marriage wardrobe in lieu of the unpaid debt."[21]

Consequently, while most of the providers in Lourdes worked as shepherds, farmers, millers, forestry workers, and quarrymen, François Soubirous worked at none of these professions. He was now a day worker, a person of no fixed employment who supported the social hierarchy from the bottom and who "sought the crust from whatever was going."[22] Employment opportunities were scarce. One day he served a local baker as a carter and the next a groom in a posting establishment, but most of the time he sat idle. Louise worked the fields for a pittance, washed clothes or cleaned houses, a task referred to as charing. Even this work was scarce, however, and much of the family's time was spent in the forest gathering sticks that could be sold to buy bread. Still, times were very difficult, and the children seldom had enough to eat.

Bernadette, meanwhile, grew weaker and François was seemingly becoming desperate. It may have been his poverty or perhaps the assumption of his desperation that led to the accusation. Regardless, the result was that François was arrested and charged with stealing a bag of wheat from his employer. Despite the hardships, the hunger, and the sickness, Bernadette didn't whine. She ate what was offered and dealt with the effects of her illness in silence, prompting one that knew her to comment, "She never complained of anything. Always docile, never a sassy answer."[23]

As the prospects of homelessness drew closer to reality, François appealed to his cousin, André Sajous, a stone-cutter by profession, for help with temporary lodging. Perhaps out of a sense of familial loyalty, Sajous offered his cousins rent-free living arrangements. Sajous had just converted a former prison to his home. In it he had a spare room that he had tried to rent with little success. The *cachot*, as this room was called, was the prison's former dungeon. It occupied the lowest floor and constituted the filthiest of rooms in the transformed prison, but it still presented a better alternative than the streets. Consequently, François accepted the charitable overture. The government had abandoned the facility as a jail some years earlier "because of its damp, unhygienic condition."[24] One state official described the room as "a dark, noisome den."[25] As noted earlier, Sajous had in fact tried to rent the room several times, but other than the occasional homeless laborer, the room went mostly empty. With its low black ceiling, the space was fairly grim. It had a large chimney, a slate floor, the pieces of which did not quite fit together, and two small windows, one of which was still barred, a reminder that it was a place of incarceration. The windows overlooked a small, high-

15

walled courtyard which was used to store an ample pile of manure. But while the windows may have allowed the smell of manure to permeate the room, direct sunlight eluded their direction, making the 16' x 13' room rather dark and dank.

Furnishings were sparse and consisted of a table, a trunk, some old chairs, and three beds, one for the parents, one for the two girls, and one for the two boys. The cupboards were relatively bare, holding some cheap dinner plates and a few cooking utensils. The otherwise empty walls were decorated with a crucifix and some other religious pictures.

Regardless, this room would become the domicile for all six members of the Soubirous family. Accepting lodging, however, did not diminish François's pride, which prevented the Soubirouses from accepting handouts of millet bread often offered to the family by André's wife.

Humiliation seemed François's lot at this time and sometimes his own seemingly harmless actions were misinterpreted as intentional mischief. Take for example the day in which there was no kindling material in the cachot with which to start a fire. François took to the streets in search of some type of tinder. As he walked along the roadside he spotted an otherwise worthless plank which he at once took up and carried home. The gesture was cause for his arrest and imprisonment. He remained for eight days in custody before the charges were withdrawn.

It was during some of these most difficult times that Bernarde, Bernadette's godmother and aunt, would step up. As a diversion from the misery of poverty at home, and perhaps to provide a little money, she often would take Bernadette with her to a tavern she managed at the corner of Rue du Bourg, not far from the Lacadé and Boly mills. There Bernadette would tend bar, often displaying a natural generosity while pouring wine for a patron when her aunt wasn't looking. Marie Camps and Jeanne-Marie Caudeban were beneficiaries of this generosity and would often receive good measure when they arrived at the tavern. Emile Zola witnessed this on many occasions, noting in his journal, "When her little friend came for a liter, and her aunt's back was turned, she said to her friend: 'Here! Quick! Take a good drink: my aunt isn't looking.' This showed a kind heart,"[26] he wrote. It may also have betrayed a somewhat mischievous side to young Bernadette.

Bernadette as she appeared in a photo taken by Viron on July 2, 1866.

1857-1858

Bernadette, meanwhile, found a formal education elusive. Though occasionally attending school, her absences significantly outnumbered her days in the classroom and the girl remained relatively ignorant, while her siblings attended class regularly. By age fourteen, Bernadette did know her common prayers, though she could neither read nor write. She did, however, have a burning desire to make her First Communion and inquired about taking formal catechetical instruction toward that end. "The priest in charge of the special catechism class, however, believed, because of her tininess, that she was still too young for admission to it, and Bernadette was, as yet, too retiring to press her claim."[27]

Regardless, Bernadette, "from about the age of six, had a pronounced tendency to piety,"[28] though there was nothing out of the ordinary about it. She enjoyed evening prayers with the family and, according to Sajous, shouted the prayers so loudly that he could hear her from the next room. Even her behavior at church was rather ordinary for a child, as she would often turn around while at Mass to see what was going on around her.

Still impoverished, the children continued to struggle to fill their stomachs, causing them a great deal of suffering. Little Jean-Marie, Bernadette's young brother, actually scraped from the floor, and "nibbled the wax from the church candles to fill his empty stomach."[29] Emmanuélite Estrade, the sister of the local tax collector, happened to be praying in church when the sound of someone rattling the votive candle stand annoyed her. Turning to remonstrate the perpetrator, she discovered a small boy "eating the wax drippings from the burnt-out candles. Being a charitable soul, she was duly horrified, took the boy home and fed him a slice of bread and butter. He was tongue-tied to the point of dumbness and refused to give his name, but at her invitation he came daily and devoured what she gave him in the passage of the foot of the stairs. It would be months before Emmanuélite, while visiting the home of Bernadette, discovered that her 'little pensioner,' as she called him, was Jean-Marie Soubirous, the eldest brother of" Bernadette.[30]

September 1857

In September 1857 Marie Lagues dispatched a servant girl to the Soubirouses' home with a proposal for Louise. Marie needed assistance caring for her eight children, doing the housework and watching the sheep, and wanted Bernadette to "return to the Lagues' farm"[31] in Bartrès to help manage that charge. Perhaps Louise and François found Marie's promise to send Bernadette to school and to catechism classes appealing. Perhaps they were repaying a debt to the woman who served as the surrogate wet nurse when Louise was unable to perform such duties. Or maybe it was as simple as reducing by one the number of hungry mouths that needed to be fed in the cachot. Whatever the reason, the Soubirouses found the proposal difficult to refuse. So, despite her failing health, Bernadette worked as the Lagueses' servant for the next four months. But if there was a benefit to the Soubirouses in the arrangement, that benefit didn't transfer to Bernadette. While in their servitude, "Bernadette suffered the harsh and laborious conditions of a child servant."[32] Her diet was limited to meal cakes, eliminating the occasional treat of wheat bread provided by her parents. "At Bartrès, wheat bread was only for the masters."[33]

Bernadette was also affected by the lack of companionship and would sometimes invite Jeanne-Marie Caudeban, another servant child, to help tend the sheep in the Arribans' meadow and the tranquil hillside. More often, however, she would tend the sheep in solitude, a loneliness that afforded Bernadette the opportunity to learn to pray the Rosary.

For her part, Marie Lagues and her husband were having second thoughts about promises Marie had made to the Soubirouses, deciding that sending Bernadette to school and catechism class would leave the sheep without a shepherd for a portion of the day. So, despite her promise to the Soubirouses, Marie reneged on the offer and elected to herself act as Bernadette's teacher, despite having neither the skill nor the patience to undertake such a task. This made the chore of learning a very difficult exercise for Bernadette. If she didn't immediately grasp a lesson, something she did with little frequency, Lagues would lose her temper, ending the lesson by "throwing the book across the room shouting, 'You'll never know anything.'"[34]

Late December 1857
to Early January 1858

Though never complaining about the poor quality of the food, the long workday, or the lack of a formal education, Bernadette did have a desire for the opportunity to receive the Blessed Sacrament at Holy Mass. Sometime in late December 1857, or early January 1858, Bernadette began to send messages to her parents through emissaries such as her good friend Jeanne-Marie Garros, begging for her return to Lourdes. When those messages went unanswered, Bernadette decided to leave Bartrès and return to Lourdes to speak with her parents.

Sunday, January 17, 1858

On Sunday, January 17, 1858, she informed Monsieur and Madame Lagues of her decision. They naturally worried, instructing her to return by the following day. But Bernadette didn't return until Wednesday, January 20 and informed her worried employers that "the parish priest wants me to make my First Communion, and if I go back to Lourdes, I'll make it."[35] This was a proposition that Bernadette gave considerable thought.

Wednesday, January 27, 1858

The Grotto as it appeared at the time that Bernadette encountered the Virgin Mary.

Just ten days later, Bernadette informed Mrs. Lagues that she was leaving Bartrès for good and returning to Lourdes. The very next day she set out on foot, alone, for the cachot. She traveled the old road, scenic and serene. To her right was the beautiful valley and to her left the peaceful waters of the Gave River, rolling along at the foot of the mountains that were sprinkled with the rock ledges of the Masse-Vieille also known as the Massabielle. This "steep cliff stood at the edge of the

Gave in the shadow of the north slope."[36] Bernadette could not have known during that lonely, albeit peaceful journey home, that a small grotto within that shadow would change her life, the lives of all that knew her, and the lives of those who would come to know her, forever.

The rocks of Massabielle formed a solitary spot in Lourdes. There the serenity of the stream, artificially diverted to power the mill, rejoined the flowing white waters of the Gave River through a meandering path along the valley. On the bank of the stream, in front of the Ile du Chalet, formed by the Gave and the canal, stood a rock formation pierced by several holes, cave-like in appearance. The largest of these stood at ground level with an arched entrance that stood about thirteen to fifteen feet in height. Its breadth and depth surpassed, by over three times, its height. Slightly right, and about fourteen feet above this cave were two additional fissures, oval in appearance and each "about the size of a window in a house or a niche in a church."[37] The first of these was about six feet deep and forked with one of the branches extending to the larger grotto beneath and the other turning back on itself and forming the second of the upper caves. This cave also formed a light source for the others. From the base of this orifice a wild rose bush grew from a fissure in the rock, and climbing shrubs formed a curtain over the opening. Ivy, box, heather, and moss grew around tangled brambles, hazels, and a few trees. These caves were known as the Grotto of Massabielle.

Rocks that had fallen from the mountains lay at the base of the caves, causing the gentle water of the mill stream to rush over them in a chaotic manner, seemingly breaking nature's serenity as the stream raced to merge with the waters of the Gave about fifteen feet below.

Farther down the banks of the Gave was a group of rocks belonging to the commune of Lourdes. Here the town's poor would bring their pigs to feed, occasionally taking shelter in the grotto from the extremities of the weather. Though rain, usually driven by a westerly wind, would find its way into the cave on the right side, the other side remained relatively dry, though even that side of the cave tended toward dampness during such weather events.

Thursday, February 11, 1858
Between 9:00 AM and 11:00 AM
Sexagesima Week

Bernadette had been home for only about two weeks and her parents were deeply concerned about her health. Since her return, Bernadette realized her dream of attending school regularly though her asthma worsened, and her general appearance caused the family much anxiety. For her were preserved the warmer clothes and she was often confined to the cachot, denied the opportunity for fresh air even as her siblings were told to work and play outdoors. François, still without work and the ability to provide a stable means of support, "remained in bed to blunt the edge of his appetite."[38]

This day was different, however. It was 'Shrove Thursday,' the first day of the pre-Lent carnival and there was no school. Consequently, it was Bernadette who first noticed that there was no wood for burning. Toinette protested that wood was just gathered the day prior. In fact, Toinette and Louise had gathered wood at four o'clock the prior morning, but that was sold for six *sous*,* enough to purchase their daily bread. Perhaps a bit annoyed with her husband's apparent depression, Louise had a notion to go to the forest to gather some firewood, but was interrupted when Toinette's class-mate, Jeanne Abadie, arrived. Nicknamed "Baloume" because of her rather large size, Jeanne immediately suggested that she, Toinette, and Bernadette take on the task of gathering the timber, enabling Louise to do other things in the cachot. It was only Bernadette's unusual assertiveness that overcame the initial objections of her mother, who eventually consented to the girls' supplications, but not without a stern warning for Bernadette to protect herself from the elements so as not to catch a cold. "Clad in a worn-out and patched black dress, her delicate visage framed in the white capulet which covered her head, and fell back on her shoulders, with stockings and coarse *sabots* on her feet, she displayed an innocent and rustic grace which charmed the heart even more than the eye."[39]

A sou is a copper coin of very little value. The plural is "sous."

22

Approximately 11:00 AM

The cold, damp air exaggerated by the overcast and foggy skies would not prevent the inhabitants of Lourdes from absorbing their rich local custom. For years, the week before the austerities of the Lenten season was reserved for "profane enjoyments." For many of means, not even the occasional few drops of rain permeating the otherwise stillness of the day could dampen the spirits. Today was the celebration of the feast of the illustrious Shepherdess of Saint Genevieve and the faithful from the diocese of Tarbes would not be denied.

The bells of the parish of Lourdes announced the time: eleven o'clock in the morning. "While joyful assemblies and parties were almost everywhere in preparation,"[40] the poor families, at least those lucky enough to have food, were forced to scavenge for wood for cooking. For others, the wood gathered was for the more critical need of warmth.

Elated with her newfound freedom, Bernadette, her sister, and their friend had departed the cachot in search of firewood. Along the way, the girls met Pascale Lavit, an older woman who lived in the common. The girls inquired of her where they might find some wood and bones. Lavit directed them to the bank of Massabielle. Once outside the town, they trod along "the rough road which sloped steeply to the old hog-backed bridge which the Romans had built on three massive stones"[41] that spanned the Gave. The girls crossed the bridge and continued along the forest road until reaching their destination at the mill via "its footbridge over the canal into fields owned by a Monsieur Lafitee."[42] There was plenty of timber from the freshly cut trees that Lafitee had cut down a few days prior, but Bernadette warned against taking any for fear that they might be taken as thieves. Instead, something prompted Bernadette to suggest following the mill-stream to its end. Despite Toinette's brief demur, Bernadette hurried toward the swollen canal, leaving the others behind. Before long, the girls "found themselves, for the first time, at the Grotto of Massabielle, half a mile west of the town."[43] This area is located about one mile west of Lourdes. The name Massabielle literally means "old rocks."

12:00 Noon

Now, standing on a narrow tip of land at the end of the mill-stream, the children eyed plenty of branches scattered on the opposite bank. Despite the bitterly cold water fed from the melting snow of the mountains, Jeanne removed her wooden clogs from her stocking-less feet and tossed them over the canal. Toinette carried her sabots as the two girls carefully waded across the knee-high waters of the stream. Thinking of her mother's admonition against needless risk-taking, Bernadette hesitated, then tried to toss stones into the water, hoping to be able to walk over them without removing her stockings, but the water was too deep. She then asked the two girls to help toss larger stones into the river, but that request was met with ridicule. Toinette offered to carry Bernadette across, though Bernadette knew that Toinette would not be able to carry her that distance. Eventually she asked Jeanne to carry her across, a plea that was roundly refused.

Once on the other side, Toinette and Jeanne wailed from the cold water and bent to wrap their petticoats around their feet to warm them. Then, putting their sabots on, they disappeared into the wooded area in search of wood. Normally, the waters would be flowing swiftly to power the mill, but on this day, the mill of Savy was undergoing repairs that required the waters to be turned off, making the canal shallow, relatively still, and very easy to cross. Bernadette was left momentarily alone to reflect. She didn't want to disobey her mother, who had given implicit instruction to do nothing that would cause unnecessary risk, but she also wanted desperately to be with the other girls and gather her fair share of fire wood.

Bernadette was a bit shorter than most her age, standing only four feet seven inches. Her tanned face, a remnant of her time tending sheep in the fields and doing other chores at Bartrès, was not enough to erase the childish features of her countenance. Her nose was straight, her lips well-formed, and her hands small and soft. Her flowing black hair was mostly covered by her white capulet, something her mother had insisted she wear over the customary handkerchief that most peasant women in the south wrapped around their head. Bernadette's was knotted to one side, and the capulet, "a very becoming article of dress, serving as both a hood over the head and a mantle over the shoulders reaching nearly all the way down the back,"[44] would provide greater warmth and protection from illness, Louise reasoned. Bernadette's dress was an old frock of coarse black material that resembled a patch quilt.

Part III

The Time of the Apparitions

The First Apparition

Suddenly alone, Bernadette went a little farther to see if she could cross dry-shod, but finding that she could not, returned to the area in front of the Grotto to remove her stockings. The wall of rocks in which the Grotto is carved reaches to an enormous height and is partially covered with box, ivy, fern, brambles, and moss. At the bottom of that formation is the cave which forms the Grotto and opens from ground level rising to a height of about fourteen feet. Its width spans about three times that. Two openings stand above the cave. The principal opening is oval-shaped, is about eight feet off the ground, and is just about tall enough for a person to stand upright.

The mid-day air was calm, and Bernadette resolved to cross the stream to rejoin her companions. As she was bending down, the sound of a blast of wind seemed to engulf her causing her to stop and look about. As she did, she noticed that not one of the heart-shaped leaves covering the tall poplar trees was moving, but looking toward the Grotto, she noticed a wild rose bush, which hung down at the sides of it, swinging about."

Without a second thought, she once more reached down to remove her stockings but again was stopped by the sound of rustling wind. Once more she looked up to gaze at the trees, and again, observed their eerie stillness. Glancing toward the Grotto, she noticed a gentle sway in the rose bush and the adjacent brambles. Further, "A golden cloud hovered around the niche, a nimbus of brilliant light filled it, and in the midst of the light stood a young girl, whose feet rested on the bush, and who extended her arms towards Bernadette and saluted her with a gentle inclination of the head and a smile of wonderful sweetness."

The light surrounding the Lady, though bright, did not hurt Bernadette's eyes, but rather "invited the sight to repose in it with inexpressible delight." Unable to speak, Bernadette rubbed her brown eyes in disbelief, but the Vision remained. Bernadette was terribly frightened, but it was not a fear she had ever experienced before. She had no thoughts to flee. Rather, she fell to her knees with an intense desire to look at the Lady. The Vision of the girl standing upright was of middle stature. She appeared to Bernadette to be less than twenty years of age, perhaps sixteen or seventeen, and was of incomparable splendor. To Bernadette, the girl's beauty was heavenly. Her blue eyes authenticated a look of sweetness, which melted Bernadette's heart. She wore a dress of purest white with a "white veil upon her head which fell down her back in ample folds as low as her robe. She had a blue girdle tied loosely round her waist and falling in two bands almost as far down as her robe." On each bare foot rested a golden-colored rose, the same color as the chain of the rosary whose white beads draped over her right arm.

Bernadette stared into the Lady's blue eyes and instinctively pulled the rosary from her pocket. She tried to make the sign of the cross but was unable to raise her right arm. It was as though paralyzed. Not until the Lady initiated the ritualistic blessing with the cross of her own rosary, was Bernadette able to lift her arm to her forehead. The temporary paralysis was now gone. With the duel blessing, Bernadette's fear and apprehension were vanquished.

Bernadette recited the Rosary, and though the Vision's lips did not move, the Lady passed the individual large white beads through Her fingers as though keeping silent count of the prayers said. Upon completion of the Rosary, the Lady smiled lovingly and beckoned with her finger for Bernadette to come closer. When Bernadette remained still, the Vision "extended her hands, bowed, smiled and disappeared into the niche." All that remained was the brilliant light, which though radiant, did not hurt Bernadette's eyes. Then at once, the niche again became cold and grey.

Just about this time, Toinette and Jeanne were returning to the Grotto and from a distance, saw Bernadette on her knees and staring at the niche. Toinette called to her three times, but Bernadette remained silent and continued to look straight ahead. As the girls got nearer, Toinette threw two small stones at Bernadette, hitting her once on the shoulder. Still Bernadette did not move. She appeared white and Toinette feared she might be dead until Jeanne pointed out that a dead person would be lying down, not kneeling in prayer.

I am the Immaculate Conception

Bernadette initially felt dazed and, looking around, spotted her companions. Then, regaining her composure, Bernadette removed her cabots and stockings and crossed the stream. To her surprise, she found the water somewhat warm, not at all like the glacial waters described by the girls earlier. Bernadette called to her companions asking why they had made such a fuss about the water temperature when they had crossed. "Did you see anything?" Bernadette inquired of them. Despite having observed Bernadette on her knees in prayer, they had seen nothing of the vision. Neither did Bernadette reveal to them what she had just experienced. The girls gathered their wood together and departed for their return trip to Lourdes.

Jeanne seemed agitated with Bernadette for not gathering as much wood as she had, and she began to walk home ahead of the others [dragging] the heavy load of faggot and the bones" she collected. The sisters tied their bundles and began to walk up the steep hill along the path behind the niche. Though stronger than Bernadette, Toinette could not carry her bundle and threw it down three times along the way. Bernadette, however, carried her bundle straight to the top and then returned to carry Toinette's. Once atop the hill, the two girls continued home carrying their bundles atop their heads.

Along the way Bernadette said, "I am going to tell you something, but I don't want you to talk about it at home, because mother would scold me." With assurances that Toinette would tell no one, and despite her previous secrecy, Bernadette now told her sister of the vision. Rather than the calmness experienced by Bernadette, Toinette was frightened and warned against going there again for fear that the vision might do them harm. As they continued their journey, Toinette's fear seemed to turn to jealousy and then rage as she began to think of all her older sister was allowed. Bernadette was "entitled to wear stockings, eat wheat bread and exercise authority," none of which Toinette was allowed to do. She snapped her disbelief at her "visionary" sister and, taking a stick from her bundle, began to strike Bernadette with it.

Once home, the girls tossed their faggots against the door and each ate a morsel of bread, after which Louise began to comb Toinette's hair. As if forgetting about, or perhaps simply ignoring, her promise to keep Bernadette's secret, she told her disbelieving mother of her sister's

31

vision. In turn, Louise questioned Bernadette who reluctantly told her what she had seen. Louise reached for the stick used to stretch the blankets, and "a good beating followed for the two girls, with Bernadette receiving the lighter of the blows. 'Your eyes deceived you! You saw only a white stone,' her mother insisted," but Bernadette persisted. From his bed, Francois scolded his eldest daughter whom he loved dearly. Bernadette remained silent. Perhaps what hurt Louise more than the perceived fable itself, was the fact that Bernadette would persist in her lie. Louise had never known her daughter to lie before, yet this was such an incredulous tale that it belied reason. Why would she choose to make her first lie such a preposterous story? Or, could there be truth in what Bernadette was saying? It might just be that, for Louise, the possibility of truth was an even more frightening prospect.

Late Afternoon/Early Evening

The chores required for the balance of the day brought about an end to the discussion as Louise and her daughters went about selling the firewood, buying the daily bread, and doing the other required things.

That evening, when their prayers were completed, "Bernadette said the Rosary out loud, concluding with the words, '*Oh Mary, conceived without sin, pray for us who trust in you.*' As she said this she went pale, as she had done at the Grotto, and burst into tears."[45] The sobbing became so intense that she was momentarily unable to speak. Louise grew frightened and very concerned, and went upstairs to seek the advice of her neighbor, Romaine, who lived there with her five children. Once back in the Soubirous home, Louise and Romaine confronted the visionary and were at once both frightened and astonished. They "grilled and lectured Bernadette."[46] Knowing Bernadette was not accustomed to fabrication, Louise believed that her daughter saw something, but feared it might be evil. She insisted on Bernadette's word that she would not return to Massabielle. Despite her intense desire to look upon the beautiful vision again, Bernadette promised to stay away, perhaps realizing that "a privilege such as she had received must be paid for in pain."[47]

Friday, February 12, 1858

Though Bernadette did not speak of it, the extraordinary events of the prior day at the Grotto of Massabielle swirled in her mind and dominated the conversation with her sister Toinette. Bernadette felt an intense desire to return and, no longer able to remain silent, told her mother that "Something is pushing me to go to Massabielle."[48] Louise, however, would have none of it, admonishing the child to "Get to work!"[49]

Meanwhile, the story of Bernadette's vision began to circulate the town.

Saturday, February 13, 1858
Late Morning/Early Afternoon

Abbé Pomian, the chaplain at the Hospice School, was just about to hear another confession at the parish church. There was but one more person in line after this one. But this one would not be a typical confession. Drawing the curtain closed, he heard the penitent say, "I saw something white, having the form of a lady."[50] Pomian was not easily rattled by what he heard in the confessional and calmly probed the person kneeling on the other side of the curtain for more information. Gaining confidence, Bernadette, who by now had revealed her name, grew more excited and her voice began to increase in volume. The last penitent in line was Eleonor Perard. Despite trying not to overhear, she was able to discern every word of the young girl's revelation, prompting her to run away so as not to hear the remainder of Bernadette's confession.

Abbé Pomian was struck by the words of Bernadette, particularly the phrase, "A sound like a gust of wind." Was this a biblical coincidence? Was this similar to the wind that revealed God to the prophet Elijah, hidden in the cave? Was it like the mighty wind of Pentecost? Or was it simply the tone in which Bernadette told him the story that deeply impressed him?"[51] He was unable to identify the cause for his consternation but did ask Bernadette's permission to discuss the matter with the pastor, a permission that Bernadette eagerly granted.

Later that evening Pomian met with Curé (Pastor) Peyramale and briefly explained what he heard in confession. The curé seemed disinterested, telling Pomian, "We'll have to wait"[52] to see what comes of it.

Sunday, February 14, 1858
Quinquagesima Sunday

Since Saturday, Toinette had been spreading word of Bernadette's vision to other charity students at the Hospice School. The school was run by the Sisters of Nevers and Bernadette had been attending for a few weeks. So, on this beautiful Sunday morning, curiosity among the children, particularly among Bernadette's classmates, was high.

Approximately 9:45 AM to 11:30 AM
The Second Apparition

That interest piqued at impromptu meetings of the children with Bernadette both before and after the ten o'clock High Mass on this last Sunday before Lent - the Quinquagesima - also known in Lourdes as "forty hours Sunday." Bernadette wanted badly to go back to the Grotto but wouldn't do so without first gaining her mother's approval, something she vowed to do in concert with the other children as soon as she returned home. Shortly after lunch, the girls made their request of Louise.

Her initial reaction was not the favorable one for which the girls had hoped. The rocks of Massabielle, dampened by the waters of the Gave, were slick and dangerous, she reasoned. Besides, if you go you will be late for Vespers, the late-day prayer services recited together with church officials and the faithful. And all this nonsense is childish, Louise concluded. But all pleaded, promising to be careful in their journey and to be home for Vespers. Perhaps not wanting to be the source of such disappointment to her child, Louise instructed Bernadette to ask her father.

François was working at Cazenave's stable at the time and the children eagerly tracked him down, only to be disappointed with his immediate denial of their request. François' boss, however, sided with the children, noting that a lady praying the Rosary couldn't possibly be of evil origins. François was forced to relent. Crying at this point, François told Bernadette that she could have only fifteen minutes at the Grotto. Bernadette pleaded for more time and François finally agreed.

The group of girls ran back to the cachot to inform Louise of François' decision. While there, "Bernadette took a flask from the mantlepiece. When [they] got outside, she said, 'Let's go and get some holy water.' [They] all went to the church to fill the flask from the holy water stoup; then [they] went down to Massabielle by the rue du Baous and the path through the wood."[53] The canal that was passable on the Thursday prior was now at normal depth. The children "had to approach the Grotto by the wood road. When they were opposite the top of the rock of Massabielle, they turned right and climbed down the steep path cut by the swine-herd."[54]

At this point Bernadette started to run, easily outdistancing the pack of girls that had now swelled to twenty. She was already kneeling next to a rock at the base of the Grotto when the others arrived. To their surprise, Bernadette, who was now praying the Rosary aloud, was not at a loss for breath. She told the others to pray the Rosary. Toinette reached for the beads that Bernadette had purchased for her in Betharram for two French sous and each of the girls began to say the Rosary individually.

As she concluded one of the decades of the Rosary, Bernadette exclaimed, "Now it's getting brighter." A moment later she continued, "Look there, she has a rosary on her right arm...She is looking at you."[55] The Lady was dressed as she was the prior Thursday with her feet resting on a rock of the niche.

Approximately 1:00 PM

As had been preordained by the young girls, Bernadette stood, approached the rocks which held the niche in which the Lady stood, and "said a prayer of exorcism while sprinkling holy water as high as she could toward the Lady. 'If you come from God, advance; but if not...'"[56] The Lady "bent forward and came almost to the edge of the rock, smiling at the precautions of Bernadette."[57] The child repeated the words but was unable to complete the sentence in the presence of a Lady so beautiful and seemingly gracious. She again inquired of her friends their ability to see what she so clearly saw, but their eyes could not behold the sight. Just then the Lady began to make the sign of the cross and Bernadette again fell to her knees in prayerful rapture.

Jeanne Abadie, who arrived late with some friends, decided to give Bernadette a fright. She climbed to the top of the cliff and slammed a rock about the size of a loaf of bread down from above. The rock struck the rock against which Bernadette knelt, and exploded into several pieces with some of the fragments rolling into the canal.

Bernadette didn't flinch, but many of the others dispersed in panic and fear. Still others tried to drag Bernadette to safety, but she was immovable and like dead weight, and appeared as in a trance. Bernadette had fallen into a state of ecstasy, something of which none of the girls were familiar. During such a state, as described in Catholic mysticism, "the soul becomes so absorbed in what it sees that it seems to leave the body. The external senses are in consequence suspended, with a resultant corporeal insensibility, slowing down of physical life and lowering of vital heat, and this condition leads to pallor of countenance and, ordinarily, immobility of body."[58] It is understandable then that Bernadette's friends were in fear for her safety and well-being.

Though Bernadette was pale in appearance, her eyes remained fixed on the niche in which the Lady stood. The child completed the Rosary aloud as the Lady silently fingered her beads. As the prayers concluded, the Lady vanished just as she had at the conclusion of the first apparition.

I am the Immaculate Conception

While Bernadette was deeply ensconced in ecstasy, the girls, who had dispersed in fear, returned with the mother and aunt of twenty-eight-year-old Antoine Nicolau, a miller employed at the Savy mill. The mill was only about 300 yards from the Grotto. "The two sisters went to the Grotto and tried to drag Bernadette away, but they could not manage it,"[59] so they went back to the mill to get Antoine, who was dressing to go to a pub in town. Without finishing, he followed his mother and aunt to the Grotto. He arrived to find only three or four other girls with Bernadette who "was kneeling down, her face deathly pale, her eyes wide open and fixed on the niche, her hands joined and her rosary between her fingers. Tears were streaming from her eyes, yet she was smiling, and her face was beautiful – more beautiful than anything [he] had ever seen."[60] All were spellbound. They just stood and gazed at her for a few moments. Only an occasional whisper from the girls broke the stillness of the silence. At his mother's urging, however, he tugged at Bernadette. She resisted his gentle pull as she was still focused on the Lady. Antoine exerted more force to pry Bernadette from her position, but it was only after the vision ended that he met with any success, leading her first up the steep path and then down the wooded lane toward the Savy mill. His mother held Bernadette's other arm as they walked, though Bernadette still looked upward and ahead as if seeing something. She remained focused, somewhat dazed as she had not yet fully emerged from the ecstasy and did not speak even when questioned. Tears continued to roll off her cheeks.

Upon entering the mill, Bernadette bowed her head. She was now aware of her surroundings as her cheeks were restored to their formerly rosy color. She felt no trace of fatigue and could now see the frightened faces of the others. The Nicolau family led Bernadette to the kitchen where she had a seat. Perhaps more from worry than a sense of humor, the miller began to joke with her. "Did you see something ugly?" he asked Bernadette. "Oh, no! I saw a beautiful young girl with a rosary on her arm." As she said this, Bernadette clasped her hands flat together in a praying motion. Nicolau left for the pub where he told Bernadette's godmother Bernarde the entire story.

Toinette had not followed the other girls to the Savy mill, but rather, overcome with fear for her older sister's safety, ran home to get her mother. "In tears, but with all the vehemence and urgency of a frightened child, she poured out the story of what had happened,"[61] explaining that Bernadette was nearly dead. Louise grabbed a small stick and ran toward the Grotto with an entourage in tow. When they reached the mill, they were told Bernadette was inside and appeared normal. Both relieved and upset, Louise raised the stick, no doubt intending to use it on Bernadette in a gesture of authority. "What's all this again? You little hussy, do you want to have the whole town laughing at us?"[62] Bernadette was spared the beating only at Nicolau's mother's insistence. She intoned, "Don't hit the child, she's a little angel."[63] Overcome, Louise dropped the stick and began to cry. Together, they returned home.

Approximately 3:00 PM

The hour was now close to three o'clock in the afternoon and Vespers were about to begin. As they did, Bernadette tried without success to erase the day's events at the Grotto from her mind and concentrate on her prayers. She was unable to do so. Neither was she able to prevent word of the vision from spreading throughout the village.

At the conclusion of the prayers, many town residents took advantage of the beautiful weather by taking an extended, late afternoon stroll, trying to enjoy the last rays of sun on this spring-like winter's day. As they did, many recounted the day's strange happenings. Rumors began to circulate with some believing and others discounting the apparitions of this otherwise ignorant peasant girl. Some merely laughed while still others refused to take the time to discuss it.

Louise's friend, Cyprine Gesta, stopped by the Soubirous home to ask Bernadette to validate the story already spreading throughout the village. François and Louise, regardless of the varied reactions of the villagers, were "fully convinced of their child's sincerity, but regarded the apparition as an illusion,"[64] perhaps even the trickery of the devil.

Monday, February 15, 1858

With only two days remaining before Ash Wednesday, there was much to do. Mere Ursule Fardes, Mother Superior of the children's school at Hospice, was inspecting the student class. As she approached Bernadette, she inquired, "Are you all through with your shenanigans?"[65] Mother Fardes earnestly believed that what Bernadette was experiencing was a dream-like illusion and was not something on which anyone should dwell. Regardless how badly these words made Bernadette feel, her day was about to get a whole lot worse. Upon leaving the school, Sophie Pailhasson approached her. The gaunt woman of about forty reached out and slapped Bernadette in the face, saying to Sister Anastasie, "Look! Here she is, the clown!"[66] The sister then grabbed Bernadette by the arm, shook her and said, "Clown! Clown! If you go back to the Grotto, they'll lock you up."[67] At this, many of Bernadette's classmates began snickering at her.

Bernadette seemed confused. Although feeling no bitterness toward her attackers, she couldn't understand why she was being treated this way. She would soon learn that this state of affairs was her new normal.

In the afternoon Bernadette attended sewing class. She was adept at this skill and took pleasure in the fruits of her work. The good-natured Sister Damien Calmels presided over the class and was totally unaware of the visions to which Bernadette had been privileged. Her classmates thought this a good time to tease Bernadette and taunted her to tell Sister Calmels all about the apparitions. When Bernadette refused, the other girls began to recount the stories in a most inaccurate way. As Bernadette began to correct their misstated facts, Sister Calmels interrupted, telling her not to repeat this to anyone for fear that she will become the butt of ridicule. It was too late for such warnings, however, as Bernadette's classmates began chants of "The swine of Massabielle, barefoot tramp, the pig's cave, and the lady without shoes."[68] These taunts would go on for months, making Bernadette regret ever having told anyone of her visions.

Tuesday, February 16, 1858

As she left the confines of the Hospice School during a morning break, Bernadette was approached by a servant girl carrying a message from her boss. Most villagers knew of her boss even if they hadn't met Madame Milhet in person. She was a middle-aged woman, a former servant girl herself who had the good fortune of marrying her employer, Monsieur Milhet. She dressed in a rather bizarre fashion with clothes she made herself with the help of Antoinette Peyret. She also was one of the few women who offered Louise Soubirous some work and for that reason, she was free to call on Louise with every reasonable expectation of being granted her wish. In fact, Madame Milhet always got her way, or at least it seemed so to most who knew her.

A former servant girl, Madame Milhet had the good fortune to marry her employer. In her new position she occasionally employed Louise Soubirous. By leveraging that connection, she was able to accompany Bernadette to the Grotto on February 18, 1858 enabling her to witness the third Apparition of Mary to Bernadette.

Thinking that Milhet wanted only to inquire about the events of the Grotto, Bernadette told the servant girl that she had no desire to speak with anyone and the servant girl returned to Madame Milhet with

40

the unfortunate news. Later that afternoon, however, as Bernadette was leaving school for the day, the servant girl reemerged, this time informing Bernadette that her own mother wanted her to stop by Madame Milhet's before coming home.

The Milhets lived in a rather wealthy area on Rue Saint-Pierre, next to the home of the police commissioner. As Bernadette answered Madame Milhet's questions regarding her vision of the lady, the older woman became all the more intrigued by her story, suggesting that they go to the Grotto together. Bernadette, however, explained that she was no longer allowed to go to Massabielle, to which Milhet replied, "Yes, yes, that will have to be straightened out. I'll take you home. I know your mother well. She won't be able to refuse me."[69]

Wednesday, February 17, 1858
Ash Wednesday

The children who had accompanied Bernadette to the Grotto a few days prior did a pretty good job of spreading their version of the story of the events of Sunday around Lourdes. Most simply dismissed the stories as children's fantasies, but others believed something was going on even if they couldn't agree as to what exactly it might be.

Madame Milhet, meanwhile, had already secured permission from Louise Soubirous to accompany Bernadette to the Grotto. Louise was obviously still upset about the entire affair when Madame Milhet suggested that the child may actually be seeing something. Louise was in no position to make her displeasure known. Clearly at wit's end, she first protested that they would be made into laughingstocks, but eventually relented saying, "Do what you like, I think I'm going off my head."[70]

Milhet assured her that the trip would be done in such a way as to maintain secrecy and that only her confidante, Antoinette Peyret, would join them at the Grotto. Peyret was a member of a group called the Children of Mary. She was also intrigued by Bernadette's stories and believed that the vision might be that of the group's deceased former

41

president, Elisa Latapie, who was now returning to ask for prayers. Latapie had perished the year prior "in circumstances that had impressed the parishioners. A few hours before she died, she asked to be dressed for burial in simple garments: her sodalist's dress, without any lace or ribbons. The pastor gave her funeral 'the greatest splendor and pomp possible.'"[71] Milhet and Peyret now decided to return to Massabielle at a time when no one else would be present. That would give them an opportunity to determine the truth.

Thursday, February 18, 1858
The Third Apparition
Approximately 5:00 AM

Bernadette and the two women met at the cachot early enough to attend the morning Mass at 5:30 and then headed directly to the Grotto of Massabielle. Madame Milhet, the only one of the group who was married, carried a candle that had been blessed at the Feast of the Purification, the same candle that she lit in her room during bad storms or on the feast days of the Blessed Virgin. Antoinette, the daughter of a bailiff, carried a pen and paper under her coat hoping that Bernadette could convince the Lady to write down on paper exactly what she wanted.

Upon arriving at the summit of Massabielle, Bernadette, as she had in prior visits, could not contain herself and ran down the hill toward the Grotto, her asthmatic condition all but gone for the moment. Unlike the circumstances of the first apparition that had caused the waters of the millstream to become shallow, the mill repairs were now complete, and the mill was operational once again. The waters of the stream were, therefore, restored to the original height which made passage near impossible. Rather, it was now necessary to climb up one side of the Espelugues hill and down the other.

The two women, even the younger Antoinette, had a great deal of trouble with their descent and lagged quite a distance behind. Bernadette was already steeped in prayer, however, and saw the bright light that she had come to associate with the onset of her visions. The Lady was there. She leaned forward toward the child, "with her countenance beaming with eternal brightness; and with her hand she made a sign to her to come nearer."[72]

At that very moment, Antoinette and Madame Milhet arrived slightly spent from their decent of the hill. They could clearly see that Bernadette's entire countenance had changed, but still the child was able to see and hear them. Bernadette told the women that the Lady was present and motioning for her to approach.

As she did this, the Lady came down from the niche and moved into the cave of the Grotto to meet the child. The two women followed close behind Bernadette until the Lady motioned to Bernadette to ask them to stop. Without looking back, Bernadette raised her hand in a halting gesture and Madame Milhet and Antoinette stopped. Milhet immediately felt the hurt of rejection. The feeling was one not unfamiliar to Milhet. Despite the new social status that her marriage brought, her prior station in life left her an outcast among the socialites, and her new-found social status caused those in the lower-class to abandon her. "Ask your lady if my presence offends her," Milhet directed Bernadette. "It does not,"[73] she replied. The two women then knelt down by the child's side and lit the blessed candle they had taken with them.

The women were not finished yet and handed Bernadette a pencil and paper that they had taken with them. "'Go up to her,' they said, 'as she calls you and makes a sign to you to come. Ask her who she is, and why she comes here; whether she is a soul from Purgatory begging prayers and Masses to be said for her. Ask her to write upon this paper what she wants. We are ready to do whatever she wishes, and what is necessary for her to be at rest.'"[74] A compliant Bernadette moved toward the Grotto and offered the pen and paper to the Lady, but with each step that Bernadette took forward, the Lady took a step backward until she was near the back of the cave. Bernadette stopped her advance and temporarily lost sight of the Lady, but then saw her standing slightly above and much closer than she had been before. "Miss, will you be so good as to write down what you want from me?"[75] Bernadette asked. The Lady smiled and for the first time in three apparitions, spoke to Bernadette, *"It is not necessary for me to put down in writing what I have to say to you.*[76]

The two women could hear nothing but noticed that Bernadette was still listening. *"Will you have the kindness to come here for a fortnight?"* the Lady asked. Bernadette agreed, subject to her parents' approval.

Bernadette asked the Lady her name, but rather than answer, she "inclined her head and smiled,"[77] instructing Bernadette instead to *"Go and tell the priests that a chapel must be built here."*[78] Then the Lady concluded, *"I cannot make you happy in this world, but I promise to do so in the next."*

Bernadette retreated toward the two women but kept her eyes focused on the Lady, who followed the child with her eyes. She "looked for some time very benevolently upon Antoinette Peyret."[79] Bernadette told the women what the Lady said, to which the women asked Bernadette to ask the Lady if they may accompany the child to the Grotto each day of the fifteen. Bernadette complied, and the Lady responded, *"They may come with you, they and others too. I wish to see many come."*[80] As she spoke these words, she disappeared, leaving behind only the light which eventually dissipated as well. The entire event lasted about an hour.

While walking home, the two women bombarded Bernadette with questions, to which Bernadette provided answers. There was a period of silence before Bernadette took hold of Antoinette's arm and said, "You know, Antoinette, the Lady looked at you for a long time and smiled at you." The excitement of hearing those words was something that Antoinette would never forget.

On her arrival home, Bernadette recounted the entire story to her family while Antoinette and Madame Milhet told everyone they met about what they had witnessed. They were convinced that Bernadette was seeing the Lady and that provided hope to many people of Lourdes. Upon hearing of the account, Louise decided that she would no longer oppose Bernadette in keeping the promise she had made to the Lady.

Thursday was also market day in Lourdes. Consequently, there were many strangers in town that also were exposed to the story of the apparitions for the first time. By nightfall, the story had spread over the mountains and all the way to the coast.

Friday, February 19, 1858
Morning – The Fourth Apparition

Reaction to the young girl's vision was certainly mixed throughout the area, though clearly "an electric current, and irresistible power from which no one could escape, appeared to have roused up the entire population at the word of an ignorant shepherd girl."[81]

Aunt Bernarde was not enthralled by Madame Milhet's sudden interest in her godchild but remained relatively silent about her feelings, instead suggesting that Bernadette bring something blessed with her to the Grotto. Bernadette asked her aunt if she would ask Aunt Lucile for her sodalist's candle. Bernarde complied and the child decided to carry the candle to the Grotto on each of the remaining days.

Bernadette had unwittingly become the talk of the town. "Nothing else was talked of anywhere, in the streets, in the taverns, in family circles, in public assemblies, among the poor and the rich, the clergy and laity; and, of course, there were all sorts of opinions about those wonderful events."[82]

Largely unaware of the talk around town, Bernadette walked to church and by 5:30 AM was seated in the pew attending daily Mass. Following Mass, Bernadette, Bernarde, and Louise stopped by Madame Milhet's house and from there they all left for Massabielle. By the time they arrived at the Grotto, at least a hundred people were already assembled. Louise "was much perturbed when she saw how many people had taken the trouble to come there on account of her daughter."[83] Bernadette simply knelt on a flat rock and began to pray the Rosary, falling into ecstasy as soon as she gazed upon the vision of the Lady. Those present witnessed "waves of joy" passing over her face and "thrills of happiness" that made her entire body tremble.[84] Bernadette "always began by making most graceful salutations before the Apparition; then she made the sign of the cross in a manner so noble, respectful and devout, that those who saw her said it was only in heaven that the sign of the cross was made like that. She then clasped her hands together and said her beads. The crowd of people contemplated with astonishment her striking loveliness. She did not look at all like herself. Her face was white and shining with glory; her looks seemed eager to penetrate the hollow of the rock. Now and then two tears would fall from her eyes upon her cheeks. The crowd could look at nothing but her: but they kept exclaiming; 'she sees!' She did see, but her eyes were fixed only on the Lady, who appeared just the same as she did the first time, with her white dress and veil, her blue girdle or sash, with the yellow roses on her bare feet, and with a look of unspeakable tenderness. She bowed her head and smiled, then made the sign of the cross with the golden crucifix hanging from the rosary, and with her hands clasped together, appeared to tell the beads."[85]

Bernadette leaned forward with her arms spread wide. Her lips moved, and a smile appeared on her face. It was then that she "heard shouting, confused voices that challenged each other and clashed together. It was like a thousand angry people shouting. It was horrible. The loudest voice shouted, 'Save yourself! Save yourself!' ...The Lady raised her head and frowned, looking in the direction of the river. Then the voices fled in all directions."[86]

Satan is God's antithesis and as such he despises Jesus. Moreover, Satan fears Mary, the mother of Jesus, the woman who will ultimately destroy him. That message was delivered at the beginning of time and is noted in the Book of Genesis. At the very instant of the fall of Adam and Eve, God foretold that Satan's ultimate defeat will come at the hands of a woman. "I will put enmity between you and the woman, and between your offspring and hers..."[87] God continued, "the woman will crush your head." The devil, therefore, fears Mary and "loathes the fact that his ultimate defeat will come at the hands of a lowly handmaiden."[88] In a sense, Mary, the Queen of Humility, has replaced the prideful Lucifer in God's Kingdom, and now on earth, even a glance and a frown from Heaven's Queen sends the devil scurrying.

Louise grew frightened, shouting, "Oh, God! Please don't take my child."[89] Still others commented at the child's radiant beauty. *The Lady thanked Bernadette for coming and promised to have revelations*

46

for her during future visits. The experience lasted about a half hour and Bernadette, rubbing her eyes as she emerged from ecstasy, rose, "went up to her mother and flung herself into her arms."[90]

Evening

By this time, even some newspapers began to carry accounts of Bernadette's visions. Though many of the major papers of Paris were more occupied with coverage of the impending trial of Felice Orsini, the Italian revolutionary and leader of the Carbonari who attempted to assassinate French Emperor Napoleon III, local papers began to report on the events taking place at the Grotto. The evening edition of the *Lavedan*, an anti-clerical newspaper widely circulated in Lourdes, created its own account of the events, blending fact with fiction. The paper described Bernadette and her companions as petty thieves who, when caught by the landowner trying to steal wood from his property, ran to the confines of the Grotto to escape prosecution. The same article, however, did not mention "buffoonery or comedy" when describing the visions. It reported, "We do not propose to repeat the dozen and one versions which are already current on the matter. Let us say only that every morning the young girl goes to pray at the entrance to the Grotto, carrying a candle in her hand and escorted by more than five hundred people. There one can watch her passing from a state of contemplation and gentle smiles into a state of pronounced ecstasy. Tears roll from her motionless eyes, which remain fixed on that spot at the Grotto where she believes she sees the Blessed Virgin. We propose to keep our readers informed concerning the progress of this affair, which finds new believers every day." [91]

While unable to suggest outright buffoonery, the writer was content to suggest that Bernadette may have suffered from a mental illness and settled on an overall tone of sympathy towards her. The *Lavedan* referred to Bernadette as "this poor visionary" and wrote "All indications suggest that this poor young girl is suffering from catalepsy."[92]

Scientifically, catalepsy is a medical condition characterized by a trance or seizure with a loss of sensation and consciousness accompanied by rigidity of the body. The free thought of materialism popularized at the time, however, inspired a fierce hope that science could explain everything, even things of the supernatural.

Other than sow seeds of gossip, the article neither discouraged those who were predisposed to believe in the reality of Bernadette's visions, nor change the minds of those who believed her to be insane. Many of them went to Massabielle to either pray or be entertained. Rather than look objectively at the facts, the gossip-mongers considered any type of investigation a waste of time. Even fifty-year-old Abbé Dominique Peyramale, who was urged by his parishioners to go to the Grotto, steadfastly refused, saying, "We do not yet know whether it is a miracle, imagination or deceit. The presence of a priest at Massabielle now would be premature. We should risk deceiving the people. We must wait."[93] Monseigneur Bertrand Laurence, Bishop of Tarbes, would later approve of Abbé Peyramale's decision as prudent.

Abbe Dominique Peyramale – Pastor of Bernadette's church in Lourdes. It was Peyramale who asked Bernadette to ask the name of the Lady who Bernadette claimed was appearing to her. Her answer, I am the Immaculate Conception, sent shivers through his body.

Those who sought the truth rather than participate in gossip, however, took note of the events of the past week and decided to investigate the case. Among the latter group were Dr. Pierre-Romaine Dozous, attorney Dufo, and Magistrate Pougat. Skeptical but honest, they agreed to examine the facts "with scrupulous objectivity."[94]

The Grotto Affair, as the recent events were now known, even drew the attention of the civil authorities. Monsieur Vital Dutour, the Imperial Prosecutor; Monsieur Gerald August Lacadé, the Mayor of Lourdes; Monsieur Dominique Jacomet, the Police Commissioner; and Monsieur Baron Massy, Prefect of the Department, followed the affair with the deepest concern and agreed to dispatch a number of "observers" to the Grotto with the intention of detaining Bernadette if she threatened the peace in any way.

Saturday, February 20, 1858
The Fifth Apparition
Early Morning

Jean-Baptiste Estrade and Henri Lasserre arrived at the Grotto at Massabielle at about dawn and were surprised to see that about four to five hundred people were waiting for the girl to arrive in anticipation of the day's vision. There was a steady din of private conversation which turned silent upon the arrival of Bernadette.

Approximately 6:30 AM

Louise accompanied her visionary daughter to the Grotto, arriving at approximately 6:30 in the morning. Bernadette was unfazed by the size of the crowd approaching, as if she herself was a mere spectator to the events about to unfold. Arriving at the Grotto, she simply reached for her rosary and began to pray. Soon, however, a transfiguration seemed to take place within her. Bernadette trembled as she appeared in conversation with an invisible friend. Many in the crowd heard nothing and her mother, standing nearby, began to cry. "I don't recognize my own child anymore," she mumbled through her tears. "I don't know where my head is…"[95]

As her vision of the Lady faded, Bernadette "seemed to awaken from a dazzling dream,"[96] and immediately, albeit hurriedly, began to reply to the many questions from the assembled. "Yes, the Lady spoke to me," Bernadette said. *"She was kind enough to teach me word by word a certain prayer specially for her."* When pressed to repeat the prayer that others might recite it, the visionary replied with "charming embarrassment, 'No, I can't do that. I don't think the Lady would allow it.'"[97]

Bernadette was happy and carefree as she walked home. She was greeted by her aunt, Basile Casterot, who expressed displeasure at the number of people talking about her niece. She warned the child not to return to the Grotto, but Bernadette said that she was not concerned about the talk and she invited Aunt Basile to accompany her to Massabielle the following day. It was the invitation for which Basile waited and she tried hard not to let the excitement of the invite show. "All right," Basile replied, "but let's go earlier or later, when there are not so many people."[98]

Sunday, February 21, 1858
The Sixth Apparition

Even before the sun could fully illuminate the dawn, hundreds, perhaps as many as one thousand people, awaited the arrival of Bernadette to the Grotto. They included the faithful and the curious alike. Many jockeyed for a position that would afford the greatest opportunity to see the child. Others simply huddled to protect themselves from the chilly morning air. The more adventurous rested on tree limbs or clung to rocks while the less spirited found a seat on the mist-dampened slopes of Massabielle. A steady din of prayer or idle chatter arose from the crowd and many grew impatient from the inconvenience of waiting on the glacial landscape in the morning chill.

It may have seemed a long time for the anticipatory crowd, but it was only a matter of minutes before Bernadette arrived, accompanied by her mother. Wearing her white hooded mantle, the child seemed to ignore the crowd, striding naturally through the assembled, which parted to allow for her unmolested passage. She approached the Grotto, knelt on her flat rock and began to pray before the massive rock formation. Bernadette moved the beads of her rosary through the fingers of her left hand, while in her right she held her aunt's lighted candle. Within a few moments she became radiant, alerting the crowd to the presence of the Lady. Bernadette's mouth was half opened with admiration and her eyes fixed on the vision before her. Though she was "wholly absorbed in contemplating the apparition, she was in some degree conscious of what passed around her. Thus, it happened at one time that her wax candle went out, and she immediately held it to the person nearest her to light it again."[99]

Someone in the crowd reached to touch with a stick the wild rose bush that adorned the rock formation near which the Lady stood. With a look of alarm, Bernadette quickly made a sign for him to stop, thinking that the Lady might be hurt. The onlooker complied.

What to the crowd seemed like a young girl in quiet conversation with herself was, in reality, a miraculous vision with the power to transform Bernadette visibly and emotionally. As before, the Lady's arrival was announced to Bernadette by the light, always the light, visible only to Bernadette and which seemed to softly illuminate the niche and the rock like gold. The light became the vision, standing upright with her feet resting on the wild briar. On that morning, as she had before, the Lady smiled a reassuring smile and bowed. Then, making the sign of the cross, led the child in prayer.

Within the crowd, Henri Lasserre noticed a distinct difference in Bernadette's appearance from the moment before to the moment that the vision appeared. "It's like the dawn at Bastsurgueres," he noted. "At first we cannot see the sun because it is hidden by the Jer, but we see its reflection on our slopes and we know that it is there."[100]

51

Among the spectators on that chilly morning was Dr. Dozous, who had come once again with the hope of using science to "demolish with a well-chosen word or two all this puerile set-up of pathological mysticity."[101] He observed Bernadette's every move as if conducting a scientific experiment on human behavior and took meticulous notes of his observations. The doctor took particular note of Bernadette's facial transformation noticed by all that were close enough to her and indicating that she was now in touch with the apparition. Dr. Dozous wrote, "I was now studying Bernadette's every movement with the closest attention. In particular I wanted to know the state of her circulation and the state of her respiration during the trance. I therefore took one of her arms and placed my finger on the radial artery: the pulse was steady and the respiration was normal. There was nothing in her condition to indicate any abnormal excitement of a hysterical character. When I released her arm, Bernadette rose and went forward a little towards the Grotto. Soon I saw that her face, which, up to then, had shown nothing but perfect happiness, was now clouded over..."[102]

The Lady's eyes left Bernadette for a moment and focused her gaze above the child's head and into the crowd in the distance. "Why are you so sad," Bernadette asked in a faltering voice when the Lady's eyes returned to her. The Lady's sadness touched Bernadette deeply and a tear rolled from each of her eyes, resting on her cheeks. *"Pray for sinners,"* was all the Lady said, though the expression of goodness and peace on her face was enough to reassure Bernadette, whose countenance brightened once again. Then the Lady was gone.

Bernadette's features returned to normal and the crowd of people rushed Bernadette hoping for a first-hand account of what took place during the vision. One woman asked, "Is she as beautiful as that?" pointing to some stunning women from her group. "Oh! They cannot compare with her!" Bernadette responded without hesitation but with the innocence of a child.

Those who made up the majority of the crowd spoke among themselves of the morning's events. Though each had his own opinion of what took place, the number of skeptics among them began to diminish. Once dispersed, they went from door-to-door telling about the miraculous happenings at the Grotto of Massabielle. The reaction was mixed and the debate over what had occurred continued.

Evening
The First Interrogations

Bernadette, Toinette, and Louise spoke of the Lady for the balance of the morning and that evening the family attended Vespers. As they departed the church, Bernadette, who wore a white cloak which, along with her other clothing, was clean and respectable even though of poor quality, was swarmed by people asking questions. In the midst of the confusion Bernadette tried to make her way home, but as she moved slowly through the crowd, the child felt a hard tap on her shoulder. Turning around, she saw that it was Constable Callet, an armed police officer. "What do you want with me,"[103] the child asked. "Bernadette Soubirous, I have orders to take you to the home of the Commissioner of Police. Follow me,"[104] The crowd around Bernadette at once grew indignant. They followed the child and her captor to the home of the Commissioner, which was just a short distance from the church.

The first to greet Bernadette was a woman. *"Abbé Pène wants to see you,"* she told the child. Bernadette insisted that she did not know him, but the woman replied simply, "He's a priest, you must obey him."[105] Abbé Pène lived in the Commissioner's house and was first to question Bernadette. She was confused as to why a priest would be living in the same house as the Commissioner who jailed her father a year earlier for allegedly stealing a bag of flour. For his part, Abbé Pène thought he might trip Bernadette up so that he could prove she was lying about her visions. Speaking of the Lady's promise to grant Bernadette happiness in the next life, a promise that the Lady made to Bernadette three days earlier, Pène said, "So Bernadette, now you can play all you want. You can put on airs. You can do what you want and not be afraid about your salvation." The child smiled. "Oh, that's not it at all. She'll make me happy only if I'm good," she replied.[106] The curate questioned

Bernadette further and was rather impressed with her responses. He was unable to confuse her as he anticipated he might.

Police Commissioner Dominique Jacomet was an impressive man. At thirty-six years of age, he was tall and thin, but with a rather athletic build. The last time Bernadette had seen Jacomet he wore his uniform and arrested her father after François was falsely accused of stealing flour. Today, however, he was dressed in civilian clothing. "Follow me," he bellowed as he grabbed Bernadette by the arm, leading her outside and around the corner toward the town hall. "We're going to show you the inside of a prison..." Bernadette was surprisingly calm and showed no fear as they entered the town hall. Jacomet locked the door behind them. "So you're the one who goes to Massabielle every day?" he said rather warmly.

Initially, Commissioner Jacomet treated Bernadette with benevolence, believing that his interrogation methods were superior to those of others. Jacomet was highly intelligent and most conscientious. He was also arrogant and cunning. He had no tolerance for matters of faith, believing instead only in things that he could see and prove. "So it seems that you see a beautiful Lady at the Massabielle Grotto. Tell me all about it."[107] It was at this time that a tax inspector, Jean-Baptiste Estrade entered the room and sat quietly to observe the interrogation. Described by some as one of the most important and intelligent personages in Lourdes, Estrade, the District Customs and Excise Officer for Lourdes, exhumed an air of confidence. His coiffured mustache and imperial bestowed a look of significance. Further, Estrade lived with Jacomet and the two had developed a friendship that enabled Estrade to act as the unofficial entrée to the Commissariat.

Bernadette sat with her hands crossed on her knees and her head bent slightly forward. To Estrade, the child appeared to be about ten or eleven years old. He noticed a plumpness to her face as well as a glance that "suggested both great simplicity and great gentleness." As Bernadette began retelling the story of the first vision, her voice seemed to Estrade both loud and sympathetic while her story was remarkably detailed. The two men questioned Bernadette even longer. Their pace was quick and their questions thorough. There was also an occasional kick on the door, some more violent than others. Each was followed by a voice threatening to break the door down if Bernadette wasn't released. The interruptions only strengthened the inquisitor's resolve.

Jacomet questioned the girl on every aspect of her apparitions, her reactions, and those of her family, the Lady's appearance and dress, the comments of others who accompanied her to the Grotto and many other questions. For about an hour he questioned her, recording every word on his note pad. Like Abbé Pène before him, he tried to trip her up, change her answers, catch her in a lie, but after an hour he couldn't and that frustrated him. He began to approach his questions with more determination, taking on a very different tone than he had prior; referring to the child as a flirt and a harlot.

Jacomet very often feigned anger, playing good cop, bad cop with his colleague who typically joined in on such questioning. But this was different. The Commissioner was truly angry. It wasn't a sham. "This little snip of a girl was irritating! Her simplicity left nothing to get a hold on. Jacomet hated to lose. He threatened with his eyes and with his hands: 'You make everyone chase after you. You want to become a little wh...'"[108] All the while, Estrade listened and "observed with more and more astonishment, the modest and invincible self-possession of this little girl. She was naturally very timid and confused before strangers; but in all that concerned the apparitions, she showed very unusual strength of mind and determined affirmation."[109]

Referring to his notes, Jacomet repeated many of the same questions, hoping to catch Bernadette in a lie or at least an inconsistent answer. He pretended to read her answers from his notes, creating discrepancies from the recorded word. Bernadette, however, corrected him each time, insisting that she had in fact said something else. "No, sir. You've got that down wrong. I said a white robe with a blue sash," or "No, sir. I said sixteen or seventeen years old."[110]

Jacomet grew even more frustrated with his inability to trip up his young detainee and his agitation became more pronounced. "I know what you're up to, young lady. This story of yours is pure invention. You've learned it by heart."[111] His accusations confused Bernadette. Jacomet continued, "What! Do you mean to say that no one told you on the sly to say that the Virgin had appeared to you at Massabielle?"[112] "No, sir, no one,"[113] Bernadette replied. The Commissioner then ordered

Bernadette to stay away from the Grotto, but the child resisted. "No, sir. I can't promise you that. I have already promised the Lady I would go back."[114]

The defiance caused Jacomet to jump to his feet shouting, "Very well, if you don't promise me not to return to Massabielle, I will call my *gendarmes* [armed police officers] and have you put in prison."[115] Bernadette said nothing. At this, Estrade took his turn interrogating the child, concluding with similar results.

"Outside, the crowd that had followed Bernadette to the town hall, including several quarrymen, became indignant and, not knowing what was happening to the child, spoke in a menacing manner. François Soubirous had joined those waiting outside the town hall. The others goaded him into kicking in the door. He worked himself up to a frenzy at the words of the crowd. 'The Commissioner is wrong,' they said. 'He hasn't the right to question your daughter without you being present!' All the while they pushed him closer to the front near the door saying, 'Go on in, if you're a man!'"[116] Soubirous kicked on the door, many times, hard until it opened.

The Commissioner, meanwhile, was just about finished with Bernadette, telling her she could go as he walked her to the door. That is when François Soubirous came face-to-face with Jacomet, simultaneously losing his nerve. Responding to Jacomet's command, Soubirous identified himself as the little girl's father. Jacomet was in luck. "Oh, it's you, is it? I was just about to send for you." He warned François to see to it that this foolishness stop. Soubirous explained his position noting that he too wished for a stop to the affair. "For three or four days now our house hasn't been our own, sir," he said. "We don't know how to get rid of the people. My wife and I are both sick and tired of it. We'll certainly take good care that Bernadette doesn't go to Massabielle again."[117]

Once alone, Jacomet and Estrade marveled at the extraordinary nature of the child's story. Though to Jacomet, the vividness of her recall still conjured a sense that the story was contrived and memorized. Regardless of the merits of the young girl's story, Jacomet did celebrate his success in frightening François Soubirous into agreeing to prevent Bernadette from going to the Grotto. Still, his profession had instilled in him a certain skepticism that made him distrust everyone and everything.

Despite Estrade's favorable impression of Bernadette, who was quick to point out that the child's words never showed contradiction but rather implied sincerity, Jacomet ordered his officers to keep an eye on the child's every move.

As they returned home, François forbade Bernadette to go to the Grotto again. "But Father, she said, when I go there, it is not entirely of my own accord. At certain times there is something within me which calls and draws me irresistibly thither."[118] But François persisted, explaining that Commissioner Jacomet was an all-powerful man that would send the entire family to prison. "Now don't disobey me for the first time in your life,"[119] François intoned.

Monday, February 22, 1858
Morning

Bernadette's disappointment at once again being prohibited from keeping her promise to the Lady must have been obvious, because as she prepared to leave for school, her parents felt it necessary to issue another stern warning. "Go straight to school without straying off the path either to left or right."[120] The well-defined implication was that under no circumstances was Bernadette allowed to go to the Grotto. François knew all too well how easy it was to land in jail and he had no predisposition to go back there. Saddened by the knowledge that no matter who she obeyed, she would have to disappoint somebody, the child departed the cachot and went directly to school.

If Bernadette didn't sense annoyance from her parents, her greeting from the Sisters at the Hospice School certainly left no doubt. Not only were they disturbed by the stories of visions at the Grotto, but they suspected that the entire affair might be the work of the Devil. When Bernadette offered a strenuous defense of the reality of her visions, the nuns called her a liar. One of the nuns said, "You are a wicked child, you are keeping up a disgraceful carnival there, in the holy time of Lent,"[121] embarrassing Bernadette in front of all her schoolmates. Embarrassment was the least of Bernadette's problems, however. The real dilemma was whether Bernadette should obey her parents by refraining from going to the Grotto or keep her promise to the Lady by returning.

About 12:00 Noon

When the signal came indicating the lunch dismissal, Bernadette began her walk home as she did most days. Though, unlike most days, she did so that day with a heavy heart. As the church bells tolled out the Angelus, Bernadette was overcome with the irresistible urge to go to the Grotto. She was figuratively stopped by what she could only describe as "an invisible barrier"[122] that overcame her and directed her toward the Grotto. Bernadette's change of direction was not lost on the men that Jacomet dispatched to watch her every move and they encountered her near the mill in which she was born, demanding to know her destination. She answered simply, "To the Grotto."[123] The child walked, even ran some of the way, overcome with hope and joy. Still, the closer she got to her destination, the more those feelings diminished.

Many of the throngs that had assembled that morning in antici-pation of her visit had left, but a great many remained at this crossroad, hoping for the child's arrival. They were not disappointed as they saw Bernadette walking down the path toward them. Now accompanied by two of Jacomet's policemen and a group of children, the young visionary did not seem at all nervous, prompting one observer to remark, "She walks as though she were quite alone."

At the Grotto, Bernadette immediately fell to her knees and prayed for a very long time, all the while keeping her eyes fixed on the niche, but there was no vision of the Lady. No one in the disappointed crowd would see Bernadette's face glow this day. About one hundred people watched as a clearly heartbroken Bernadette stood, her eyes red from crying. She left for home saying, "I don't know how I've failed the Lady."[124]

The distraught child was invited to rest at the Savy mill. Em-manuélite Estrade, the tax inspector's sister, was one of the last to leave the Grotto. She stopped by the mill and questioned the disappointed visionary. Now, a skeptic might have reasoned, if the child "had been an imposter, she could as easily have pretended to see the apparition then, as before."[125] If that thought crossed anyone's mind, however, no one bothered to give it voice.

Upon Bernadette's return home, François sternly asked where she had been, never really doubting the answer. The child candidly spoke of all that had taken place, noting that it was the same power that drew her to the Grotto. Her parents were not so quick to dismiss her though, retreating instead to deep thought. Finally, François broke the uncomfortable silence. "Well, as it is so, and as some superior power has carried you on, I will not forbid you any longer to go to the Grotto, and I leave you quite free."[126] Bernadette was overjoyed as she returned to school for the afternoon session.

While Louise thought about what had just occurred at home, the perspiration on her brow became very visible. "Some laugh at us; others say my daughter's mad. Some even say we're getting paid for it. And there are people who talk about prosecuting us," Louise cried to no one in particular. But while she lamented, many in the community took the opportunity of the Lady of the Grotto's absence to tout the power of Jacomet, chiding that when the Lady found out the police were involved, she thought "she better make herself scarce and find another rock."[127] Jacomet and other officials were aware of the talk in the village and knew that they needed to keep the pressure on the Soubirouses if they wanted to achieve their goal of keeping the child from the Grotto. They immediately dispatched a police officer to the cachot to deliver word of a summons. François was still in Tarbes, so Louise responded to the knock at the door. "'The Imperial Prosecutor asks Bernadette Soubirous to appear at his house at six o'clock this evening,' the man announced."[128] Louise ran to get her cousin Sajous, who quickly dressed in his best attire and accompanied Louise and her daughter to the Maison Claverie where the Prosecutor lived.

6:00 PM
Second Interrogation

He rang the doorbell and stepped back as if afraid of who might appear. It was precisely six o'clock and Sajous was a bit concerned, but before he could utter a word, the maid opened the door. Sajous asked for the Prosecutor, noting that Bernadette and her mother were with him. Unsure of their purpose, the maid left them outside the door and fetched Vital Dutour. The prosecutor arrived a moment later, bearing a somewhat standoffish look about him. Normally a rather authoritative figure, tonight Dutour looked a bit nervous. His curly hair was fluffed and parted on the right side. It extended to his sideburns, which widened toward the earlobe forming a close-cut beard that covered his square chin. "'Are you her father?' Dutour inquired of Sajous. 'No, I'm her uncle and the owner of the house where she lives.' At that, Dutour directed Bernadette and Louise to follow him. To Sajous he said, 'You, stay here a while. They'll be released.'"[129] Indignant, Sajous walked to a nearby cafe. The vantage point allowed him an opportunity to relax and keep an eye on the window of the Prosecutor's office for any signs of the Soubirouses' release.

Imperial Prosecutor Vital Dutour was known to have a great respect for law and order. Austere and unbending, he fully intended to break Bernadette. He lit some candles in his office as he began his interrogation, which followed a prescribed plan intended to expose Bernadette's insincerity and convince her to refrain from going to the Grotto. He stood before them in full uniform while standing under a picture of French Emperor Napoleon III. Next to Dutour stood the Commander of the Gendarmerie.

The demonstration was meant to be intimidating and Dutour felt that the situation did not call for niceties. Looking directly at Bernadette, Dutour barked, "'People are beginning to talk about you, young lady. Is it your intention to continue your visits to the Grotto?' 'Yes, sir, I promised the Lady I would,' Bernadette responded boldly. 'I shall go there about twelve times still,' she continued. Dutour tried to convince Bernadette that her Lady didn't exist, but Bernadette's defense was immediate. 'I'm quite certain that she does, because I have seen her several times, and, then, she talked to me.' Becoming frustrated, Dutour's tone began to change, suggesting that the Sisters at the Hospice must be lying then when they claimed that Bernadette's visions were simply a child's imagination. 'If the Sisters at the Hospice had seen what I saw, they would believe just as I believe,'"[130] Bernadette retorted.

Louise was standing and shook with fear but Bernadette, also standing, calmly responded to each question as Dutour dutifully recorded her words with his fountain pen on a solitary piece of his office stationary. Then he re-read her words, which Bernadette found unrecognizable. "Sir, I did not tell you that,"[131] she protested. They argued, after which Dutour admitted that he might have been mistaken. This process was repeated continuously for an hour with the Prosecutor intentionally adding errors each time he recounted her words. He even pulled from a green case what he claimed were the notes the Police Commissioner took during his interrogation of Bernadette. Reading from that paper, Dutour tried the same trick, but the result was unaffected each time.

7:00 PM

Outside, Sajous grew tired of waiting idly and decided to take some action, the only action he felt he could take. He spoke to some quarrymen, explaining that Louise and Bernadette had been detained at the home of the Prosecutor. A large group was quickly assembled and together they walked back to Dutour's office, where they protested loudly outside his window.

Inside Dutour was thinking that he had misjudged the girl, having thought her a mere idiot before the interview began. She was, instead, cunning and self-assured, remaining calm even while under attack and facing threats. The Prosecutor was the one now under pressure and recognized that he was beginning to forget his skills. Failing in his plan to expose her as a fraud and a liar, he quickly shifted gears and resorted to plan B: examine motives and determine outside influences.

He questioned the money she received, but there was none. The special favors then. Still none. The hospitality offered by others. Nothing there. Dutour was beyond frustrated. He knew deep down that Bernadette, like François in the flour-theft incident, was guilty, but he was unable to prove his feeling. Everything else proving inadequate, Dutour turned to intimidation. It was all he had left. "'You are going to promise me not to return to the Grotto,' he yelled. 'I promised to go for two weeks,' the child replied. 'That promise, made to a woman no one has seen, means nothing. You mustn't go,' he quickly responded. On it went for another hour until finally Dutour, determined to win, summoned his wife who responded at once. 'Send word to the Commissioner to come fetch this little girl to have her sleep in jail,'"[132] he bluffed. Louise, whose sniffs and sobs had previously gone undetected by Dutour, now burst out with uncontrollable sobs. Dutour looked with surprise as Bernadette walked to her and whispered, "You are very kind to weep because we are going to jail. We haven't done anything wrong." Louise seemed to not hear. She was exhausted from standing for two hours and could take no more. She staggered and appeared to be falling when Dutour, in a condescending voice, offered them a chair. "'No,' Bernadette retorted, having detected the condescension in his tone, 'we would dirty them.'"[133] Louise was too weary to comprehend what was happening and took the chair that was offered. Bernadette, however, showed no such weakness as she sat cross-legged on the floor.

While Bernadette and her mother suffered the indignities within the Prosecutor's office, the noise generated by Sajous and the quarrymen that gathered outside in protest to Bernadette's detention was louder than before. They were now shouting, "Let them out!" while knocking on the windows and banging on the door. Dutour opened his window, leaned out and said, "Easy there! Come on!" Hardly words the crowd found intimidating. They continued to protest even louder.

Turning his attention back to Bernadette he warned that she was exciting the crowds, saying that the child must stop them from going to the Grotto. Not giving an inch, Bernadette replied, "'I don't ask them to come.' 'But you go!' he said in frustration. 'Yes,' she answered, 'but I made a promise.'"[134]

Dutour had nowhere to bring this conversation. He was back to where they had started and could take no more. He knew that he had no grounds on which to arrest the child, so he left his office for a moment, collected his thoughts, calmed his nerves and returned. "The Commissioner hasn't the time," he said. "This case is postponed till tomorrow. But it is understood, you are not to go back to that Grotto." "Sir," the child retorted, "I do not promise you that." In complete frustration, Dutour released them.

As they left the Prosecutor's house Sajous and the quarrymen wanted to know what had taken place. Together they walked to the cafe where the quarrymen offered to buy her a glass of white wine, as she preferred white to red.

Extraordinary, Dutour thought as he watched them disappear into the cafe. Tearing up his notes from the just-concluded interrogation, he took advantage of the opportunity to preserve whatever dignity he had left. He vowed to use Louise's "drunkenness" as the basis for his report that was due on March 1.

> "Bernadette belongs to a poor family," he wrote. "Her father was arrested in 1857 for aggravated theft. The moral character of the mother is just as questionable. It is common knowledge that this woman is a drunkard. The combination of these miserable people - their language, especially their morals and their reputation - was certainly of a nature to destroy all attractiveness; they inspire not only doubt but disgust. They are indeed unworthy go-betweens for her who is considered the pre-eminently pure being."

Even now, the nightmare had not ended. As they left the cafe, someone of the group noticed officer Callet, a decent policeman who lacked the arrogance of most public officials. He announced to the group of quarrymen that he was on his way to get Bernadette to bring her to the police station. When finally convinced that the case had been continued to Friday, Bernadette and her mother were allowed to return home.

The questioning continued at the cachot, as several people were assembled awaiting word of the evening's events. Elsewhere, word of what had taken place at the Prosecutor's home began to spread and become exaggerated. But things being said around town didn't concern the Soubirouses. They retired for the night, putting off tomorrow's problems until tomorrow.

Tuesday, February 23, 1858
The Seventh Apparition
Morning

Following morning Mass, Bernadette went immediately to the Grotto. Though still before sunrise, a crowd had already gathered and was even larger than it had been previously. Many in the crowd gasped as they saw Bernadette appear and they silently parted as she approached, allowing her to pass through unmolested. She wore her white capulet of coarse cloth and her black frock, replete with its patches, and was seemingly unaware of the mass of people as she made her way to the Grotto, knelt on her rock, and took her rosary from her pocket.

The rosary was firmly affixed between the fingers of her right hand and she held the lighted candle with her other. She blessed herself and almost immediately became "transfixed by a thrill of admiration and seemed to be born into a second life."[135] After that, sheer joy as her face was illuminated with various expressions. Though the masses could see and hear nothing, the women fell to their knees and the men removed their hats. Bernadette, however, for the seventh time could see the Lady clearly. The miraculous Vision looked down upon the child with "inexpressible sweetness and tenderness, [and] called her by her name, *'Bernadette!'* 'Here I am,' answered the happy child. *'I have a secret to tell you,'* said the Lady, *'which is for you alone, and concerns you alone. Will you promise me never to tell it to anyone in this world?'* 'I do promise you,' said Bernadette,'"[136] and the Lady imparted her secret. The Lady was not yet finished. *"And now, my child, go and tell the priests that I wish to have a chapel built here in my honor."*[137] With these words, the Lady vanished, leaving behind just a glow of light. Those observing saw that Bernadette's face resumed its usual appearance and they crowded around her hoping to find out what had transpired. Bernadette explained that the Lady had imparted a secret that she was not at liberty to disclose but that concerned only her. The other, she said, is for the priests and "I am going at once to tell it to them."[138]

Bernadette hurried back to town and went immediately to the house of Abbé Dominique Peyramale, her parish priest. Louise walked with Bernadette to the rectory and a small group from the Grotto followed them, curious as to what the child might tell the priest, but Bernadette alone entered the house.

Peyramale had not met Bernadette, but someone had pointed her out to him only a day or two prior. Though never having made her acquaintance, he was certainly aware of all the ruckus that she had been causing and was rather annoyed at her visit. "Are you not Bernadette, the daughter of the miller Soubirous?"[139] he asked in a rather stern voice. Bernadette acknowledged the fact and told him that she was sent by the Lady who appears to her at the Grotto of Massabielle. At the priest's request she recounted all the things that had occurred there, including the conversation that had taken place between her and the Lady just a short time ago. As she spoke, Peyramale couldn't help but admire the truthfulness of her character and her innocence, but did not allow his facial expressions to betray his innermost sense about her. Rather, he was indignant that the child would dare ask that he build a chapel at Massabielle based on the request of some unknown entity, even if the Lady wasn't a mere figment of the child's imagination.

"Those who believe you, imagine that [you are seeing] the Blessed Virgin Mary,"[140] he said, implying that he himself did not believe her. Bernadette was hurt but soldiered on. "'I do not know,' she responded, 'if it is the Blessed Virgin, but I see the vision as plainly as I see you, and she speaks to me as plainly as you do. And I come now to tell you from her, that she wishes a chapel to be built in her honor, at the rocks of Massabielle, where she appears to me.'"[141]

Abbé Peyramale did not know what to believe. He didn't want to discount the possibility that something miraculous was taking place, regardless of how unlikely it was. He also didn't want to encourage a child who, though sincere, might simply be deluded. The priest remained silent for a moment then said, "'If the Lady you tell me about is really the Queen of heaven, I shall be happy to do all in my power towards building her a chapel: but your word is no security. I am not obliged to believe you. I don't know who this Lady is; and before I can set about complying with her request, I want to know what right she has to make it. Ask her then to give me some proof of her power. You tell me that there is a wild rose bush under the feet of the apparition, which grows out of the rocks. We are now in the month of February. Tell her from me, to make that rose bush blossom, if she wishes for the chapel.'"[142] With that, he walked Bernadette to the door.

The priest's words to Bernadette, the demands that he made of the Lady on that day, were not unlike the demands made by the Bishop of Guadalupe, Mexico to Juan Diego some 357 years earlier. The response he would receive from the Lady was very much like the response of Jesus when a group of Jews asked the son of God to prove his divinity by offering a sign from heaven. No sign was given them. Neither was a sign given when they taunted Christ to "come down from the cross, and we will believe in you." Though more than eighteen hundred years have passed, does man still dare to prescribe the terms on which we shall condescend to believe? Is it any wonder then, that Peyramale's words would fuel the actions of Jacomet and many other government officials?

Afternoon

Bernadette headed off to school while Louise went straight home. Once there she was put off by the many visitors that were descending upon the cachot. One after another they arrived, asking questions about the young girl and her visions. Bernadette too was unable to find peace.

As she left school for the day, she was accosted by Anna Dupas, the wife of the town's hat maker. She told the child that her husband Dupas wanted a word with her and led Bernadette to their shop, where the hatter proceeded to berate the visionary in the back room. Anna's friends, meanwhile, gathered in the front of the shop. Unlike Dupas, they admired Bernadette and just hoped to talk to her. Anna, aware of Bernadette's frailty, offered her an apple, but the child politely and steadfastly refused, despite Anna's insistence.

From the hat shop, Bernadette was whisked to Place Marcadeal, the home of Eugenie Reval. Eugenie was the sister of Germaine, the foster-child at Bartrès that Bernadette friended. At Place Marcadeal there were new faces and more questions about the visions. As it became evident that Bernadette was growing wearier she was allowed to leave.

François had been at work at the stable a bit earlier in the afternoon when Dominiquette Cazenave, the sister of François' boss, "ordered" him to bring his daughter to see her. From her tone, François knew he had no choice. Dominiquette was troubled by the apparitions and intended to expose Bernadette as a fraud.

François had been waiting impatiently for the child to arrive home and as soon as she entered the cachot, he led her to see his employer's sister. Dominiquette met them in the narrow alley leading to her home. Once inside, she began to question Bernadette in a hostile manner, not allowing the child to fully answer her questions before cutting her off with a new one. That suited Bernadette, who by this time was very tired and providing very short answers anyway. After just a few minutes, Bernadette tuned out. On short-order, Dominiquette dismissed both the child and François, wondering why anyone would bother to listen to "that clown."

Wednesday, February 24, 1858
The Eighth Apparition
Morning

In addition to the throngs of women who routinely gathered at the Grotto each morning, there were many men who came to observe the Grotto proceedings. On that day, they included Jean-Baptiste Estrade, who came with his sister Emmanuélite, Dr. Dozous, Town Councilor Dufo and retired army officer Monsieur de La Fitte, along with a host of others. Estrade, the tax official who had interrogated Bernadette at the Police Commissioner's office just a few days earlier, had sensed a sincerity about the child and was determined to go to the Grotto to see for himself what his sister and so many others in town had been reporting. He arrived well before dawn and maneuvered to a spot as close to the child's rock as possible.

Bernadette arrived at the Grotto and once again found a large crowd already assembled. She moved through it with ease, locating the stone on which she would pray. She knelt on this same stone each time she went to the Grotto and it had by this time become an object of respect by the large crowds that gathered each day. As on each of the prior visits, Bernadette knelt, and reached into her pocket for her beads. Holding her lighted candle, she began to pray the Rosary, falling into a state of ecstasy very soon thereafter when the Lady appeared to her.

Jean-Baptiste Estrade took note as the child's appearance dramatically altered. Her face "lighted up with some unknown brightness; and she kept her eyes, filled with joy and happiness, upon the niche in the rock."[143] Estrade also looked up but saw nothing unusual. "Yet, when he beheld the transfiguration of the child, all his prejudices and objections at once passed away, and he felt certain that some mysterious being was there. Bernadette was no longer like herself. Her posture, her gestures, the way she made the sign of the cross, all had a certain dignity and grandeur about them more than human."[144] Estrade strained to hear the conversation that Bernadette was having with the invisible being. He even held his breath so as to hear better. Though he heard nothing, "Bernadette listened almost with adoration, mixed with unbounded joy and delight. Sometimes, however, a shade of sadness passed over her countenance, but the prevailing expression was that of great joy."[145]

Bernadette told the Lady that the parish priest asked for proof of Her authority in the form of a blossoming rose bush. The Lady smiled but rather than answer, said, *"Pray for sinners."*[146] Then she ordered Bernadette *"to climb up to the farthest end of the Grotto."*[147] As Bernadette moved forward, the Lady cried out *"Penance, penance, penance."*[148] Bernadette repeated her words as she walked the fifteen feet to the end of the Grotto on her knees. Once there, the Lady told Bernadette another secret meant only for her. The Lady asked Bernadette if she would kindly *"get down on her knees and kiss the ground as a penance for sinners."* Many people heard Bernadette respond, "yes," though no one else in the crowd heard the question. Then the Lady asked, *"if this would bother her?"* to which the young girl replied "no." Once again, no one heard the question.

Suddenly "a great sadness seemed to come over the face of the child, and those present could see tears running down her cheeks as the Lady told her to *'pray to God for the conversion of sinners.'*"[149] Then, with tears still welled up in her eyes, the visionary's mood lightened. "She burst out in sweet sounding ripples of laughter,"[150] according to bystander Jacquette Pène, the sister of curate Pène.

Without hesitation, Bernadette walked along on her knees, falling prostrate on her face, kissing the earth. As she rose to a kneeling position, Aunt Lucile cried out and fainted, interrupting Bernadette, who was just about to bow to the ground once again. Turning to Lucile, the child said in a reassuring yet reproved tone, "Aunt, it's not good to get all worked up like that!"[151] Bernadette turned back toward the Grotto, but her Lady was no longer there.

Bernadette arose, filled with disappointment at the premature departure of the Lady. She looked around the back of the Grotto hoping to find something resembling a blooming rose bush. There was nothing but a few blades of grass and the rocks. She rejoined her family and began to walk off with them, telling Lucile that she shouldn't accompany her to Massabielle anymore. After taking only a few steps, Bernadette's admonition was interrupted by the booming voice of a man yelling, "Make way!"

At that moment, "a sergeant from the Lourdes garrison pushed his way through the crowd and tapped Bernadette on the shoulder. 'What do you think you're up to, my little joker,'"[152] he shouted in a voice loud enough to be heard by many of the onlookers. Bernadette didn't reply, acknowledging the officer's presence neither by word nor glance. Not one to be ignored, particularly by a child and in the presence of such a large crowd, the officer turned to his men saying, "To think that this is the nineteenth century and to see such stupidity!"[153]

Immediately Bernadette departed the Grotto with her family. She needed to report to Abbé Peyramale the events of the morning. It seemed to Bernadette that the Abbé was concerned only with the Lady's response to his request for a blooming rose bush and Bernadette had to deliver the unfortunate news that she had received no response to his request.

Late Morning to Afternoon

Many onlookers and other curious townspeople made their way to Bernadette's home where, once again, the Soubirouses had a house full of visitors awaiting the arrival of Bernadette. Bernadette's walk home, however, was once again interrupted many times by the curious and faithful alike calling her into their houses where they would ask all types of questions about the Apparitions. One such man, Mr. Dufo, was one of the most eminent lawyers in Lourdes. He invited the child into his home, asking many questions about the Lady.

Bernadette finally arrived home hoping to get some rest, but those that awaited barraged her with hundreds of questions. Tired though she was, the child patiently responded to each query.

When all except a neighbor and a relative had gone, a stranger came to the cachot and questioned Bernadette most specifically, wanting to know every detail. He could tell by the sparse surroundings and broken furniture that the family was indeed very poor and was moved that such a favored child would have so little. "I am rich," he said, "allow me to help you."[154] He opened his purse on the table, exposing a great deal of gold. Bernadette was very upset. "I will have nothing, Sir, take that back again,"[155] she said, pushing the purse towards him. When he noted that the donation was for her parents, François said sternly, "Neither Berna-dette nor ourselves will take anything."[156] The more the stranger insisted, the more steadfast the Soubirouses became in their refusal.

No one knew this generous man, but it is highly likely that he was an agent of the government hoping to prove that the Soubirouses were profiting from all this talk of a Lady. If that was the intent, however, the government was surely disappointed with the outcome! François and Louise were equally exhausted by the pace of recent events, and, when finally left alone, Louise simply burst into tears.

Thursday, February 25, 1858
The Ninth Apparition
Morning

There was nary a person left in Lourdes that had not heard of the strange happenings at the Grotto causing a constant stream of people to gather there each day in anticipation of Bernadette's visit. Most hoped for a miracle though none had been promised. All witnessed the expression of utter joy that swept the young girl's face each time her vision appeared.

Though today would be another disappointment in terms of delivering a miraculous rose bloom, it did deliver a powerful display, perhaps one even foretold in the Psalm sung at Mass earlier that morning. "Thou art the God that doest wonders. Thou hast made thy power known among the nations....The waters saw thee, O God, the waters saw thee; and they were afraid, and the depths were troubled."[157]

Bernadette arrived at the Grotto at the usual pre-dawn hour. Thousands lined the route and filled the Grotto area and each appeared thrilled at first sight of the child. The men removed their hats as she passed and virtually all knelt at the same time that Bernadette knelt on her rock to pray. Immediately, she fell into a state of rapturous ecstasy at the sight of the Lady, who, as usual, stood in the niche above the cave opening, Her feet resting on the wild rose bush. *"'My child,'* she said to Bernadette, *'I am going to confide a last secret to you, for yourself, and concerning yourself alone, which you must never tell to anyone in the world, any more than the two others.'"*[158] After imparting the third secret to Bernadette, the Lady continued, *" 'Go and drink and wash yourself at the spring and eat the green you will find growing there.' "*[159]

Without taking her eyes off the Lady, the child began to walk toward the Gave River to an area where the waters were rushing over stones and broken rocks, since the balance of the site had no water flowing. The distressed look on Bernadette's face was obvious to all that could see her, when suddenly the Lady interrupted her stride, redirecting her to a different spot on the dry land. *" 'Don't go there,'* She said, *'I did not tell you to drink at the Gave; go to the fountain, it is here.' "*[160] At that, the Lady stretched forth her powerful hand and pointed to the same corner of the Grotto to which Bernadette had climbed upon her knees the day before. The child could see no spring, but immediately obeyed. She stooped and began scraping the dry, dusty earth with her fingers, making a small hole in the ground. A little moisture appeared in the hole. Bernadette continued to dig until the moisture became muddy water. She scooped a bit with her hand and tried to drink but spit it out. Someone shouted, *"'That's enough now. It ought to be stopped,'"*[161] but Bernadette didn't hear. Again, she tried to drink the muddy water and again was repulsed by its taste. Determined to obey the Lady's command, she tried a third and finally a fourth time until she was able to forcibly swallow some of the watery mud.

Bernadette then scooped more of the dirty water and smeared it on her face. Then, rising, the child walked over to the golden saxifrage plant that was growing wildly a couple of steps away, plucked a few leaves and ate them. Satisfied that she had complied with the Lady's instructions, she turned, faced the crowd and descended from the Grotto.

The crowd was appalled. This was such a departure from serene events of days past. Some in the crowd called for her arrest. Many sobbed while others simply laughed at her, causing her Aunt Bernarde to wipe the mud from the child's face with a handkerchief and to escort her away from the disbelieving crowd and back to safety.

On the way back home, Bernarde and Louise questioned the child, not knowing what to make of these latest antics. Bernadette explained that the Lady asked her to drink water from the spring, to wash in it and to eat the plants. The child said she initially thought the Lady wanted her to wash in the river and eat the grass along the banks since there was no spring in the area, but "'she beckoned with her finger for me to go under the rock. I went and found a little muddy water, almost too little for me to hold in the hollow of my hand. Three times I threw it away, it was so dirty. On my fourth try I succeeded.'"[162]

Afternoon/Early Evening

Bernadette's departure from the Grotto did not bring an end to the strange events of the day. She was questioned by many people about her antics, on the way home and at the cachot. She was even summoned to the town hall, where Abbé Pène and Jean-Baptiste Estrade questioned her some more, pointing out that many people thought she was crazy. Bernadette's answers were consistent and precise. In short, she knew that sin is the saddest thing on earth and was willing to do anything the Lady asked to atone for it. To her, nothing after that mattered.

That afternoon, several people who remained in prayer at the Grotto at Massabielle noticed that a stream of water was flowing from the very spot where Bernadette had dug. Some of them tried to scoop and drink the water, which was leaving a clear mark in the dirt as it trickled toward the Gave eventually becoming one with the river. Each person was amazed as they had not noticed this stream before and yet, right before their disbelieving eyes, the flow of the water actually increased as they watched. By early evening, the trickle had become a rather substantial stream of clear water flowing freely into the Gave River. Word of the stream spread, and other folks visited the area, filling bottles that they carried back to town. Jeanne Montat offered some to her sick father. He and others who drank of it were overcome with a peaceful feeling.

Friday, February 26, 1858

Bernadette felt attracted to the Grotto, but Louise and François had renewed concern based on the latest warning from the authorities and the wild talk throughout the village about miraculous happenings resulting from the waters of Bernadette's spring. Louise in particular felt the order should be obeyed but refused to forbid Bernadette from going to the Grotto. Suddenly, Aunt Bernarde interjected, noting that she would herself attend if she were Bernadette. That is all the encouragement the child needed. She grabbed her hood and departed the cachot for the morning's pre-dawn Mass. It was the first Friday of Lent and the scripture reading, for the second straight day, could not have been more poignant to the events taking place at the Grotto. The words from the Book of Zechariah read, "On that day a fountain will be opened for the house of David and the inhabitants of Jerusalem, to purify from sin and uncleanness."[163]

Bernadette left for the Grotto immediately following Mass. The usual crowd followed her, and, once again, thousands were already assembled upon her arrival. Some called out to her saying, "'Here comes the saint!' Many even tried to touch her garments, considering everything holy that belonged to this privileged being."[164] She knelt on her rock to pray, holding her candle and her beads, but much to her chagrin, there was no apparition. The child was once again uncontrollably grief-stricken. While Bernadette lamented, trying to think of what she had done to offend the Lady, Louise worried out loud. "They're going to put us in jail."[165]

Though the Lady did not appear to Bernadette as the child had hoped, "it would seem as if the wonderful fountain was that day to bear witness by itself alone."[166] Word of the new freshwater stream was spreading quickly throughout Lourdes and the surrounding areas. Those who had hoped for a miracle were convinced that they had received one and were in a state of exaltation. The more skeptical of Lourdes were simply in disbelief and had no scientific explanation to offer that would justify the almost instantaneous creation of a new spring. Their mood was simply one of exasperation.

To this latter group belonged Commissioner Jacomet and Prosecutor Dutour. In fact, they were beyond exasperated, they were furious when they were told that the new stream that "suddenly welled up at the spot where Bernadette had scraped out her hollow was producing about 25,000 gallons of water every twenty-four hours."[167]

While authorities were trying to figure out how to control the uproar in Lourdes, more serious events began to unfold. It seemed Lourdes was beginning to unravel. Children of Bernadette's age were going "into hysterics at the Grotto. Certain inhabitants of Lourdes and the surrounding countryside seemed to have developed mental troubles. A peasant swore that he had 'heard voices' on returning to his cottage, whilst an innkeeper's servant was pretending to go into ecstasies."[168]

Though the Lady had not appeared at the Grotto that morning, Bernadette's story was still causing anxiety to others. Abbé Pomian, Fathers Serre and Pène, cantonal vicar Father Peyramale, and the parish priests of the district were being unreservedly assaulted. Those who believed in Bernadette's visions wanted them to immediately spread the word publicly throughout the region and beyond, while the disbelievers urged them to bring about an end to the babble by publicly denouncing the story. Though Father Peyramale knew that Bernadette was sincere, he still wondered if there was something else at play, hysteria perhaps, that was tricking the child. He called a meeting of the other priests, suggesting they adopt a position of "prudent reserve. 'It would be inopportune and very regrettable,' he said, 'if any of us were to show ourselves near the Grotto at the moment. If later on these apparitions should be confirmed as real, there will be people who will not hesitate to suggest that our premature taking of sides had something to do with the decision. If, on the other hand, the final decision goes against the reality of the apparitions, then people will laugh at what they call our discomfiture. Do not compromise yourselves one way or the other therefore, and guard against impulsive words.'"[169]

Meanwhile, a well-known quarryman by the name of Louis Bourriette heard of the miraculous spring flowing from the ground at the Grotto and asked his daughter to go get him some of the water from it. Almost twenty years prior, the fifty-four-year-old Bourriette had suffered damage to his right eye as the result of an injury sustained on the job when a blasting operation went horribly wrong.

Bourriette was severely injured but was actually rather lucky. His brother Joseph, who had been standing by Bourriette's side at the time of the mining blast, was killed instantly. Over the years Louis suffered great agonies of pain, and though his health was relatively restored, his eyesight worsened until he was essentially blind in his right eye. Bourriette lived in constant fear that he would lose the use of his left eye as well.

Dr. Dozous had been treating Bourriette since the 1839 accident and knew his eyesight would never be restored, and in fact suggested his condition would only get worse, adding to Bourriette's fears of one day being completely blind. "It is a well-known fact, corroborated by science," the doctor wrote in his notes, "that whenever an eye is injured by a flying object in an explosion, the shock engendered is always sufficient to lead to incurable blindness. Often it happens that the other eye, unable to escape the repercussion of that shock due to the sympathy which exists between the two eyes, is itself weakened and ends up blind too."[170] Since the day of the accident, because he had experienced further deterioration of the sight in his left eye with each passing year, Bourriette worried constantly about this possibility.

He also vowed, "as soon as Bernadette had scratched the soil of the Grotto leading to the appearance of the spring...that [he] would try and see if this water would cure [his] eye."

When his daughter finally arrived back home with the muddy water from the spring and handed it to him he knew his chance had come. As he bathed his damaged eye with the cool fountain water, Bourriette began to pray to "Our Lady of the Grotto," and humbly begged her to be with him as he did so. Almost immediately, Louis saw light, though it still appeared as though his eye was covered with a thin mist that prevented him from seeing clearly. He continued to bathe his eyes and before long, his sight was restored, and he could see perfectly, not only from his left eye, but also from his damaged right eye as well. Louis trembled all over.

Saturday, February 27, 1858
The Tenth Apparition
Morning

The crowd assembled at the Grotto was the largest yet. Bernadette arrived, hoping beyond hope that she would see the Lady. She prayed as always, kneeling upon her large flat rock. Among the crowd of onlookers was Antoine Clarens, the director of the secondary school in Lourdes. Curiosity was the reason for his first appearance. He witnessed the ecstasy but heard and saw nothing, save the glorious expression on Bernadette's face.

Back in town, Bourriette awoke from his night's sleep excited that the sight in both his eyes was still perfect. He was most grateful that the events of the prior evening and the restoration of his sight had not simply been a dream. He quickly dressed and rushed outside to the public square where he met Dr. Dozous. "I'm cured! I'm cured!"[171] he yelled. People began to gather around. Dr. Dozous was in a state of disbelief, noting that the medication he had prescribed for Bourriette was meant only to try to maintain the little sight that remained and not to cure his blindness. Bourriette, however, insisted. Dozous took a piece of paper from his pocket and penned some words on it, instructing Bourriette to cover his "good eye" and read the words with the damaged right eye. Without hesitation, Bourriette read what the doctor had written: "This patient is suffering from an incurable amaurosis."[172] Dozous was incredulous. Bourriette, hardly able to contain his excitement, explained that it was not Dr. Dozous who had cured him, but rather the Lady who produced the spring. He told Dozous that the day prior, he bathed his eyes with water from the miraculous spring of Massabielle and it was "the water from the Grotto [that] has cured me after all."[173]*

* While most sources indicate that this first miracle associated with the spring at Lourdes occurred on February 27, 1858, there are some that indicate that the first miracle did not take place until early March 1858.

Afternoon

The doctor stood dumbfounded. He could not believe what he was hearing. As a man of science, he knew that curing an injury such as the one from which Bourriette suffered was not possible, particularly in the manner in which Bourriette had described. Yet, he had seen it with his own eyes. Dozous consulted with Dr. Venez of Tarbes who simply raised his arms toward heaven.

The news of the cure spread rapidly throughout Lourdes and many began to refer to it as "the miracle, raising great hopes amongst those who were sick or suffered from some chronic disability."[174] Jeanne Crassus, a woman whose hand had been crippled for at least ten years, heard of the Bourriette miracle and immediately ventured to the Grotto. She approached the spring and placed her crippled hand into the cool water. In an instant, her hand was restored, and its full use regained, all through the simple action of dipping her hand into the water.

Evening

With the word of each miraculous story spreading, enthusiasm grew, turning Massabielle into a campground of bustling activity. By evening, hundreds of people crowded the Grotto area, some curiosity seekers, some to offer prayer, some hoping for a cure of their own, and some simply pursuing the solace of a place deemed worthy enough to merit several visits by a Lady who they believed to be Mary, the Mother of God.

Bourriette, and a great many quarrymen belonging to the company for which he once worked, along with some municipal workers, ventured to the Grotto and made a path up the rugged ascent so that visitors could more readily avail themselves to the site. They also "placed a wooden gutter before the spring which was already very strong, and under this they dug a small oval place, about half a yard deep, to receive the water, of about the size and shape of a child's cradle."[175] They worked without a word of explanation, until their task was achieved. Then they quietly left. Only Mayor Lacadé knew the reason for their clandestine work.

In addition to continuing the surveillance activities they ordered on Bernadette and the parish priests, Commissioner Jacomet and Prosecutor Dutour also met with Mr. Lacadé, the mayor of Lourdes, in an effort to convince him to institute an order that would prevent public access to the Grotto. But rather than agreeing to prohibit access, Lacadé suggested profiting from it. With the hysteria over the miraculous properties of the spring water following the alleged cures of Crassus and Bourriette, Lacadé figured there would be a market for the spring water. In fact, in addition to the sale of "Lacadé water," his entrepreneurial plan, for which he had already drafted a prospectus, also included the concept of providing thermal baths for those willing to pay the price.

Sunday, February 28, 1858
The Eleventh Apparition
Morning

The waters from the spring continued to bubble up and overflow into the Gave. On Sunday, thousands gathered in the area of the Grotto in awe of the site of the miraculous water. Included among them was Commandant Renault, a police official who had come out of concern for public safety in the face of such a large gathering.

The masses eagerly awaited the arrival of the child seer. Many had spent the night with little to no sleep, just hoping for a closer spot from which to watch Bernadette. Mr. Estrade took up a position at the crest of the hill, giving him a bird's-eye view of Bernadette as she passed by him very closely, rosary in hand, praying as she walked. From that vantage point it looked like a "sea of human heads one over the other, their owners bending forward in order to see better."[176]

Bernadette continued down the hill, walking through the crowd until she found her rock. She knelt, made the sign of the cross, and immediately fell into a state of ecstasy. The peaceful expression of joy overtaking the child's face indicated to the crowd that the Lady was present. Among the spectators were two soldiers from the fort. They were so moved by the sight of Bernadette that they took it upon themselves to push the crowd back in order to leave sufficient space between them and the praying child. Though Bernadette conversed with the Lady, her words were inaudible to the onlookers. At one point, however, Bernadette moved to the interior of the Grotto and drank of the waters of the spring.

Late Morning
The Third Interrogation

Bernadette had just left the church after attending high Mass when she was stopped by Inspector Latapie, the Lourdes official responsible for springs and fountains. He intercepted the child on her way to the Grotto to bring her before the judge for interrogation. Latapie was not a very impressive man and certainly didn't intimidate Bernadette, who teased him saying, "Hang on to me or I might slip away!"[177] Even the interrogations were no longer frightening to her. These too were becoming relatively routine to Bernadette. Seldom were the questions new, and the answers were always short, accurate and, above all, consistent.

The questioning frequently started with a threat and this day was no different. "'We're going to lock you up,' the judge said. 'What do you do at the Grotto? Is someone pushing you to do this? We're going to put you in prison.'"[178] The child no longer feared arrest and was quick to reply, "I'm ready, put me in, but it better be strong and locked up tight or I'll escape. I'm telling you."[179]

The judge warned her not to go to the Grotto again, but in the end, the Commissioner had to admit that there was no basis to hold her and Bernadette was once again released.

The child seer was constantly questioned about the Lady everywhere she went, and complete strangers would ask her to present requests to her invisible Virgin. Even a friend, Pauline Sous, asked

Bernadette to use her rosary when praying before the Lady on the following day. Pauline was a very devout woman who believed in the child's apparitions. She was just too ill to make a journey to Massabielle.

There was simply no privacy, no peaceful moments other than those spent in ecstasy before the Lady. Antoine Clarens, who was in attendance at the Grotto on prior days, didn't go to the Grotto on that Sunday, but that didn't mean that what he considered imaginary events weren't paramount on his mind. He visited the cachot out of a sense of duty to convince Bernadette to stay away from the Grotto. Rather than achieving his objective, he noted that Bernadette seemed unfazed by the hysteria and excitement found in many of the people of Lourdes and he was taken by the child's sincerity. Slowly, his own opinion of the matter began to change.

Monday, March 1, 1858
The Twelfth Apparition
Morning

The emotional tide sweeping the region caused a stir in tens of thousands, some of whom gathered at the Grotto in anticipation of Bernadette's arrival. By now the site was the subject of a pilgrimage that created a flow of people that seemed as constant and endless as the waters of the spring opened by Bernadette. Many routinely camped out at the site overnight. Despite the young girl's desire for anonymity, she had become somewhat of a celebrity to those who travelled quite a distance to be there.

Murmurs turned to cheers as Bernadette arrived in the area. Making her way to the rock, she knelt, looked upward, and began to pray. She was oblivious to the thousands of eyes staring at her, watching her every move and marveling at the radiance of her face when she achieved ecstasy. As she had before, Bernadette walked on her knees to the spring to drink of its water and as she returned, she remembered the request to pray using Pauline Sous' rosary. The child put her own rosary back into her pocket and removed Pauline's instead.

Before resuming her prayer, she raised the rosary about eye height to show it to the Lady. Seeing this, a great many of the onlookers thought that Bernadette was blessing the rosary and copied her every move, lifting their own rosaries into the air. The Lady stopped Bernadette and the child's arm was stilled. *"You have made a mistake,"* the Lady said, *"That rosary is not yours."* Without hesitation, Bernadette put Pauline's rosary back into her pocket, removing her own rosary at the same time, and presented it to the Lady. Satisfied that the child now held her own rosary, the Lady allowed Bernadette to continue the sign of the cross. Bernadette and the Lady prayed. Though in ecstasy, the young girl was still unmindful of the thousands that were cheering her on and was rather taken aback by the aftermath.

Jean-Baptiste Estrade and his sister Emmanuélite, both present at the Grotto during Bernadette's ecstasy, reported the incident with the rosary to Abbé Pène who seemed upset that the child might be performing blessings. Immediately he sent for Bernadette to put a quick end to this abuse. "So you're blessing rosaries now," Pène barked. Laughing, Bernadette asked, "Do I wear a stole?" "What did you do then," he demanded? Though Bernadette's description of the rosary exchange satisfied any concern that Abbé Pène may have had, rumors still spread rapidly throughout Lourdes.

Tuesday, March 2, 1858
The Thirteenth Apparition
Morning

The crowds once again began arriving early to claim a choice spot near the Grotto, some staking their position shortly after midnight. Witnesses estimated the crowd to be one of the largest yet. They cheered to acknowledge Bernadette's arrival at the Grotto. Ignoring the spectacle, Bernadette knelt on her rock and began to pray, and as on previous occasions, the Lady appeared in the niche carved within the wall of the cavern.

When prayers were completed, the Lady once again asked Bernadette to *"Go back to the priest and tell him that I want a chapel built at Massabielle. Tell him also to bring people here in procession."* When Bernadette emerged from ecstasy, according to one of the on-lookers, she was "obviously preoccupied."[180]

"What did she say?" many of the onlookers asked Bernadette as she lifted herself to her feet. Bernadette was nervous at the prospect of approaching the priest a second time with the Lady's request and wanted to leave as soon as possible to address the matter. She told me "To go tell the priest that people are to come here in procession,"[181] she quickly responded, revealing only part of the message.* Then she hurried from the Grotto to deliver the message to Abbé Peyramale as instructed. Upon doing so, he reiterated his requests for a miracle; a blooming rose bush, and for the identity of the Lady.

Bernadette did not reveal the entire message because she was anxious to meet with the pastor before forgetting the words of the Lady.

Wednesday, March 3, 1858
Morning
Approximately 6:00 AM
The Fourteenth Apparition*

Bernadette arrived at the usual time to meet with the Lady. There were hordes of curiosity seekers intermingled with the faithful, each there

Some contend that there was an Apparition on this day. While eyewitnesses indicate that there were no signs of ecstasy this day, Bernadette herself noted that only twice in the fifteen days in which the Lady asked her to go to the Grotto, did she not appear. Those days were Monday February 22nd and Friday February 26th. If there was an Apparition on this day, then the total number of Apparitions would equal eighteen and not the seventeen confirmed in this book. There is no hard evidence of such an apparition however.

hoping for just a chance to see the Lady, witness a miracle, or at least touch or speak with Bernadette. Many thousands of people squeezed between the towering wall of the Grotto and the Gave River, making it very difficult for Bernadette to make her way to the rock on which she prayed. The people pushed and shoved the others, hoping for a better view.

Making her way through the crowd on her approach to her rock, the candle that the child always carried to the Grotto was somehow broken. Unfazed, Bernadette took the rosary from her pocket and began to pray, but no words were spoken. There was no indication of ecstasy and seemingly to the onlookers, no Apparition. Many in the crowd began to grumble. Some said the child saw nothing, blaming the lack of Apparition on the broken candle. Others insisted that she did see the Lady. Still others said the Lady didn't appear because some visitors desecrated the site. Bernadette rose from prayer, however, and quickly left the area, leaving behind the masses, many of whom began to depart the Grotto as well.

Afternoon

Later in the afternoon, Bernadette would learn of the passing of François's sister Jeanne Soubirous. Her aunt died at five o'clock in the morning just about the time Bernadette prepared to go to the Grotto. Naturally, the child was distraught at hearing the news, but was drawn by a sense of obligation to return to the rectory to let Abbé Peyramale know that she still had no information relative to the Lady's identity.

She knew that Abby Peyramale would be waiting to find out how the Lady identified herself. She also knew that her lack of adequate reply would anger her pastor. The child was shown in but had to wait for Peyramale, who was expected to return from Tarbes shortly.

It was late when Bernadette delivered the bad news and left the rectory. Consequently, she knew that she had missed her supper.

Fortunately, she ran into Dominiquette, who invited her to her house for a bite of codfish. As they dined, the stagecoach owner, Jean-Marie Cazenave, "Ganco," as he was known to locals, arrived with a coachful of people from Bagnères. Many of the riders were there to attend the Grotto on the following day, the last on which the Lady had asked Bernadette to return.

At thirty years old, Jean-Marie was a tall man of immense confidence. He was accustomed to barking orders to horses, passengers, and other coachmen who blocked his path. He had already heard the rumors of the disappointing morning at the Grotto. While Jean-Marie intimidated many people, including Bernadette's father, she was not afraid of him. In fact, she thought his size and confidence might be just the thing she needed to help her navigate the expected crowd at the Grotto in the morning. She asked, and Ganco gladly accepted the invitation to accompany her to the Grotto for the much-anticipated appearance of the Lady.

Soon François Soubirous arrived to get his child, informing her that her aunt and cousin Jeanne Vedere had just arrived for the funeral of Aunt Jeanne and to accompany her to the Grotto the following morning. The two hurried back to the cachot.

Jeanne Vedere was a schoolteacher in Momeres and Bernadette was particularly fond of her. Jeanne's brother, Jean-Marie Vedere, was Bernadette's godfather and an army sergeant stationed in Lyons with the fifth infantry. He was the very first person about whom Bernadette inquired when she saw her cousin. Though they wanted badly to catch up, they hardly had an opportunity to speak to each other due to the curiosity seekers who had gathered at the cachot.

The hour was getting late and all the visitors, family excluded, were asked to leave, finally allowing Bernadette the opportunity to speak with her cousin, telling her of all the day's events. When exhaustion overtook them, they slept.

Thursday, March 4, 1858
The Fifteenth Apparition
Morning

Bernadette arose early in anticipation of a big day at the Grotto and she was not alone in her enthusiasm. Thousands of pilgrims were already on their way to the Grotto and thousands more had camped out at the site the night prior to secure a good position close to Bernadette's rock. Henri Lasserre estimated the crowd at no less than 20,000. Bernadette, however, was unaware of the crowd as she began her day at a Mass celebrated for the repose of the soul of her Aunt Jeanne.

Though saddened by her aunt's passing, Bernadette's excitement for the Lady's anticipated appearance was difficult to contain. Shortly before the end of Mass, Bernadette slipped out of the church to begin her journey to Massabielle. Her cousin Jeanne Vedere had seen Bernadette walk out of the church, however, and went after her, catching up with her in the church square. François, his sister Thecle, Aunt Bernarde, and Ganco the stage coachman, all met her there and together they silently departed for the Grotto. They took the route by the foot of the castle, suggested by Uncle Sajous, hoping that it would be a road less traveled.

As they began their approach to the Grotto, Jeanne pressed close to her cousin for fear that they might be separated. Bernadette promised her that she would be right next to her when the Lady appeared, but as she spoke the words, she was interrupted by "an old mountaineer, bent beneath the weight of years, and venerable as a patriarch, supporting himself with his trembling hands upon his enormous staff, shod with iron."[182] His name was Monsieur Troy and he had traveled some twenty-three miles with his family from Barèges of the Canton of Luz. A woman, tanned and wrinkled, stood beside him with a flowing black-hooded cloak lined with red. His youngest boy stood nearby on the tip of his toes to better observe Bernadette. Troy presented his daughter and implored Bernadette to pray for his little girl who was blind. Bernadette's eyes slowly left the man's face and focused on the small child standing next to him. The child wore a red-hooded cape and had bandages covering her eyes both to "conceal the ugliness of her diseased eyelids and to shield her eyes from the light, which hurt them."[183] She looks so frail, Bernadette thought to herself, not quite knowing what to do.

The girl appeared to be about Bernadette's age, though she looked so unhappy. Ganco studied the girl and the father, noting that they looked familiar. In fact, they had ridden in Ganco's stagecoach just the day before on their way to Lourdes. Bernadette was filled with affection toward the little one, an affection so deep that it could be seen in her eyes and heard in her voice. Sensing the affection, Ganco suggested that Bernadette kiss the child. Bernadette walked toward the child, took her hands and kissed her on the cheek. The little girl felt reborn and both she and Bernadette burst into laughter. Bernadette kissed her again on the other cheek and without even asking her name, told the man to take the girl to the spring and have her wash there. The man departed with his daughter Eugenie and family in tow. Bernadette turned and continued on her journey.

Not too much farther, however, Bernadette was accosted once again, this time by a woman. The woman was accompanied by her servant, who carried in her arms a lame and mute child. The child seemed to Bernadette to be around three or four years old. Holding out a candle, the woman said, "Take this candle. Offer it to the Virgin for my child."[184] Bernadette offered her prayers and gently, but firmly, instructed the woman to leave the candle at the Grotto or in church herself. This was an authoritative side of Bernadette that her cousin Jeanne had never before witnessed, perhaps a confidence gained at the hands of the countless interrogations experienced over the past two weeks.

Word of the apparitions of a Lady to Bernadette of Lourdes had been news throughout the region for two weeks now, and newspapers had been reporting the facts of the happenings as they occurred, but reports began to take on a new dimension of vitriol. The day's edition of a freethinking newspaper in Paris ran a story about the events that occurred in the Grotto three days earlier on March 1st. The story read in part:

> *"This morning, March 1, the little comedian of the miller*
> *of Lourdes again gathered an audience of about two*

*thousand simple-minded souls around her at the Massa-
bielle rock. The stupidity and mental cretinism of her fol-
lowers is impossible to describe. The little visionary treats
them like a band of monkeys, getting them to perform all
sorts of mummeries. Having no taste for inspiration this
morning, the Pytoness of Lourdes could think of nothing
better for a change than to constitute herself priestess.
Adopting a solemn air of authority, she called on the sanc-
timonious audience to present their rosaries which she
then blessed in bulk.*"[185]

The reaction of this writer was slowly becoming the norm of
many news outlets as disdain for young Bernadette and her claims of
seeing a Lady clearly annoyed the press as well as the politicians of the
area. Soon there were even more dangerous reactions and, "in certain
influential circles it was rumored that Bernadette was out of her mind."[186]

*Bishop Laurence of Tarbes assembled a Commission to explore the events of
Lourdes. The Commission concluded that Bernadette had seen the Virgin Mary
and that the spring water flowing from the dry earth that Bernadette dug at the
direction of the Virgin was indeed regular water with miraculous properties.*

Abbé Peyramale, the Cantonal Vicar of Lourdes, and their curates refused to take an official position and refused to go to the Grotto. Even Bishop Bertrand Severe Laurence of Tarbes kept his distance.

Bishop Laurence had the temperament of a fighter. The general expression of this man in his upper sixties, the lines in his face and his determined mouth, made him appear hard, but the serenity in his eyes revealed a softer side. He could appear a rather cold spirit, but that was not to imply that he wasn't meditative and honest. Overall, he appeared very austere.

In general, authoritarians within the church were getting very anxious over the situation. Baron Massy, the Prefect of the Hautes-Pyrenees, was annoyed. It was not that he didn't believe in biblical miracles, he just didn't put much faith in Bernadette's miracle. Now that the credulous masses had come into movement, be believed that addressing the matter fell within his authority. Ordering a round-the-clock watch on the Grotto, he issued a statement that read in part:

> *"If I had been Prefect of the Isere at the time of the alleged visions of La Salette, I should soon have put a stop to the whole affair. And, as for this fantastic business at Lourdes, that must stop, too."*[187]

Those already gathered when Bernadette arrived numbered about twenty thousand and the number kept increasing as people entered from all sides. They stood at the crest of the hill, sat along both banks of the Gave River or took a place anywhere in between that enabled them to be within at least distant sight of the child. Some climbed trees and hung to vines hanging from the rocks. The constant movement of people created waves of sound that ebbed and flowed in the Grotto. Mingled in the crowd were many men, varied and of all professions and backgrounds. There were lawyers and judges, shopkeepers and notaries, doctors and clerks. They displayed "forms less rough but at the same time less marked, more humble or more polished, more distinguished in the opinion of some, more vulgar in that of others."[188] The ladies, in bonnets and veils, with their hands buried in their muffs, seemed, in spite of all their precautions, to suffer from the frosty morning air and adjusted their position frequently in a hopeless attempt to stay warm. Many of the children had fallen asleep on the ground, no doubt fatigued from their travels or bored from the wait.

Among the spectators that day were Imperial Prosecutor Dutour and Police Commissioner Jacomet. Standing on a small protrusion in the landscape, they carefully surveyed the scene, prepared to take rigorous measures at the slightest appearance of disorder, but their attention was redirected when someone shouted, "There she is! There she is! The saint!"[189]

Almost every head lifted and looked around as Bernadette appeared on the quarry path. The hearts of many in the crowd, even the coldest, were stirred with emotion. The child, aided by Ganco and accompanied by her family, made her way to her rock via an "aisle" that the commissioner's men had created using girders. Before kneeling, however, Bernadette noticed that her cousin Jeanne had become separated from her and, looking around, could see no sign of her.

From her position many yards behind Bernadette, Jeanne's fears of separation were realized despite the reassuring words of her cousin that she would be at her side during the Apparition. Jeanne had just about resigned herself to the fact that she would not be reunited with Bernadette in time for the appearance of the Lady, when she heard a booming voice yell out, "The little one is asking for one of her cousins."[190] "'I'm here,' Jeanne cried out, 'but I can't move ahead.'"[191] The commissioner and one of his men collected the girl and took her to Bernadette. Once the visionary child verified that this was indeed the cousin for whom she was asking, Bernadette knelt on her rock and began to pray. Jeanne did likewise.

The crowd in the immediate area followed their lead. Bernadette raised and extended her arms toward the Grotto, and the crowd mimicked her again in choreographic fashion. Then the seer fell into ecstasy and the onlookers noticed a certain joy luminate her face. Bernadette raised her arm in an attempt to make the sign of the cross but was unable to do so. Three times she tried, succeeding only on her third attempt when she was led in prayer by the Lady. At one point, the Lady relocated to the ground-level crevice that formed the Grotto. Bernadette rose and walked a few steps forward into the hole and continued in conversation from a vantage point so close that Bernadette could have reached out and touched the Lady, though she dared not. Bernadette asked the Lady her name in compliance with the request from Abbé Peyramale. The Lady provided no answer. She did, however, as she had in the past, instruct the child to *"drink at and wash herself in the fountain, and to eat of the plant"*[192] from which she had eaten in days prior. Throughout the course of the hour-long ecstasy, Bernadette's expression ranged from happy to sad, mirroring the emotion being transmitted by the Lady, who once again instructed Bernadette to tell the priests to build a chapel on the site and arrange processions in her honor. Finally, the child's expression returned to normal and she rose from her ecstasy.

Over the course of that hour, the commissioner dutifully recorded her every action in his notebook, even keeping a tally of the number of times Bernadette bowed, smiled, or frowned, but there was no miracle. Nothing to prove to anyone that the child had actually seen anything.

Bernadette was disappointed that there was no miracle and though she conversed with the Lady, the child was troubled that the Lady didn't respond when asked her name. In fact, the Lady didn't even say goodbye before she vanished for what Bernadette felt could be the last time she would see her.

There was no time for self-pity, however. Bernadette needed to depart the Grotto before she was rushed by the dissatisfied crowd. Ganco took hold of her right hand and with the others from her small entourage in tow, led her up the hill toward home. Ganco used his free hand to wave off the crowd as they walked.

Along the way, cousin Jeanne had a great many questions for Bernadette, including one that she had not heard before. ""'And why were you talking so softly that I couldn't hear a thing?' Bernadette looked surprised. 'We were talking the way I'm talking to you now,'"[193] she said.

Mid to Late Morning

A large crowd followed Bernadette and her family back to the cachot. Even more people stood outside, eagerly awaiting their arrival. All wanted to speak with Bernadette. The family entered, closing the door behind them, but the crowd grew larger and called out for Bernadette. Several times Bernadette peered out the second-floor window of Sajous' apartment where she fled to get some rest, but that made the crowd even more anxious to see her. Finally, François opened the door and several people rushed in, pushing their way up the staircase to the second floor from which they had seen Bernadette at the window. Jeanne Adrian, a schoolteacher from Gavarnie, was among the first to reach Bernadette. She had spent the entire night at the Grotto and wanted only to hug the child. Satisfied, she left the cachot and departed for her village. Tens, perhaps hundreds, made their way upstairs, trapping Bernadette so that she was unable to leave. Each kissed and/or hugged her - men, women, and children. For some, a hug was not enough. They wanted Bernadette to touch their rosaries or to press their rosary beads to Bernadette's. Others went even further, taking out a pair of scissors that they had carried for this purpose and cutting a piece of the lining of Bernadette's dress to take home for a souvenir.

Bernadette was beside herself. Why did all these people want to touch her or cut her clothing as if she had some magical powers. As new people arrived, replacing those who had left, Bernadette feared that the ritual might continue well into the night. Even cousin Jeanne stood in line, caught up in the emotion or excitement. She too wanted something to take back home with her that day and held out three rosaries for Bernadette to touch: the rosary of the Seven Sorrows, the Camaldolese rosary, and the rosary of Saint Dominic. "'You too!' Bernadette said when she saw Jeanne. 'What do you want me to do to them? I'm not a priest!'"[194] In the end, Bernadette took the rosaries and pressed them to her own with which she prayed in the Grotto. For Bernadette, the gesture was more than ritualistic. It was a symbolic recognition that it was the Lady and not Bernadette that deserved credit for the things that occurred at the Grotto, though that symbolism may have been lost on Jeanne.

Afternoon

The crowd thinned by dinner time and Bernadette was able to share a meal, albeit a quick one, with her exhausted family. It was afternoon and the child knew that Abbé Peyramale was awaiting news of the Lady's identity. On very short order, Bernadette was off again to the rectory.

"'What did the Lady say,' Peyramale asked with great hope in his voice. 'I asked her name...,' Bernadette responded, 'She smiled. I asked her to make the rosebush bloom and she smiled again. But she still wants her chapel.' 'Do you have money to build this chapel?' the priest snapped. 'Me neither. Tell the Lady to give you some.' Then he added almost as an afterthought, 'She didn't tell you to come back?' Bernadette answered his question saying, 'She did not say.'"[195] Bernadette empathized with Peyramale's disappointment as he turned his back and walked slowly away, but took some solace in the fact that she at least delivered the Lady's message.

As she departed the rectory, she recalled that Clarens, the director of the Lourdes secondary school, had invited her to his house, one he shared with Isidore Baudean, the candle-maker. Clarens thought that, at his house, the child might find respite from the crowds that hounded her. In fact, she did and immediately joined the director's children in some games, forgetting, at least for the moment, the radical responsibility that had been thrust upon her.

Evening

As Bernadette enjoyed the diversion, people in Lourdes were talking about "the 'miracle' of the blind girl with the red-hooded cape."[196] In their disappointment at the lack of an explicit miracle at the Grotto that morning, they were eager to latch on to anything and used little Eugenie Troy as their paradigm. An excited crowd descended upon the cachot once again. The street was jammed at both the Soubirouses' home and that of the Clarenses. François had a difficult time working his way through the crowds; nevertheless, he was able to get to the Clarenses' house and accompany his daughter back to the cachot, where a waiting line had already formed. Hundreds, maybe thousands, waited to kiss the visionary. After hours, Bernadette was exhausted and found it difficult to breathe. The asthma that had not bothered her for three weeks returned, and the child begged her mother to lock the door. But that was not to happen.

Later that night, as Bernadette slipped into the restful sleep she so desperately needed, the crowds of people began to return to their homes in villages both near and far. Many witnessed strange and "miraculous lights" illuminate the dark sky. "One group, returning to Angles, saw a bright light pierce the darkness, 'Like a fire in the air.'"[197] Another group of about six or seven people returning to Saint-Pe reported "something glowing" opposite the Grotto. Among this group was Monsieur Lacoste, the bailiff. They chalked it up to a weather event or some other "freakish occurrence," but "Capitayne, the poacher, was stunned. He stopped at the first shelter and didn't leave until daybreak."[198]

Friday, March 5, 1858

During the period of time encompassing the apparitions, there was a stretch of weather that included the most magnificent experienced in Lourdes during the winter months in many years. On March 5 that changed. The weather became much colder and overcast, eventually dumping a heavy snow in the region. More than the disappointment inflicted on the masses because of the lack of a miracle the day prior, the snow was probably the chief culprit in the great diminution in the number of visitors to the Grotto.

While not adversely impacting the faithful of Lourdes, the disappointment of the

"miracle-less Thursday was lost on neither the government officials nor their agents in the secular press. Even

94

some of those who so desperately tried to find a miracle using the examples of the blind girl or the lame, mute child, were coming to grips with the fact that no miracle had taken place. Their sentiments were fueled by press statements such as the one written in the morning edition of the *Lavedan:* '*What fakery!"* the article began, *"How many naive believers have been humiliated. How many! People have finally understood too late, alas! The foolishness of their behavior and now deplore their extreme gullibility...'"*

For her part, Bernadette was unimpressed by the fickle chatter or the official newspaper accounts. She knew full well what she had experienced and, though wishing to see the Lady again, was rather glad the experience was behind her. She was clearly disappointed at not being able to determine who the Lady was, but wanted nothing more than to resume play with other children and regain some normalcy in her life. She no longer felt an attraction to Massabielle, at least not the irresistible urge that had overtaken her in previous weeks.

She was, in fact, preparing to make her First Communion, something she had long hoped to do, but she continued to struggle to learn her catechism. Even nine-year-old Julie Garros, whom the sisters at the Hospice School had hand-picked to tutor Bernadette, was of no help to the poor child, despite having committed the prayers and answers to the catechetical questions to her own memory. The nuns, who felt little pity for Bernadette, quipped that she might have been better off had she asked the Lady for help with her catechism.

Despite the press reports and the lack of a miracle, many faithful continued to believe that Bernadette had miraculous visions of the Blessed Virgin Mary. They were not discouraged in their faith but rather continued to flock in large numbers to the Grotto of Massabielle and to the cachot. In fact, as word of the visions continued to spread far beyond Lourdes to places like Begore and Bearn, the parade of spectators traveling through the area toward Massabielle grew larger and the noise they made became louder. There remained an atmosphere of joy and fervor among the people and the

Soubirouses' house continued to be beleaguered, causing Louise to complain, "We never have the place to ourselves anymore."[199]

Some of the curious souvenir seekers took rocks from the Grotto, while some of the faithful constructed a small altar there and placed a statue of the Blessed Virgin on it. Many left religious medals, holy images, and other religious objects there. Similar objects were left littered around the Soubirous home as well. This was the new life to which the Soubirouses had to grow accustomed. They didn't know when, or even if, it would change, but for now, this was just how it would be.

Tuesday, March 9, 1858
Mid Afternoon

Though she tried to be a normal child, Bernadette was both revered and reviled at the same time. Her classmates were as divided on the issue of the authenticity of Bernadette's claims as the village adults whose conversations may have helped form the children's opinions. There were classmates who believed that she had miraculous visions while others felt she was deeply disturbed. Joséphine Doucet may have fallen into the former group of classmates when she politely approached Bernadette outside of school after classes to ask if she would be so kind as to stop by her house to visit her little brother Jean-Marie. "'[He] would like to see you,' she said. 'He's been sick a few days. He thinks only of seeing you.'"[200] Bernadette promised that she would accompany Joséphine home to visit her brother during the lunch break on the following day.

Despite the misgivings from government officials and attacks from the secular media, there were some possessing the power of the ink that supported and believed in Bernadette's visions. Among this more select group was Romain Capdevielle, a prominent attorney who was engaged to the beautiful Marie Dufo. Capdevielle published an article in *Memorial de Pau* acclaiming the blessings of the little visionary of Lourdes. His words sparked a resurgence of daily visitors to the Grotto, many leaving candles and other trinkets in their wake.

Wednesday, March 10, 1858
11:00 AM to 1:00 PM

Joséphine could hardly wait for school to be dismissed for the lunch break. She so wanted to please her brother by bringing Bernadette home to visit him. During break, the two met in the school yard to begin the five-minute trek up the hill to the Piqué Farm in Bartrès. Bernadette sensed the smell of sheep and hay that permeated the air even before spotting the square house bordered by two small sheds and hidden among the trees. Joséphine rushed ahead to open the door leading to the living room. Bernadette's eye was immediately drawn to the fireplace where sat nine-and-a-half-year-old Jean-Marie. He was a dreadful site. "A huge mouth, open wide like an oven. It seemed to be devouring the face of a sickly child, seated near the fire in some sort of cradle."[201]

This disease, or whatever it was, came on suddenly, around Christmastime. For the past ten or eleven weeks, Jean-Marie had not walked. His mouth rarely closed, only enough to take an occasional morsel of food, and he spoke only in horrific sounds which Bernadette could not understand without interpretation from the boy's mother. As if not scourge enough, the boy's body wrenched uncontrollably and without warning.

The child had been seen by several physicians including Doctors Lacrampe, Peyrus, and Borderes, each of whom had never seen the likes of that condition before. None could offer any help, and each thought it to be some type of incurable neuralgic disorder. Regardless of what it was that ailed the boy, he "yelped" with joy upon seeing Bernadette. To her, it sounded like the shrill cry of a dog, but it was simply the excited sound that emanated from the boy's gaping mouth. Despite his appearance, Bernadette noticed that "he had a sharp eye and a fresh, rosy complexion"[202] yet she was hardly able to turn her gaze away from that mouth and the saliva that drooled from it, all the way down to his knees.

Bernadette's heart broke watching the child's body jerk as it did, but she wouldn't let her heartache show. "How are you?" Bernadette asked. Jean-Marie yelped something that his mother translated as "Not too good." She turned her attention to some drawings that hung in a makeshift chapel near the fireplace. "Are you the one who made this?" Bernadette asked, pointing to the one of the sketches. He indicated that he was. Drawing colorful pictures provided comfort, busied his mind, and helped lift his spirits a little, so he was encouraged by his family to do it. They spoke about that for a short time but as the hour drew close to one o'clock when school would resume, Bernadette and Joséphine had to cut the visit short. As she turned to walk out, the boy said something that his mother interpreted as "You must come back." Bernadette promised to return as she disappeared from his view and into the chilly air.

At once the boy's lips trembled. He yawned three times and his mouth closed. Looking at his mother, Jean-Marie said in a voice as crisp and clear as it had ever been, "Now I'd like something to eat and drink."[203] His mother could believe neither her ears nor her eyes as an immense joy overtook her. For months she could think of nothing but the loss of her child and just like that, he returned to normal. For at least the moment, she believed a miracle had taken place, a miracle performed at the hand of Bernadette.

But if a miracle had taken place, its relief was to last only for a brief time. "The meal was barely over when all the torments began again with the same violence as before,"[204] and from that night on, Jean-Marie could neither close his mouth nor eat and drink.

In fact, with the exception of a moment or two around noontime on the following day, during which time he took a small snack, the boy's mouth did not close again for two days. The brevity of the "miracle" didn't stop Joséphine from spreading the news of it throughout the school. Bernadette humbly downplayed her own significance in the matter.

Friday, March 12, 1858

Whether or not Bernadette believed that a miracle had taken place, however briefly, she received a certain joy in being able to brighten little Jean-Marie's mood. So, Bernadette agreed to return for a second visit. This time, however, she would not visit alone, owing to the fact that the classmates that heard Joséphine's story of the miracle wanted to accompany her.

Bernadette greeted the boy as she had before and added, "Are you hungry?" He answered in the affirmative. "Well, force yourself to close your mouth and eat!" Bernadette ordered. Without hesitation, the boy yawned several times and, as had happened two days prior, his mouth closed. The boy had a meal for the first time in two days and for quite a while spoke to Bernadette about the visions she had at the Grotto of Massabielle. Before the visit was over, however, his mouth returned to its formerly open position.

Saturday, March 13, 1858
11:30 AM – 4:00 PM

Bernadette and her classmates paid another visit to Jean-Marie. This time, however, Bernadette was determined to be firm in her handling of the boy. She was taught at a rather young age that children need not be coddled in their affliction, especially when they seem to be succumbing to self-pity. In fact, this attitude of self-reliance seemed instinctive to both the Soubirous and Casterot families.

After greeting the boy, Bernadette said, "So, you never want to get up. It's always up to me to come and see you!" "Oh, if I could get up, I really would, really!" the boy responded. "Oh, you are a lazybones; otherwise, you would get up. And you would dance around the room. Look, you're a rascal. You act sick to get good food to eat. Well, as for me, I don't like you anymore, because you're a lazybones."[205] Jean-Marie's mother caught on to Bernadette's tactic and encouraged her, noting that the boy hadn't eaten anything that day. "Well now, eat, lazybones," Bernadette said as she spoon-fed her friend. He ate without a fuss.

While Bernadette was spending time with her new friend, Joséphine and the other girls ran an errand for Madame Doucet, thinking

99

they would be back in plenty of time to return to school before classes resumed at one o'clock. They didn't figure on the nasty weather, however, as what started out as a light snow became a downpour. The girls returned home sometime after classes had already begun and they didn't need too much coaxing from Madame Doucet to skip the afternoon classes and remain at Piqué Farm.

Jean-Marie was most delighted of all until he realized that Bernadette was going to join the other girls at play in the barn. At three o'clock, Madame Doucet went to the barn to inform Bernadette that her son was asking for her, but in sticking to her initial plan, she stopped inside for only a moment before going back to the barn to resume play. At four o'clock, the girls left Piqué Farm for their respective homes.

Things were looking up for the Doucet family. Jean-Marie's mouth closed about twice a day now, at least allowing him to eat meals. That was a vast improvement and the Doucets attributed it to Bernadette.

Sunday, March 14, 1858
Morning

Bernadette was pleased with her approach to Jean-Marie and decided she should keep the "tough girl" mantra going for all her visits. She agreed to visit the farm twice that day and, on each visit, she scolded the boy. "All right, since you won't eat, I'm leaving. Adieu! I don't like you anymore."[206] As soon as Bernadette walked out, Jean-Marie's mouth closed. Madame Doucet raced out to tell the child, who happily returned and fed the boy, not one, but two meals over the next hour. Sunday was different, however. That time the boy's mouth did not open after the meals. It remained in a natural position and his speech was restored. It remained so all day and, for the first time in months, the boy enjoyed four full meals.

Monday, March 15, 1858

Fueled by the Doucets' reveling, a new miracle was proclaimed by the people around Lourdes. Word even spread to the rectory, where Abbés Peyramale, Pomian, and Pène took particular interest. Together they visited Piqué Farm and checked on the boy themselves. They were intrigued if not confused by what they experienced. The case of the "cured blind girl" proved to be false, but to their untrained eyes, this case seemed more substantial. Returning to the rectory, Abbé Peyramale penned a letter to Bishop Laurence of Tarbes. "An interesting case," he wrote. "Quite an improvement. If he is thoroughly healed we can say with Saint Augustine: *Causa finita est.*,"[207] translated, case closed.

While the men and women of the local church were practically ready to proclaim a miracle, Prefect Baron Massy was concerned. He was in the prime of his life. He was both a crafty politician and a worthy administrator. He was known in political and governmental circles as a hard worker, always willing to accept responsibility. Although a bit authoritarian in style, he had a capacity for cutting through bureaucratic red tape and solving problems. He had been described as a proud man, perhaps even to the point of vanity, and once he made a decision, he stuck by it even to the point of stubbornness when shown that he might have erred in judgement. He was at once both courteous and cold and resisted opposition vehemently.

He was also a good Christian, one on whom Pope Pius IX bestowed the honor of Commander of the Order of St. Gregory the Great. He considered the problem of Bernadette and her visions to be "the burning problem of the moment." He knew he needed to control the flames lest all the officials of Lourdes scorch their fingers at it.

Tuesday, March 16, 1858

By now, stories of the "miracle at Pique" were circulated well beyond Lourdes. Villagers talked about a little boy cured of his horrible affliction while some marveled at the healing powers of Bernadette. Romain Capdevielle published a second article in *Memorial de Pau* in support of Bernadette, and the authorities, who thought that Bernadette's hoax was finally exposed following the lack of a miracle on the fourth of March, began to worry anew as they found themselves ensconced in a new movement that was reaching into the highest levels of society.

Imperial Prosecutor Dutour, for example, had been receiving reports of ranking officials cavorting with Bernadette and her family. Monsieur Dufo, who served as both town councilor and president at the bar, was rumored to have "kissed [Bernadette's] hand and called her the saint."[208] It got worse! Tribunal President Pougat, whose appointment to the bench was the result of high-level political connections, had been providing secret counsel to the Soubirous family, undermining the government threats against the family and reducing the threats to rather meaningless gestures.

Dutour knew he had to include an account of these occurrences in the report to the Attorney General due for submission on the following day. He was keen enough to also realize that such claims must not stand alone, but rather must be followed by an action plan that would address this impending crisis with "direct and official action."[209]

Wednesday, March 17, 1858

The Imperial Prosecutor submitted his report to the Attorney General in Pau on schedule, handling an awkward situation by tempering his comments with a smooth blend of blunt accusation and political skill. He "tried in veiled terms to denounce the scandal.... After mentioning the Dufo case, he wrote on his rough copy, 'I could mention other men whose position is even higher....' But he stopped there."[210]

Thursday, March 18, 1858
The Fourth Interrogation

The officials were ready to take on the issue once again. Bernadette was summoned to the Commissioner's Office to meet with a host of officials that included the Attorney General, who had reviewed Dutour's report; Police Commissioner Dominique Jacomet; Imperial Prosecutor Vital Dutour; Mayor Gerald-August Lacadé; and Joanas, the Mayor's secretary, who dutifully notated the official minutes of the interrogation.

Bernadette had grown accustomed to this type of grilling and was able to remain much calmer under the intense questioning than she had under similar circumstances just a month earlier. The inquisitors asked her about the details of the Capdevielle article and Bernadette confirmed that the Lady did indeed ask that the priests build a chapel at the Grotto. She also confirmed that the Lady imparted secrets to her, but refused to disclose what they were. Explaining that those secrets were meant only for her, she assured the officials that they didn't contain anything of which they should be frightened. She was asked to describe her visits with Jean-Marie Doucet, which she did ever so briefly, swearing to them that she had not visited any other sick people. Bernadette did acknowledge under questioning that one sick person was brought to her, however, that being the daughter of Monsieur Sempolis. Then she remembered "the apple given to the half-paralyzed child on March 4, and concluded, 'The child left the way she came.'"[211]

The inquisitors turned their attention to the "blind" girl with the red cape whose cure had been exaggerated. This prompted Bernadette to respond very clearly and precisely, "I don't think I've cured anyone whatsoever, and besides I haven't done anything for that reason."[212]

Finally, the officials asked Bernadette to recount the apparitions, including the exact dress of the Lady and all her mannerisms, which the child did in exceptional detail, and with uncanny consistency to the previous responses she had been giving since the very first apparition.

Bernadette believed that the Lady was now gone for good and said that she had no desire to return to the Grotto. She was exacerbated and wanted nothing more than to resume a life of normalcy where she could play youthful games with other children. She expressed this desire as the interrogation was being wrapped up saying, "I don't know whether I'll go back to the Grotto again."[213] The sincerity of the statement alone was enough to imply conviction and her conciliatory tone gave the Prosecutor the confidence to interpret her words noting, "She promised not to go back, nor to invite the abuse which credulity and bad faith make of her actions and of her person."[214] The officials were comforted by these words and were optimistic that this affair regarding the Apparitions, the Lady and the miracles, would finally be behind them.

Wednesday, March 24, 1858
Evening

We've all experienced it at some point in our lives. That inner feeling deep down in our souls. That sixth sense that gives us direction, encouraging our belief that it is the voice of God or his angels imparting a message, perhaps even asking of us a task. It's that silent voice that tells you to take a different route to work or to avoid a particular event, only to find out later that something terrible happened to those less inclined to go with the feeling. Well, on Wednesday evening Bernadette felt something similar. A stirring inside her - perhaps an intense feeling, but she was confident that it was a message from the Lady. Unable to sleep, she counted the minutes to morning.

Thursday, March 25, 1858
The Sixteenth Apparition
Between 4:00 AM and 6:00 AM

Bernadette arose at 4:00 AM, well before sunrise, and hurriedly dressed in total darkness. She listened patiently for the first signs of life from her parents' room and then hurried to confide to her mother and father that something big was going to happen at the Grotto that day. Despite their misgivings, Bernadette held firm, telling them with complete assurance about the happiness awaiting her at the Grotto. Louise worried about her child's health, reminding Bernadette that she had recently been experiencing an asthma flare-up, but the young one assured her mother that she was better and needed to be at the Grotto right away. At least "'wait until sunup,' Louise pleaded. 'No, I must go and go quickly.'"[215] After a quick discussion in which her parents reasoned that the spontaneity of the trip would mean that no crowd would be at the site, they consented. Louise and François dressed quickly and just before 5:00 AM the three left for the Grotto of Massabielle.

Louise and François had underestimated the enthusiasm that the feast of the Annunciation would generate at the Grotto. They also were not aware of the false rumors that had been circulating around Lourdes, rumors that Bernadette and the Bishop were to leave for Rome on Friday March 26 and would visit the Grotto on the great holy day before their departure. Commissioner Jacomet was certainly aware of the rumor and he was one of over one hundred people standing at the Grotto even before the sun made its appearance in the sky.

Bernadette was confident that the Lady would appear to her that morning and she knew that she could not let the opportunity pass without getting an answer to the burning question that Abbé Peyramale and others had demanded of her. For weeks, since last she saw the Lady, Bernadette had prepared in her mind a "beautiful, formal and reverential way of asking her question: 'Mademoiselle, would you have the kindness to tell me who you are, if you please?'"[216] She practiced the question dutifully for almost three weeks and though she knew it cold, she still repeated it to herself several times as she approached her customary place at the Grotto. Strangely, however, she noticed a glow as she advanced, "a soft and mysterious light" coming from the niche. Looking up, she saw that the Lady was already awaiting the child's arrival. Bernadette hurried to her rock, knelt, and began to pray. The crowd fell silent and would remain so.

When prayer ended, Bernadette asked forgiveness for her late arrival. The Lady made a sign with her head as if to say that there was no need for the child to excuse herself. Bernadette told the Lady how much she loved her and how happy she was to see her again. Then the child was unable to contain herself any longer and the words just slipped out. "Mademoiselle," she said, "Would you have the willingness to tell me who you are, if you please?" She practically choked on the words as they left her lips. As she had so often in rehearsal, she confused the word "willingness" (*boulentat*) for "kindness" (*bountat*). While she had trouble distinguishing the two words, she did believe the word "kindness" sounded much more respectful. The Lady bowed her head and smiled as she tenderly gazed upon the child. Bernadette began again and as she did, the Lady moved from the niche into the interior hollow. She stood close to Bernadette as she had before when she wanted to speak. Still that beautiful smile enriched her face. Bernadette kept repeating the question, determined to get an answer. She was prepared to ask ten times if necessary. On her fourth attempt, however, the beautiful, reassuring smile disappeared from the Lady's face. She "slipped Her rosary over Her right arm. She unfolded her hands and extended them toward the ground. She then folded them at her breast, raised her eyes to heaven and said, '*Que Soy Era Immaculada Conceptiou, I am the Immaculate Conception.*'"217

Bernadette did not know what that meant, but was excited just to know that finally, she had something to tell Abbé Peyramale.

6:00 AM

After about one hour the ecstasy ended, and the visionary wanted desperately to leave something at the site as a sign of her gratitude and thanksgiving. All she had taken with her, however, was her Aunt Lucile's solidarity candle, which she lit and held during the apparition. After getting her aunt's permission, she tucked it into a cavity between the rocks next to the spot where just moments before the Lady stood. Then she turned around and began to leave, excitedly repeating the Lady's words so as to be sure to remember the name she did not understand. As she passed by the crowd, several shouted to her, asking what the Lady had said. She did not answer but passed close enough to them that Jeanne-Marie Tourre was able to decipher the words that Bernadette repeated under her breath.

I am the Immaculate Conception

The sky, formerly gloomy and unmoving, was now showing signs of life as the rising sun began to brighten the darkness. Bernadette began her ascent up the partially illuminated hill when Ursule Nicolau ran up to her from behind, grabbed her arm and gave her a pleading kiss. She sensed Bernadette's happiness and asked, "'Do you know something?' 'Don't tell anyone,' Bernadette replied, 'but she said, *I am the Immaculate Conception.*'"[218]

As one might expect, Ursule shared the secret with her friend Eugenie Raval, who, despite admonitions not to say anything, told her sister Germaine, who told Dominiquette Cazenave and on and on until a great many people were abuzz with the information. With word spreading quickly among the onlookers, many broke out into prayer chanting, "Oh, Mary! Conceived without sin, Pray for us who have recourse to thee!" They had not seen, but they believed and prayed in the words imparted by Our Lady of the Miraculous Medal in her second apparition to Saint Catherine LaBoure in July 1830 in the rue du Bac, Paris, France.

Bernadette, however, was on a mission and heard none of it. She needed to let the Abbé know who the Lady was, though she herself was unaware. Reaching the rectory, she entered and yelled to Abbé Peyramale the words that the Lady had told her, "'I am the Immaculate Conception, she told me,' Bernadette said excitedly. 'Do you know what that means,' the Abbé asked. The child shook her head no. 'Then how can you say that, if you didn't understand?' the priest said. 'I repeated it all the way here,'" Bernadette answered.

Abbé Peyramale, though he didn't share his understanding with the innocent child standing before him, knew exactly what the words meant, and he couldn't prevent the tears from forming in his eyes. There was an extended silence broken only by Bernadette's murmur, "She still wants her chapel."[219] "'Go on home,' the priest said, choking back sobs, 'I'll see you another day.'"[220]

Bernadette's arrival home provided no rest. Several people had gathered. Dominiquette Cazenave, the sister of François' boss, pulled the little one aside. "Do you know the Lady's name," she inquired. Bernadette was a bit annoyed, realizing that only Ursule, in whom Bernadette confided, could have told Dominiquette that she knew the Lady's identity. Though she wanted to tell Abbé Pomian first, she shared the

107

information, but then immediately left to tell Abbé Pomian before he could hear the news from Dominiquette.

Afternoon

Abbé Pomian listened to Bernadette calmly. He was rather confused and noted that he wanted to discuss the day's events at the Grotto with Abbé Peyramale. Bernadette left but was still no wiser regarding the Lady's identity.

Confused, the child urgently needed to confide in someone who might offer an explanation. She hurried to the home of Mr. Estrade who was with his sister. She told them all about the vision, leaving out not a single detail. When she told of her boldness in pressing the Lady to identify herself she seemed a little embarrassed and lowered her head. Then, turning toward Estrade's sister she said, "'Mademoiselle, what does it mean, Immaculate Conception?' Bernadette had great difficulty even saying the word and "always pronounced it Con-chep-tion, laboriously articulating each syllable."[221] Tears filled the eyes of her audience as Bernadette demonstrated the Lady's actions and how she identified herself at the Grotto. Clearly, the innocent child had no idea that the Lady had just unmistakably identified herself as the Mother of God. Before bidding the Estrades farewell, however, she would understand the significance of the revelation and was overjoyed with the realization that she had actually been visited by the Blessed Virgin.

Friday, March 26, 1858

Many of the faithful had long believed that the Lady of Bernadette's vision was in fact the Virgin Mary, the Mother of God, but the revelation of March 25 removed any doubt and the number of people showing up each day to the Grotto was even greater than before. Marie Dufo was one of the many people that questioned Bernadette, writing down every word as the visionary patiently described the apparitions in beguiling detail.

The authorities were now more concerned than ever, wondering where all this hysteria would lead. To that end, the Prefect of Tarbes, Baron Massy, sat down to write a second letter to the Minister for Ecclesiastical Affairs, informing him of the events and seeking guidance and/or intervention.

Saturday, March 27, 1858
The Fifth Interrogation

After giving the matter significant thought, Massy came up with another plan. He summoned Bernadette to both interrogate the child regarding the latest happenings at the Grotto and perform an in-depth medical examination on her with the hope of proving that she was mentally unstable. For the latter purpose, he selected three doctors in whom he had complete confidence. They were Doctors Balencie, Lacrampe, and Peyrus. These medical professionals not only had the respect of the administrative authority of Lourdes, who governed the Hospice for which Dr. Balencie worked, but had exhibited no intent to betray the administration with false reports based on non-scientific findings. After contacting those who didn't believe in the developments at the Grotto and composing a dossier for the prosecution, the doctors were ready to conduct their examination on the child. For two hours the doctors examined Bernadette both physically and mentally.

Initially they found nothing alarming about the child noting that she was "of a delicate constitution, of a lymphatic and nervous temperament; her eyes have a vivid expression; her head is of a regular shape. But narrow, small rather than large."[222] They did note that her breathing was labored and that there was significant wheezing. This, they attributed to asthma.

The doctors then made Bernadette recount the events at the Grotto of Massabielle. They asked if the child really saw a Lady, to which she replied, "Of course, I see her as I see you. She moves, she talks to me, she holds out her arms."[223] Shaking their heads, they asked Bernadette to start at the beginning with the first time she heard the "rush of wind" that preceded the apparition. Bernadette responded in minute detail, but to the surprise of the doctors, she seemed unaware of some of the things that others had said about her and the visions. The doctors wondered amongst themselves if it was a memory issue or a sign that Bernadette had made up the entire story. They asked the child, "Aren't you afraid when you see so many people around you, throwing themselves at you?"[224] "'At those moments,' Bernadette responded calmly, 'I don't see a thing around me.'"[225] The doctors now understood that Bernadette simply did not know what others were doing or saying during her ecstasy.

Sunday, March 28, 1858
to Tuesday, March 30, 1858

Throughout the following four days, the team of doctors debated the contents of the report that was to be submitted to Baron Massy. They were confused by Bernadette and could not agree on the wording of the report. They didn't want to anger the prefect, but at the same time, they couldn't exaggerate the medical facts. Massy's questions to the doctors were clear. "Is the child suffering from a mental disorder? Is treatment necessary for her?"[226] After great debate and consternation among themselves, they finally addressed the issue with carefully crafted language. "There is nothing to indicate that Bernadette wanted to deceive the public," they wrote. "The child is of an impressionable nature and could have been a victim of a hallucination; a reflection of light, no doubt, drew her attention to the side of the grotto; her imagination, under the influence of a moral predisposition, gave it a form that impresses children. Must not the young child's state of mind have been more and more affected and her overexcitement reached its peak? What at first was a simple hallucination exercises more control. And here we find a genuine state of ecstasy, that lesion in the mind, which places the one affected under the domination of the idea that obsesses him. Examples of this type are moreover reported by the authors.

Does the ailment require treatment? We have little to say on this subject. The sickness that we believe can be assigned to Bernadette offers no risk to the health of this child within the limits observed. It is likely, on the contrary, that when Bernadette is no longer harassed by the crowd, when they no longer ask for prayers, she will stop thinking about the grotto and the wonderous events she described."[227] In short, the doctors agreed that Bernadette's "illness" was an administrative issue, not a medical one.[228]

It wasn't perfect, but Massy thought it was enough to at least open the door of opportunity. He ordered Bernadette's detention, citing the June 30, 1838 law concerning lunatics. Under the authority of that law, Massy could commit Bernadette to the hospice at Tarbes for observation. Though temporary, this observation could lead to a transfer to the lunatic asylum on a more permanent basis. He hurried to inform the mayors of the district of Lourdes, asking for their support. That support was not forthcoming.

Bernadette, meanwhile, went to school each day, lending a particular focus to her Catechism. She often went to the Grotto hoping to see the Lady. She would kneel on her rock and pray but Our Lady didn't come. From the day she gained understanding of the meaning of the Immaculate Conception, Bernadette referred to the Lady as Our Lady of the Grotto, or Our Lady of Massabielle. Her life remained essentially the same as it was prior to the first apparition. The throngs of people no longer invaded the cachot and Bernadette was able to interact with her family, attend school, play with her friends, and the like, but she now carried with her a peaceful joy at all times, despite still having to repeat her story numerous times to visitors from all sectors. She remained ever humble, more self-effacing and monotonous in her tone, leading some visitors to leave feeling rather disappointed.

On the day following the interrogation by the doctors, three sisters, Antoinette, Marie, and Theotiste Tardhivail asked Bernadette if she was afraid of the Commissioner and Prosecutor and if she feared being put in jail. Bernadette replied with a laugh that she wasn't afraid of anyone and could care less about being jailed. Bernadette now had the joy and comfort of knowing that the Blessed Virgin would protect her.

Bernadette and her family were still living in abject poverty in the cachot, a former prison closed because the building was deemed unfit even for prisoners. Throughout the period of the apparitions, many people offered the child money or other items of value. The child, however, would accept nothing. When Bernadette rejected a forty-franc piece and another worth twenty francs, offered by two gentlemen moved by the extent of the Soubirouses' poverty at the cachot, Antoinette Tardhivail was moved to write,

> "And nevertheless, they are poor as our Lord was poor when he was on this earth, and on this little girl Mary has cast her eyes, preferring her to so many rich young people, who, at this very moment, envy the lot of her whom they would have looked at with contempt. They now consider themselves lucky to be able to kiss her and touch her hand."[229]

Wednesday, April 1, 1858

Mayor Lacadé of Lourdes was one of the officials worried about the events taking place. The crowds at the Grotto were so large that he had no capacity to control them. The people were loud, they disrupted the peacefulness of the town. What if they became angry or if someone got hurt? Would he be held responsible? Many thoughts filled his head, so he sat at his desk and penned a letter to Prefect Baron Massy, hoping for guidance or at least to lighten his own burden. "The crowds at the Grotto remain as big as ever," he wrote, "in fact their numbers increased considerably over the holidays. The majority of people who go there as a matter of piety pray to God with great fervor. I assume that after the Easter holidays the numbers will begin to decrease...."[230] The Mayor may have been expressing more hope than belief when he jotted those words.

Thursday, April 2, 1858
to Sunday, April 5, 1858

For many Christians throughout the world it was Holy Week. It began with the arrival of Palm Sunday, a few days prior, commemorating Jesus' triumphant entry into Jerusalem. For Catholics, Holy Week is traditionally a week of somber reflection on the events preceding Jesus' death: His triumphant entry into Jerusalem; His betrayal by Judas; His Last Supper with his twelve apostles; His arrest, crucifixion, and death; and His burial in a tomb. All of these events culminate with His triumphant resurrection just three days later on Easter Sunday, which was to be celebrated on April 4. Because of those sacred days, rumors spread throughout Lourdes that Bernadette was going to the Grotto. So, on Good Friday, three hundred people gathered at the site. To their great disappointment, Bernadette was not there.

Prefect Baron Massy had secured the mayor's letter and now, however, had more pressing issues on his mind. He was less concerned with Holy Week and much more preoccupied with the ruckus that Bernadette was causing in his town. Consequently, he left his home to attend a meeting with Bishop Laurence of Tarbes. He hoped to discuss a strategy to address the Grotto issue that was spinning out of control; a strategy that the Bishop might be willing to support and promote. But the official concern about Bernadette and her Lady could not interfere with destiny.

Monday, April 6, 1858
10:00 AM – 4:00 PM

Unaware of all the official fuss, Bernadette and her family left Lourdes to travel to the town of Ade, located about four kilometers from their cachot. Blaise Vergez, the former mayor of Ade turned wine merchant, had long suffered from the pain of persistent rheumatism. Nicknamed Blazy, Vergez had gotten relief by washing in the icy waters of the Grotto. Blazy summoned Bernadette with the hope of meeting her and introducing her to the parish priest over lunch. The child was rather uncomfortable in this setting, however, and after having a routine lunch, she and her family quickly left Ade for the comforting, more familiar confines of Lourdes. She was accompanied by Blazy's son.

Shortly after returning to the cachot, Bernadette felt that familiar urge to go to the Grotto. First, she went to church so she could pray and go to confession. Antoinette Tardhivail happened to be in the sacristy at that time preparing the priest's vestments for Vespers. Noticing Bernadette, she "sounded the alarm in town."[231] Townspeople questioned François and Louise about the prospect of Bernadette returning to the Grotto in the face of the officials' recent actions. How would Jacomet respond if he found her there? The Soubirouses worried, but there was little time to think about the consequences.

Blazy's son proposed a scheme to bring Bernadette with him back to the village of Ade. The Soubirouses could then say honestly to any that might ask, that Bernadette was neither at the Grotto nor at the cachot. This, hopefully, would keep the officials and other curiosity seekers away. However, according to his plan, he would secretly bring Bernadette to the Grotto at daybreak the following morning, or before if it suited her. His proposal was accepted.

Antoinette Tardhivail knew nothing of the plan but was reasonably certain that Bernadette would be at the Grotto the following morning. Rather than chance sleeping through the event, she decided to stay awake, spending the entire "night 'on a trunk,' counting the hours."[232]

Tuesday, April 7, 1858
The Seventeenth Apparition
5:00 AM

True to his word, Blazy's son had Bernadette at the Grotto before sunrise. Despite the deception, about one hundred people were already gathered when the child knelt on her rock to pray. She held a large candle that Blazy provided her, but the weight of it caused Bernadette to place it on the ground, holding it at the top with cupped hands to protect the flame from the breeze.

Among the early spectators was Antoinette Tardhivail, who despite the lack of sleep, was ready to watch the child converse with Our Lady of the Grotto, the Virgin Mary. Dr. Dozous was also there, ready to chronicle the events that might take place. He was eager to learn more about Bernadette and her apparitions following the inexplicable cure of his patient, Louis Bouriette. As a man of science, he desperately wanted to find a way to explain why Louis could now see. He worked his way to the front of the crowd, providing an excellent opportunity to observe the child up close.

The Virgin appeared, and Bernadette fell into ecstasy. As she prayed, the onlookers noticed waves of joy. Her appearance was elated, her eyes lost in love and she recited the prayers of the Rosary with angelic fervor. As she had during each prior apparition during which she wanted to speak to the child, the Lady pointed her finger toward the ground. Bernadette understood that she was to walk under the arch of the ground cavern where she again could converse with her beautiful Lady, the Mother of God.

As she "began to rise from her knees, there was a sudden pause in the movement, and her right hand, coming near the left, put the flame of the large candle under the fingers of that hand, which were far enough apart from each other to allow the flame to pass between them easily. At that moment a fairly strong breeze caused the flame to flicker up, but it did not appear to produce any effect on the flesh."[233]

Dr. Dozous could not believe what he was witnessing, and a look around demonstrated that those around him were equally unnerved. The child moved toward the cavern as instructed by the Lady and they spoke for several minutes. During that time, the Virgin Mary made it clear to Bernadette that she still wanted her chapel built at the site. The entire Apparition lasted about thirty minutes.

Immediately following the ecstasy, Dr. Dozous ran to the child and examined her hands and fingers, expecting to see them charred by the flame of the candle. "'There's nothing there!' he exclaimed. 'I don't know what you see, but now I believe that you do see something,'"[234] he said breathlessly. He instructed Fourcade and Martinous, the gamekeeper Callet, the Tardhivail young ladies and the other witnesses within the range of his voice, to leave Bernadette alone, and taking his pocket watch from his vest, was able to observe her perfectly for about fifteen minutes. During these minutes he took the lit candle and placed it near the child's left hand. She immediately withdrew her hand from his grasp saying, "But you're burning me."[235]

6:00 AM – 10:00 AM

The news of "the miracle of the candle" spread like wildfire throughout the village and beyond. People began flocking to the cachot once again. To escape the drama, Bernadette fled to the protection of the home of Antoinette Tardhivail and her sisters. The three sisters questioned the child about the apparition, her discussion with the Lady, and the candle flame. "But why did you put your hand like that on the flame? Weren't you afraid of burning yourself?" The child was weary from all the questions but was surprised especially by that one. She had no idea what Antoinette was talking about. Antoinette took Bernadette's hands and examined her fingers. Nothing. They were soft to the touch. With the exception of some needle marks on her index finger caused by her sewing, the child's hands were delicate and unmarked.

Antoinette decided to perform her own experiment and asked Bernadette to cup her hands as she had earlier that morning at the Grotto. Then she slipped a lighted candle between them. The child immediately pulled them back, crying, "I'm burning myself." At that, the child got up and left. No sooner had she walked out of the door of the Tardhivail house, when she was met by Madame Garoby who was distraught for having missed the morning apparition. Having heard of "the miracle of the candle," however, she took her own candle and lit it so as to perform her own experiment. Bernadette was able to pull her hand away in time. Thinking that everyone had gone mad, Bernadette quickly ran away.

The many stories of these miracles were problematic and a cause of embarrassment to the public officials. Now, a noted and respected professional, Dr. Dozous, passed along his account of the candle incident to the newspaper. From the point of view of the officials, something needed to be done to end the madness.

Wednesday, April 8, 1858
to Thursday, April 9, 1858

An edition of *Le Lavedan*, an area newspaper, picked up the story of Bernadette and the candle, writing:

> "...A witness has assured us that whilst in ecstasy she held her hand in contact with the flame of a candle for quite a long time and that she did not feel the slightest pain. You can well imagine that people began to shout that it was a miracle...."[236]

This and other accounts of the events of Massabielle, both verbal and written, spawned even more activity at the Grotto and its appearance began to change. People were leaving flowers, both real and artificial, in vases. There were a great many ex-votos, statues, and statuettes left at the site, and candles, so many candles. The area took on the look of a junkyard. People even threw money into the hollow, several thousand francs in all, and incredibly, no one took it away.

Perhaps more surprising was the fact that the visions had occurred over the course of two separate judicial court sessions and over that time, not a crime was committed in the department or a sole criminal convicted.

Friday, April 10, 1858
The Sixth Interrogation

Monsieur de Resseguier was a representative in the legislative assembly of 1849; a member of Parliament. He was also a legitimist and one of the signers of the declaration that deposed Emperor Louis-Napoleon. To say he was a man of political influence might be an understatement, and on that day, he went to Lourdes with a gift of a chasuble for Abbé Peyramale and the church in Lahitee. A chasuble is the outermost liturgical vestment worn by the clergy of the Catholic Church for the celebration of the Eucharist. They are expensive, and it was no small gesture on the part of de Resseguier.

De Resseguier may have had an ulterior motive for his visit, however, because during his short stay at the rectory in Lourdes, he also arranged for a meeting with Bernadette. Under the watchful eye of Abbé Peyramale, he spoke with the child for a long time. In particular, de Resseguier tried to trip up Bernadette on the Lady's words of March 25 in which the Lady identified Herself as The Immaculate Conception. "That expression had not yet been introduced in Lourdes."[237] And de Resseguier was taken aback by the child's use of the name. His reaction was not surprising and mirrored Abbé Peyramale's own rejoinder when he first heard the name fall from Bernadette's lips.

Peyramale later said of the examination, "Everything about this girl struck him vividly; he subjected her to a most detailed, thorough and tricky interrogation, and this child answered all his questions with explanations beyond her years and, it seems to me, beyond her understanding."[238]

Sunday, April 12, 1858

The Minister of Ecclesiastical Affairs had been mulling over the events of Massabielle and more importantly, recalling the events of the meeting he had with, and letters he received from, Baron Massy, the Prefect of Tarbes. It is likely that they both heard the other stories coming from Lourdes. Not the tales of Bernadette's Lady and the ecstasy that followed, but those of the ghostly, evil presence around the vicinity of the Grotto. There were tales of the young girl of rue Basse who heard "a mysterious chorus of celestial voices.... Upon her return to the Grotto area, she heard gentle notes followed by "strange dissonances, by 'false and shrieking' tones which gradually rose to a cacophony. Then there was growling and the sound of combat. The young girl was so frightened that she did not want to go back to Massabielle again."[239]

There was the bizarre story that the twelve-year-old boy told of seeing the "Ugly One," while waiting at the Grotto for his friends to arrive and there were many instances of demonic possession that kept Ambulant Missionary Fr. Beluze busy in the performance of exorcisms. It was time for action and he was certain that the officials would not react without his prodding. Responding to the Prefect's pleadings, the Minister wrote:

> "I have examined the two reports that you were good enough to forward to me on March 12 and 26 respectively concerning the supposed appearance of the Virgin at the grotto in the neighborhood of Lourdes. In my view it is time to put a stop to happenings which must in the last resort compromise the real interests of Catholicism and undermine the religious feelings of the population."

He went on to discuss a particular point of law warning that, if invoked too quickly, would lead to grave difficulties. He recommended instead the use of tact, prudence, and firmness. The Minister also advised the Prefect to co-operate with Monseigneur Laurence, Bishop of Tarbes saying:

> "I authorize you to inform that prelate in my name that in my view we should not allow a state of affairs to go unhindered which cannot fail to serve as a pretext for new attacks against the clergy and against religion."

Upon reading the letter, Baron Massy was elated knowing that finally, someone with ties to the church agreed that "the Bernadette issue" posed a problem. He immediately scheduled a meeting with Bishop Laurence. After exchanging pleasantries, Massy noted "'the burning problem of the moment,' and explained the confusion created by Bernadette's stories. 'One thing or the other, Monseigneur,' Massy noted, 'either the Visions at Lourdes are authentic, in which case they should be sanctioned, or they are not, in which case they should be condemned.'"[240] The Bishop listened intently, but Massy pushed too hard by "insisting that a declaration one way or the other on the part of Monseigneur, the Bishop of Tarbes, was now 'absolutely imperative.'"[241]

Bishop Laurence was not impressed. He was strong-willed and didn't take kindly to being bullied. "'I do not share your view,' he calmly told Massy. In circumstances such as these, 'the duty of a bishop is to refrain from all personal judgement and wait until Providence has revealed the truth.'"[242]

"Your silence could become a danger to public order and tranquility, Monseigneur,"[243] Massy protested. "Again, that is not my view. They pray at the Grotto, and I have yet to be convinced that prayer represents any very serious danger,"[244] Laurence noted.

Massy saw that he was getting nowhere so decidedly changed the course of the conversation. "Public worship is taking place at the Massabielle Grotto against the express provisions of the law. The administration cannot tolerate at Lourdes what it forbids elsewhere."[245] The Bishop again reacted strongly to the threat. "Consider carefully what measures you propose to take,"[246] he said coldly. Massy concluded by telling the Bishop that he could not shirk his public duty and the two parted company.

Between Monday, April 13, 1858
and Sunday, May 3, 1858

While the church and public officials argued about how to handle the issue that Bernadette created, the Soubirouses sank deeper into poverty. Though offered a hundred thousand gold francs from a foreign family offering to adopt Bernadette, they refused. They also steadfastly refused to accept anything from the many visitors that came to their home to talk with the child visionary. Despite their refusals, the Soubirouses were still accused of enriching themselves through Bernadette's fiction.

Then things got worse! Five women visited the Grotto shortly after de Resseguier's meeting with Abbé Peyramale and Bernadette. They carried a ladder which they leaned against the Grotto wall to enable access to the upper niche in which the Lady appeared when not in conversation with Bernadette. The narrow opening was about ten feet from ground level, just right of the main opening of the Grotto. Wearing their fright and emotion on their sleeves, they reluctantly climbed the ladder until they were eye level with the niche. They then climbed a bit higher, enabling them to step inside. Walking in, they noticed, through the flickering of their candles, that the stalactite formed a "dazzling white shape, standing upright."[247] Stalactite is a calcium salt deposit created by dripping water. It hangs from the roof of caves like icicles in a tapering form. In the dimly lit darkness of the cavern, with imaginations running wild, these devout ladies believed that they too "had seen the Blessed Virgin. Thus, began the epidemic of visionaries."[248]

Meanwhile, Bernadette's health was declining. Perhaps it was the excitement, or maybe it was her asthma. Regardless of the cause, by Wednesday, April 22, it had all caught up to her and when several people called on Bernadette at the cachot over the ensuing days, they found her in bed. Several priests were among the visitors, and despite her medical condition, Bernadette was interviewed many times from bed. In some cases, translators were required for interpretation. Bernadette always told the same story the same way, making it a most tedious day.

Rising Tensions

Amidst the cures, interrogations, and disruptions to Bernadette's personal life, the heretofore subtle disagreements between Bishop Laurence and Prefect Massy over the handling of the Grotto affair reached a boiling point. However, the source of contention was not Bernadette, but rather the desecration of sacred ground by the Prefect.

Baron Massy realized that his carriage and saddle horses were in need of a new domicile. While he wished for spacious and elegant stable accommodations, he hadn't the extra land on which to build them without destroying the aesthetic nature of his courtyard. To resolve his dilemma,

Massy chose to construct his new stables on a former cemetery located between the Prefecture and the Cathedral and construction began without delay. As construction crews dug the foundations, human bones and tombstones were disrupted and the new "buildings were erected exactly opposite the ancient doors of the Cathedral, and at a very small distance from it, so that the noise of the stable was unavoidably heard by the congregation."[249]

Massy ignored Bishop Laurence's pleas, seemingly unconcerned for the desecration of consecrated ground that belonged to the church. It was not in Massy's nature to admit that he could be wrong about anything, and when challenged, he doubled down. Laurence protested loudly and even appealed to the Minister of Public Worship. This greatly annoyed the Prefect, who instructed his workmen to plow ahead with the construction.

The Minister travelled to Paris seeking support from the Council General to help stop the madness and sought legal opinions throughout the process. The battle raged for months but was eventually decided in favor of the Bishop. While the battle was won, the outcome of the war would be in doubt, as the harmonious relationship that had existed between Laurence and Massy, the Church and the government, was irreparably impaired. In fact, "this harmony was succeeded by an intense feeling of irritation. [Massy] ceased to be inclined to arrange matters amicably; perhaps his tendencies took quite the opposite direction. [Just as he] wished to encroach on the property of the Church in this miserable affair of his stables, so with regard to the question of the Apparitions, he from that time felt more inclined than before to encroach on the spiritual jurisdiction of the Bishop. The bridle, which up to that moment had kept him in check, was snapped."[250]

Monday, May 4, 1858
Mid-day

Massy had seen and heard enough and was ready to take matters of the Grotto into his own hands. The investigations initiated by Jacomet in the

Police Commissioner's office were abysmal failures and the church leaders were clearly not willing to offer any assistance, despite some supportive words from the Bishop. *This will end today*, the Prefect thought to himself. On behalf of the district, he announced the adoption of some exceedingly strong measures. "I have instructed the Commissioner of Police," Masse said, "to seize and transfer to the Town Hall all objects placed in the Grotto and to hold them there at the disposal of those who so placed them. Further, I have issued orders for the detention and transfer to Tarbes for treatment as sick persons at the expense of the Department all those who give themselves out to be visionaries. At the same time, I will prosecute as disseminators of false news all those who contribute to spreading the absurd rumors now current in the matter."[251] Based on this new mandate, Bernadette could have been arrested immediately as one who readily admitted that she had seen visions of the Immaculate Conception; and, at least initially, that was the plan.

Mayor Lacadé, who was tasked with seizing Bernadette, and Commissioner Jacomet, charged with sacking the Grotto, were less than enthused. The mayor thought it best for him and Prosecutor Dutour to visit Abby Peyramale before taking any action so as to better understand the position the church might take should Bernadette be detained. He found out on quick order. "'The Prefect has no right whatever to order the arrest of Bernadette Soubirous,' he said, hinting at anger. 'Oh, it is perfectly legal,' Dutour countered. 'It is nothing of the sort,'"[252] Peyramale said immediately, pulling himself up as he did and warning that if Bernadette was arrested, it would have to be over his dead body. Lacadé was a perceptive man, but a keen perception was not necessary to know that the good priest meant it. Further, the priest noted that the people of Lourdes, who were clearly of sound mind, were on the side of Bernadette. Their patience shouldn't be tested, he warned. Besides, Bernadette was too sick to be detained.

Evening

While Lacadé was learning exactly where the local church stood with regard to Bernadette's potential arrest, Jacomet was sacking the Grotto as instructed. The locals stood silently and did nothing to make his task easier. Four cartloads of ex-votos and other religious items were taken that day.

Meanwhile, a large crowd paraded toward Massabielle, illuminating the path with the hundreds of lighted consecrated candles that they carried. They sang hymns to the Virgin Mary as they processed. The officials watched with concern. The people took it as a sign from God when unpleasantries befell the woman who rented to Jacomet the cart that he used to haul away their pious objects from the Grotto and to the man who lent him the ax. That is when Massy decided that it might indeed be wise to abandon his plan and to leave young Bernadette alone.

Tuesday, May 5, 1858

After conferring with Lacadé, Massy was now convinced that he would not be able to arrest Bernadette, at least not without causing a major incident with the Church and exposing himself to the wrath of the public. That is, unless he was able to debunk the "myth" of the cures that had been attributed to the spring water from the Grotto.

Wednesday, May 6, 1858

A little thought and Massy believed he had the perfect way to debunk the miracle cures. He decided to have the water from the spring at the Grotto tested. The Prefect couldn't lose. If the analysis showed that the water contained some therapeutic principal that contributed to the cure of the sick and infirmed, then talk of miraculous cures would subside and he could claim the water for himself in an entrepreneurial effort to bottle and sell it. The public would have been provided with a natural explanation of the phenomena.

He entrusted the task to a chemist at the Prefecture by name of Latour. Latour, who had previously worked as a pharmacist at Trie, was given a sample of the Massabielle water for analysis. Following the analytical work, Latour would issue a report on his findings. Massy fully expected that the analysis would disclose the curative properties which represented the mineral riches of his department.

Friday, May 8, 1858

Bernadette suffered greatly from her asthmatic condition. She was so sick that sacraments of the church were administered according to ecclesiastic custom. It was suggested that Bernadette be taken to Cauterets, a small village located about 20 miles outside of Lourdes. It bordered the Pyrenees and was therefore surrounded by high mountains. Flowing from those mountains were waters that were believed to have therapeutic qualities. It was the waters of the Cauterets that formed the Thermal Baths of Cesar. The waters would do her good, it was thought. Besides, removing her from Lourdes would protect her from arrest, which under the edict of May 4, could happen at any time. Bernadette believed that concern over her illness was overstated as was the talk of any impending arrest. As she left the cachot for the healing waters of Cauterets, she said, "I fear nothing because I have always told the truth."[253] Regardless, Bernadette quietly slipped out of Lourdes to the rest and tranquility of Cauterets.

Friday, May 15, 1858

Bernadette's rest was destined to last only one week, however. That was just about how long it took the news of her departure to reach the ears of Prefect Massy. Upon hearing the news, Massy sent word to the Cauterets Police Commissioner to "Put Bernadette and those around her under a discreet surveillance and watch all their movements. Send me a report."[254]

Thursday, May 17
to Sunday, May 21, 1858

Removing the religious items from the Grotto did nothing to assuage the enthusiasm of the crowds, which continued to descend upon the Grotto in numbers that increased each day. The curious followed the faithful, having heard the stories of rocks haunted with evil spirits. Dwelling on the luridness, some worked themselves into a frenzy. Surveying the situation, Abbé Peyramale decided it was time to take control before the sensationalism took over. On Sunday, May 17, the Abbé took to his pulpit to urge his parishioners to be prudent. He intoned mothers to watch over their young children carefully and keep them from the Grotto of Massabielle. He talked of the day in which the Virgin Mother would triumph and vanquish evil, converting the Grotto to a holy place for all. But for now, he warned, the devil may have taken up residence in those rocks.

Among the parishioners that day stood two policemen whose identity was concealed in plain clothes. They were part of Jacomet's surveillance team. Fortunately for Bernadette and those who believed her visions, they misunderstand much of the sermon and reported back to Jacomet that the "clergy of Lourdes had at last disavowed the events at the Grotto and the fairy tales told by Bernadette."[255]

Despite any comfort Jacomet may have realized from the fictitious narratives provided by his men, reports of miraculous cures emanating from the spring at the Grotto continued to spread.

In late February of 1858, Catherine Latapie lived just a few miles outside of Lourdes in the town of Loubajac and was in the final months of pregnancy with her third child. Two years earlier, at the age of thirty-six, she fell from a tree, injuring her right hand. "The accident caused a subluxation of the humerus, which was easily reducible, but owning to the traumatic stretching of the brachial plexus, she was left with an ulnar type of paralysis" rendering useless the pinky and ring finger of her right hand "which were held in typical palmer flexion."[256]

During the night of the last day in February, Latapie had the sudden urge to visit the Grotto of Lourdes. So irresistible was this yearning that at three o'clock in the morning she awakened her two children and together they left for the Grotto. Latapie and her children arrived at about dawn and joined Bernadette in prayer. When the prayer had ended, Latapie bathed her hand in the small hollow where the spring water collected. Immediately her fingers "regained their movements and suppleness. She could flex and extend them with the same facility as she could before the accident."[257] Without delay, Latapie returned home. That evening, she gave birth to her third child.[258]

Henri Busquet's story is another included in the succession of miraculous cures. The fifteen-year-old boy from Nay, in the Atlantic Pyrenees, suffered. For fifteen months the boy was ill. It started as a simple fever and was initially diagnosed as typhoid. Later the diagnosis was changed to the dreaded tuberculosis. This was quickly "followed by an abscess in his neck, a purulent adenitis, which spread to the right side of his chest. Several months later, the doctor lanced the abscess to avoid fistula formation, but developments were of the most complicated kind."[259] In early 1858, Henri was admitted to a facility in the town of Cauterets for a short time, but his condition only worsened as he developed a throat ulcer and two glandular stoppages, one on either side of the ulcer. There were no signs that Henri would get any better. The boy asked his parents to take him to Lourdes, but they refused. Regardless, they did convince a neighbor to bring him some of the water from the Grotto. On the night of April 28, 1858, while his family prayed, the boy applied the water to the base of his neck. Dr. Subervielle had previously advised the boy's parents that cold water would aggravate the condition, but that didn't seem to matter now. After the self-inflicted treatment, Henri retired to his bed for the night. When he awoke the next morning, the tumors and the ulcer had completely vanished, leaving only some scar tissue in the place of the latter. All the medical experience of the time indicated that such ulcers "are specifically slow in healing-if they ever heal."[260] Astonishingly, this healing occurred overnight. Several doctors reported on the phenomenon. Professor Vergez cautiously noted that this cure "departed from the ordinary course of nature."[261]

These stories are astounding, but they represent only two of the many cures that were reported at the time. The reports led to ever increasing crowds at the Grotto, people who were comforted with the thought of having a higher power to assist in their time of troubles. To the authorities, particularly the law enforcement personnel charged with keeping the peace, it represented only a widespread sense of anxiety.

With the increased multitudes that beat a path to the Grotto daily, the local newspapers devoted more of their attention to the events. *Ere Imperiale* and *Le Lavedan* were progressive papers that went out of their way to exhibit hostility toward anything related to the events at Lourdes. Even the larger papers, such as *Les Debats* and *Le Siecle* reported that the events of Lourdes constituted a "well-staged affair."[262] They even resorted to "fake news" in an attempt to discredit Bernadette's story. The newsmen vividly recalled the sensationalized story of Rose Tamisier that occurred some seven years earlier.

In that case, Rose, a young and sickly peasant girl claimed to have had supernatural visions. She spoke of receiving the Eucharist "from celestial and luminous hands, and she also said that on certain days she bore the stigmata of Christ."[263] As if to punctuate the matter, a painting which hung in the Church of Saint-Saturnin, Rose's place of worship, a picture depicting the crucified Christ being lowered from the cross, started to bleed from Christ's wounds. Initially the bleeding took place only in the presence of Rose, but afterwards it also happened when a crowd was assembled. The believers proclaimed it a miracle, but the church elders approached it with more caution. The Bishop of Avignon instituted careful inquiries. It was during this inquisition that Rose was exposed. She had been complicit with the sacristan and the parish priest, Abbé Grand. Rose was sentenced to serve a prison term for her role.

Certainly, the authorities in Lourdes were well aware of that hoax and, because of it, even more skeptical of the local events taking place at the Grotto. They believed that, in time, Bernadette, too, would be exposed as a fraud. They simply needed time. Of course, their position on the matter belied the fact that since the spring was uncovered at the Grotto by Bernadette at the instruction of her Vision, many people were cured of long-standing, irreversible medical conditions. Those cures were apparently inconvenient truths that the authorities and the press chose to ignore.

Friday, May 22, 1858

Prefect Massy had waited patiently as rumors spread wildly throughout Lourdes. Finally, the report from the Police Commissioner of Cauterets arrived. The report detailed Bernadette's activities in the Village. "Bernadette Soubirous," the report began, "...has been the subject of a very active surveillance. This girl went regularly to bathe at the Bruzeaud baths. Several people questioned her about her so-called visions. She keeps to her original story. Several sick people spoke to her, but she limits her answers to saying that, if they believed in God, they would obtain their cure; she has always refused any remuneration."[264]

Saturday, May 23, 1858

Bernadette Soubirous as she appeared after the 1858 Apparitions, but before entering the convent at Nevers.

Bernadette was unaware of the Police Commissioner's surveillance activities and she departed Cauterets as she had arrived, with assumed anonymity. The people of Lourdes were much dismayed over Bernadette's absence and her return was greeted with a renewed vigor and a continuation of the visits to the cachot.

Tuesday, May 26, 1858

The increased activity worried the officials, prompting Police Commissioner Jacomet to write in his report, "Young Bernadette returned from Cauterets Saturday morning; they call her to various houses; they show her off to strangers; in a word, they never miss an opportunity to bring her out. For example, yesterday at nine o'clock, Mass was being said for a woman's group; it was a policeman's wife's turn to distribute the blessed bread. Do you know, Monsieur le Prefet, whom she chose to bring it to the altar in church? Bernadette, of course, who naturally attracted the attention of all the people in church. That's all it took to make Bernadette the topic of conversation for the rest of the day for those very people who had almost forgotten all about her."[265] Despite his apparent discomfort with all things Bernadette, Jacomet concluded, "No trouble. No disorder to report."[266] His words, incoherent as they were, probably reflected his anxiety.

For Catholics worldwide, May is the month of Mary. To celebrate the Queen of Heaven, Bernadette set up a makeshift altar in the front of the cachot and decorated it with flowers, a custom she had learned from her time in Bartrès. Marie Fourcade delivered a floral crown that was made by the nuns of Bagnères. Bernadette placed the crown on top of the statue of Mary that adorned the altar.

Friday, May 29, 1858

The spring weather was amazing, a fact that may have been responsible for more traffic at the cachot than usual. Among the many visitors was

Abbé Vincent Père, who was not exactly supportive of Bernadette's visions. He had actually come to Lourdes to visit his godmother but decided to take advantage of his time in Lourdes by visiting the visionary child he had heard so much about. Despite warnings from his godmother that the Bishop had recently forbidden all priests from talking to the child, he decided to go anyway. Being from Landes, he was not under the jurisdiction of the Bishop of Tarbes. So technically, he was not violating Bishop Laurence's directive. He trekked to the cachot and said sternly, "Are you the little clown who claims to see the Virgin on rocks of Massabielle?"[267] The child answered affirmatively, and Abbé Père immediately labeled her claims as a lie, for which he threatened to send her to jail. Louise burst into tears, but Bernadette remained steady, noting that it was the Blessed Virgin who instructed her on how to reply to such questions. On and on the interrogation went until Abbé Père noticed that the house was now full of visitors, laborers returning from work, who by their facial expressions, were not happy with the priest's tone. Pare understood the danger and toned it down. Still questioning the child, Abbé Pare tried to convince her that she simply imagined hearing the Blessed Virgin. "I went to the rocks of Massabielle myself yesterday," the priest said, "and I thought I heard something move. It must have been the same with you. You probably heard some bird who was hiding there, and you imagined it was the Blessed Virgin who spoke to you." "If it's a bird," Bernadette replied, "it wouldn't have spoken." Pare was floored by her response but before he could digest her reply, a workman approached Pare, holding a fist to his nose.

Pare turned to leave when he came face to face with Dr. Dozous, who said that the interchange proved without doubt that Bernadette was not lying. He requested the priest's name so that he could write up a full report that he wanted the priest to sign. But with a terse refusal, the priest left the cachot.

Wednesday, June 3, 1858

One of the more pleasurable priestly duties is the administration of the sacrament of First Communion. It is a time of rejoicing for

Catholics as the children experience the Body and Blood of their risen savior for the very first time. It is the culmination of hours of study and preparation on behalf of the children and a source of growth for the Church.

All the preparatory study is concluded with a personal interview in which the child is required to answer questions presented by the priest and a selected layperson. The questions generally center around the area of study and are used to determine the child's preparedness for reception of the sacrament.

Bernadette's questioning, however, deviated from the routine. A woman who had been dying to meet the visionary child assisted Abbé Peyramale in Bernadette's interview. Referring to Abbé Peyramale's directive that Bernadette refrain from going to the Grotto, she asked, "Monsieur le Curé [Peyramale] forbids you to go to the Grotto. Suppose the Blessed Virgin ordered you to go, what would you do?" "I would come and ask Monsieur le Curé's permission," Bernadette calmly responded. In more ways than one, Bernadette had proven herself a worthy candidate for First Communion, and her day had finally arrived.

Abbé Peyramale participated in the ceremony as he had each successive year. Bernadette was overjoyed as she arrived in the chapel of the Hospice of Lourdes for the rite. Those in attendance thought her an "angel from heaven...a little mystical rose who intoxicates us with the aroma of her innocence and simplicity."[268]

Thursday, June 4, 1858

Abbé Peyramale was very pleased with Bernadette on the day prior. She was a model of good behavior and a quality student. Because of all that had taken place, or perhaps in response to a request, Peyramale sat down to write a letter to the Bishop of Tarbes in which he described Bernadette and the First Communion exercises. He wrote, "She appeared to be fully conscious of the solemnity and significance of the occasion. During the retreat I arranged for the children. Her behavior, her meditation, and her concentration left nothing to be desired. Her development is now going forward in an astonishing fashion."[269]

As Peyramale was describing Bernadette's virtues in his letter, Emmanuélite Estrade was satisfying her own curiosity through some thoughtless questions. She asked the child if receiving the Body and Blood of Christ or speaking with the Blessed Virgin provided her the greatest pleasure. Ignoring the stupidity of the question, Bernadette replied, "I don't know which gave me most pleasure. The two things go together, and they can't be compared. All I know is that I was very happy both times."[270]

Saturday, June 6, 1858

Acbille Fould, the Imperial Minister of Finance, had been reading about the events taking place in Lourdes. His concern prompted a visit to Tarbes for the purpose of conferencing with Baron Massy. Among the topics of discussion were the incidents at the Grotto of Massabielle. The two spoke about Lourdes and no doubt Massy noted his own frustration with the Prefect's inability to convince Bishop Laurence to address it. They more than likely noted the land on which the Grotto stood was under the commune of Lourdes and therefore administered by Mr. Lacadé in his capacity as mayor of Lourdes. Regardless of the depth of the discussion, the results were clear, and action almost immediate.

Monday, June 8, 1858
The Grotto is Closed to Public Access

Prefect Massy had only a short time to consider the words of Minister Fould, knowing that patience was running thin in high places. He met with Mayor Lacadé and instructed him to issue what can be described only as a despotic order. To soften the blow, Lacadé laced the order with a number of justifications that made the directive appear more protective than punitive in nature.

The edict used phraseology such as, "In view of the fact that it is necessary in the interests of religion to put a stop to the regrettable scenes which take place at the Massabielle Grotto situated at Lourdes on the left bank of the Gave...." and "Having regard to the fact that it is the duty of the Mayor to watch over the public health in the mayoralty...."[271] Despite the flowery language, the order essentially barred the faithful and the curious alike from the Grotto. The many articles of the mayor's order forbade the drawing of water from the spring and even the crossing of the common on the Massabielle bank, and mandated the construction of a barrier to the entrance of the Grotto to prevent public access and required the erection of signage noting that entry onto the property would be strictly prohibited. The order also clearly spelled out punishments for violators.

Regardless of the deception used in justifying the order, it was a perfectly legal and enforceable directive and the mayor, and his police commissioner, knew it. It seemed that the government finally had found a solution to what had become a very large thorn in its side.

Monday, June 15, 1858
to Saturday, July 4, 1858
The People Will Not Be Denied Access

To ensure that people did not trespass at the Grotto, Mayor Lacadé ordered fences installed around the perimeter and hired some local men to construct them. The barriers might have been effective in keeping people from getting close to the Grotto and bathing in the waters of the spring, but the fence was not up long enough for its effectiveness to be tested. On that very night, the same men charged with the task of installing it tore it down under the cover of darkness.

On Sunday, June 28, Mayor Lacadé again hired some local men to erect a fence that would prevent access to the Grotto. The fence lasted only until the night of June 28, when it was torn down once again. Mayor Lacadé would not be made the fool. On July 10 he ordered the fence rebuilt and began to charge trespassers with criminal offenses.

Rather than defy the order, Bernadette refrained from going to the Grotto. Many people of Lourdes protested, and some petitioned the authorities and resisted the ban. For her part, Bernadette advised against going to the Grotto.

Sunday, July 5, 1858
to Wednesday, July 15, 1858

The odd thing about the order was that, though reducing or eliminating the crowds from gathering at the Grotto and preventing the drawing of spring water, it could not stop the miraculous cures that resulted from it. It seemed contrary to the excuse that the Grotto was being closed to protect the health of its citizens. In the minds of the multitudes, the faith and belief in the cures proved more important than the order, and many chose to defy the courts and the fines. Those people continued to cross the barriers in order to pray at the Grotto.

The police officers posted at the site to enforce the order took names of the violators to enable the magistrate to impose hefty fines, which in some cases reached five hundred francs, on the offenders. Some faithful swam across the Gave to avoid detection. All the while, Bishop Laurence and Abbé Peyramale remained silent. With each passing day, the people grew more anxious, their emotions rising to the point of rebellion. The signs prohibiting access were taken down in the night and tossed into the Gave, and nighttime prayers at the site became routine. Many collected on the right bank of the Gave, which was not government property, to pray and view the Grotto. From that vantage point they would also jeer and boo the police guard on the other bank.

It was now thermal spa season in Lourdes and visitors from far and wide were in town. Many had read about the happenings at the Grotto and made their way to the site while others sought out Bernadette to hear her own description of events. Already overburdened by visitors, Bernadette's health once again began to deteriorate. Exhausted by the constant badgering of curious and faithful alike, her asthmatic condition was heightened, rendering the child weak and frail.

Among the seasonal visitors was a famous journalist by the name of Louis Veuillot. Veuillot was also serving as editor of *L'Univers*, a paper much more favorable to religion than the others that had been reporting on the events of Lourdes. Veuillot was forty-five and a realist who wrote with refreshing directness, despite having a pure and classical style about him. He was courageous and possessed a lusty and vigorous manner enabling him to interrogate nonbelievers into submission. He used his courage and style to his advantage and this sunny day in June would prove no different as Veuillot strode, with bowed head, toward the Grotto. Two police officers standing the post watched as the rather corpulent gentleman with gray hair approached them with purpose.

"You can't go any further," the police noted upon Veuillot's arrival. He looked up, exposing his pock-marked face and glowered, responding, "We'll see about that." The officers asked his name, warning that he would be summoned if he continued. The journalist confidently identified himself as he strode ahead toward the Grotto. Veuillot had read about the events being reported at Lourdes and decided to purposely take on the cause of fighting both the mayor and his edict closing the Grotto to the public.

Bishop Laurence, by contrast, remained silent, deciding not to challenge the authorities and their edict. Amidst the chaos, he remained a voice of calm reason, neither protesting Mayor Lacadé nor supporting the throngs of people still pushing their way toward the Grotto. He did, however, pen a letter to Abbé Peyramale, noting, "I had no hand whatever in the actions of the civil authorities in connection with the Grotto and I congratulate myself on that attitude. Later on the ecclesiastical authorities will see whether there is anything to be done."[272]

Though Bishop Laurence remained calm, the quarrymen had reached a boiling point. One declared, "The police had better count their bones because before long they'll be fishing for them in the Gave."[273] The quarrymen, once excited, generally made good on threats, and most citizens of Lourdes knew that. Abbé Peyramale found it necessary, therefore, to intervene in the hope of avoiding trouble. Finding no success in the field, he took to his pulpit one Sunday. "The quarrymen must reckon with me now, not the police. I am not afraid of their hammers and their crowbars. From now on I will go to the Grotto, and woe betide anyone who tries to force his way past me! Together they could trample me underfoot, but if they come as individuals and if by any chance one of them should try conclusions with me, then I warn him here and now that he will not be on his feet when the dust settles."[274]

Peyramale had a reputation for keeping his word, consequently no quarryman put his words to the test. Bernadette had no concerns about her inability to access the Grotto, however, and was comforted by the Blessed Virgin as she prayed from home. Even a severe illness that she experienced that summer could not quell the spirit within her. One Thursday, she was visited by her cousin Jeanne Vedere, who inquired about going to the Grotto to pray. Bernadette told her to pray from her room and be patient, as soon the very authorities who closed the Grotto to public access would be told to reopen it. Her words proved to be prescient.

While Bernadette was at peace about the Prefect's "temporary" closing of the Grotto, and the Abbé was able to calm the quarrymen for the time being, the masses were quite angry. They continued to overwhelm the Grotto, forcing the magistrate to write summons after summons, ninety-four in July and early August alone, written to those who persisted in violating the order to keep out. The crowds were driven by the stories of miracles that continued to emanate from the Grotto and its extraordinary spring water.

It is uncertain why the government was not able to prevail in its case against those who had trespassed the Grotto in violation of the closure orders. Some in the community called it divine intervention while those in government just shook their collective heads in disbelief. Regardless of the cause, however, Bernadette's prediction that Cyprine Gesta, a single mother who was found guilty at the Lourdes tribunal would win her appeal before the tribunal in Pau became reality. Cyprine triumphantly returned to Lourdes just before midnight on July 15, still in disbelief.

Friday, July 16, 1858
The Eighteenth Apparition

Still basking in the glow of victory, Cyprine Gesta paid Bernadette a visit. She wanted to give her thanks once again for the child's comforting words before her appearance before the Pau tribunal, and to discuss her unlikely win before that body. It was really a win for the entire community of the Lourdes faithful.

Despite the weariness from her illness and the constant badgering of villagers and visitors alike, Bernadette graciously greeted Cyprine and the two spoke for a while, though she really looked forward to going to church in celebration of the feast of Our Lady of Mount Carmel. This is a title given to the Blessed Virgin Mary in her role as patroness to the Carmelite Order, the first of whom lived on Mount Carmel in the Holy Land during the 12th and 13th centuries.

At her first opportunity, the child hurried off to church and began to pray. It was then that Bernadette heard a compelling voice, a soft voice really, from deep within. *Go to the Grotto*, she heard the inner voice repeat over and over. Rising to her feet in a rush, she ran to the house of her Aunt Lucille where Bernadette begged her aunt to accompany her to the Grotto at Massabielle.

Lucille agreed, but advised taking the path which led across the Ribére meadows. In that way they might avoid the police and the wooden blockade that they placed at the entrance to the Grotto.

8:00 PM

The sky had just darkened at day's end when Bernadette and her aunt made their way through a number of other groups of women who were already in prayer. They knelt on the right bank of the Gave and joined the others in prayer while Bernadette kept her eyes fixed upon the rocks of the Grotto. Upon noticing that the new arrival was the young visionary, a group of people encircled her just as Bernadette's face lit up. "I see her!" she cried. "I see her! There she is!" The Lady smiled as if to greet Bernadette from beyond the barrier. Then there was silence, broken only by a long conversation between Bernadette and her Lady, though no one else could make out what was being said.

This was the eighteenth confirmed visit of Our Lady to Bernadette. "The Virgin, having looked smilingly at Bernadette for some time, gave her a last long look, inclined her head and disappeared."[275] Bernadette understood that she would not see the Blessed Mother in this world again.

Part IV

A Time of Inquiry
And the Proclamation
of a Miracle

Since February 11, the life of the little fourteen-year-old girl from Lourdes was turned upside down. Bernadette didn't ask to come face-to-face with the Mother of God, though there is little doubt that she would have traded the experience for any other in the world, and she never sought celebrity status. Regardless, she found herself an unwitting pawn in the world of local celebrity. Hundreds, if not thousands, of times she was questioned about the Appearances of Our Lady of the Grotto. The inquisitors were friends, relatives, strangers, clergy, and government officials. She was dragged from house to house and from village to village to recount the events of the Grotto. There is no way to say for sure how many times visitors asked the child about the Apparitions, but, on May 12, 1858, the Curé of Lourdes estimated that "Bernadette must have answered the questions of thirty thousand people."[276]

One such inquisitor visited the cachot from Beaune. Charles Madon was a former seminarian turned lawyer and preparing for his new role as a judge when he travelled to Lourdes to speak with Bernadette about her visions. Upon entering the cachot he was immediately taken by the conditions of extreme poverty. He would later write that despite the abject poverty, neither the child nor her family would accept the slightest amount of money or "reward" for the benefit of their time and hospitality.

Madon questioned Bernadette methodically about the Apparitions and specifically about the three secrets. Though providing a description of the Apparitions consistent with her responses in the past, the child refused to give any details about the secrets other than to say, "They concern only me."[277] She steadfastly refused to divulge any aspect of the secrets imparted to her by the Blessed Virgin and noted that she would not even if it meant that she be prevented from making her Easter duty.

Though refusing to divulge information which the Mother of God had told her in secret, Bernadette did reveal for the first time that she asked the Lady if she could see her again. She also noted that the Virgin spoke to her in her native Patois rather than in formal French.[278]

Friday, July 17, 1858
1:00 PM

Abbé Euzet, a young priest from Cauterets, stepped from the carriage as it stopped in front of the rectory, and he entered the large house. After just a few moments, he re-emerged accompanied by a very excited Abbé Peyramale. Upon seeing them, Vicar General Canon Baudasse, an older priest, exited the carriage and greeted his host. Together, the three assisted Monseigneur Thibault, Bishop of Montpellier, from the carriage.

It was the Bishop's desire to inquire about the Apparitions before his return to Cauterets, and as one who can comfortably converse in the Patois of the Pyrenees, he asked to question the child personally. Abbé Peyramale, who had summoned Bernadette to the rectory, agreed to interpret for the others. The discussion began almost immediately upon Bernadette's arrival, and though the Bishop was direct in his questioning, introducing pitfalls meant to test Bernadette's veracity, she remained polite, direct, and consistent in her responses. In fact, "the more difficult, disconcerting, or tricky the question, the more relevant was her answer."[279] Bishop Thibault was very impressed with Bernadette. He actually became emotional upon hearing the testimony of this sickly, undernourished albeit radiant child.

At one point of the discussion, the rectory maid interrupted the proceedings with an offering of a snack for the Bishop, one he immediately offered to share with Bernadette. Despite her condition, she refused to accept anything and would not be convinced otherwise. The Bishop looked at Abbé Peyramale with an expression that inquired about Bernadette's poverty. "That child is poor, isn't she," he asked. Peyramale nodded affirmatively adding, "Yes, Monseigneur, very poor." Moved by her innocence and steadfastness, Bishop Thibault took Bernadette by the hand and moved it to his rosary saying, "Oh, no Bernadette, you are not poor, you are blessed, yes, blessed!"[280]

With those words, the Bishop offered Bernadette his rosary. He desperately wanted to give her something, but Bernadette "stepped back...Thank you, I have one," the girl responded. Even when the Bishop informed her that the rosary had been given indulgences by Pius IX, she would not accept. Realizing that Bernadette would accept no offering, the Bishop suggested exchanging her rosary for his. That proffer was also rejected by the visionary, saying that she preferred her own rosary, adding, "The Blessed Virgin doesn't like vanity." Then, realizing that she may have offended the Bishop, she quickly said, "Yours is good for you. I thank you very much."[281]

3:00 PM

Bishop Thibault realized that the child was right and that his offer to exchange rosaries may have been motivated as much by his desire to own a relic of the girl than his desire to provide her with a gift. He spoke a bit longer to Abbé Peyramale, then departed the rectory, indicating that he would stop to see Bishop Laurence who, unbeknownst to Thibault, was already preparing an inquiry into the happening at Lourdes.

Monday, July 20, 1858

Bernadette was summoned to the rectory just three days later as Monseigneur Cardon de Garsignies, the Bishop of Soissons, decided to visit Abbé Peyramale's rectory. It was unclear by his demeanor if Bishop de Garsignies was trying to trap Bernadette or assisting Bishop Laurence with his inquiry. Perhaps it was both, though at least one question seemed a bit odd. "Tell me, dear child," the Bishop said, "What goes on up there in heaven? You can tell me, for I know all about it." Bernadette must have been confused by the question but simply responded, "I don't know anything, Monseigneur, I'm ignorant."[282]

As soon as Bishop de Garsignies completed his questioning, he departed the rectory and visited Bishop Laurence to fill him in on the details of his conversation with Bernadette.

Tuesday, July 21, 1858

The activity level within the church hierarchy was now in overdrive. The very next day following the meeting between Bishop Laurence and Bishop de Garsignies, the two met with the Archbishop of Salinis. The three of them discussed the events that had been occurring at the Grotto as well as other information gleaned from the many interviews with Bernadette.

Wednesday, July 22, 1858

Just one day later, the Archbishop, Bishop de Garsignies and Bishop Laurence returned to Tarbes for a meeting of the council. Louis Veuillot, the editor-in-chief of the *Univers*, the publication supportive of the church, also attended the council meeting. It should surprise no one that the council's overriding topic of discussion was all that had occurred at Massabielle.

Tuesday, July 28, 1858

Bishop Laurence had been mulling the events of the past several months in his mind. Since February 11, many things had happened in the otherwise sleepy town – strange things. The people of his parish and far beyond were transfixed by the affairs of the Grotto and the authorities from the mayor and police commissioner all the way to the Minister of Finance had become involved and taken such draconian measures that the possibility of insurrection existed. The Bishop thought it time that he release an official statement. In a pastoral letter he wrote:

> "Happenings of the utmost gravity relating to our Holy Religion and affecting both this diocese and more distant parts have been occurring in Lourdes since February 11 last.

Bernadette Soubirous, a young girl of Lourdes, aged four-teen years, claims to have had Visions in the Grotto of Massabielle which is situated to the west of the town. The Immaculate Virgin is said to have appeared to her. A spring is said to have welled out of the ground there, and the waters of this spring, when taken internally or used as a lotion, are said to have brought about a great number of cures. These cures are reputed to be of a miraculous na-ture. Great numbers of people have flocked-and still flock-to the spot, both from our diocese and from neigh-boring dioceses, to obtain cures from this water..."

The civil authority has become alarmed.

"Since last March there has been a widespread demand that the ecclesiastical authority should state its views on this spontaneous pilgrimage. To deny the possibility of supernatural happenings would be to follow in the foot-steps of an outmoded school, to impoverish the Christian religion and to plod along in the rut worn by the philo-sophic skepticism of the last century.
Thus, the systematic no-men saw themselves sternly con-demned-and in the name of that very 'progress' they claimed for themselves!"[283]

Bishop Laurence continued by rebuking "those who deny God the power to make exceptions to the general laws he has established for the governance of the world," and called for "a broad, sincere and con-scientious discussion in the light of science and progress" of the pertinent facts.

Laurence concluded by signing an eight-article ordinance creat-ing an official commission of inquiry into the Apparitions of Mary to the child Bernadette at the Grotto in Lourdes. The Commission was "charged with furnishing an official report on the authenticity and nature of events which have occurred, about six months ago, on the occasion of an Apparition, true or pretended, of the Blessed Virgin, in a Grotto, situated to the west of the town of Lourdes."[284]

The commission was to include, "among others, men well versed in the sciences of medicine, chemistry, geology and so on, in order to hear their opinions on such difficulties as lie in their province."[285]

Shortly after Mgr. Laurence completed his statement, a letter was delivered from Monsieur Rouland, the Minister for Public Instruction and Ecclesiastical Affairs, declaring "the scandalous scenes" at the Grotto "lowered religion in the eyes of the populace." He requested that Bishop Laurence "rebuke such profanations publicly."[286]

Bishop Laurence responded immediately writing, "I should be very glad, Your Excellency, if you would make your inquiries concerning what is taking place in Lourdes from reputable persons who have come to the town to see for themselves, to hear what the inhabitants have to say and to talk to the child who claims to have had the Visions, such as, for example, their Lordships the Bishops of Montpellier and Soissons, His Grace the Archbishop of Auch, M. Vene the Inspector of Thermal Establishments, Mme. Bruat [the governess of the Prince Imperial], M. Louis Veuillot, etc, etc."[287]

Laurence continued by informing Rouland that rather than condemning the Visions as false, he was instead appointing a commission of inquiry. Bishop Laurence heard nothing more from Minister Rouland.

Bernadette was unaware of all that was happening within the church but was still the one person to whom everyone wanted to speak. The poor child was again summoned to the rectory, this time by Abbé Pomian. He was taking charge in the absence of Abbé Peyramale, who was with the Archbishop and Louis Veuillot at the mineral springs at Bagnères. Abbé Pomian arranged the meeting at the request of the wife of Admiral Bruat, governess to the Imperial Prince. She was accompanied by her three daughters and Sister Saint-Antonin. Also present was Abbé Labayle, a priest from Rome, and Monsieur Lannes, who agreed to interpret for Bernadette. Lannes was a tobacco warehouse keeper and a co-tenant at the rectory but it was assumed by those present that he was a schoolteacher.

Labayle tried to trick Bernadette, noting that since the Virgin is married to St. Joseph, she must have been wearing a ring. Bernadette politely replied in the negative. The child took a particular liking to the nun, however, and the two spoke of Bernadette's great joy in seeing the Mother of God. At the conclusion of the meeting, the group visited the Grotto. Bernadette refused to accompany them, noting that she was forbidden from going there.

That did not end Bernadette's day, however, as just a few minutes after the conclusion of the meeting, she was summoned to Pailhasson's pharmacy for an interview arranged by Louis Veuillot, that functioned more like a press conference. The event was crowded but Bernadette was neither intimidated nor impressed. She recounted the events of the Apparitions slowly, allowing Abbé Pomian time to translate from her Patois to French. When she finished, Veuillot asked her questions, focusing with particular interest on the three secrets imparted to her by the Virgin Mary. Veuillot, who was indignant when the government prohibited public access to the Grotto, now treated Bernadette as though she had fabricated the entire affair.

> "'Many people think badly of this mystery,' he told her. Bernadette did not defend herself. – the secrets concerned only her. 'Have you heard about the children of La Salette?' Veuillot asked.
> 'Yes, since the visions.'
> 'If you were lying, do you know to what extent you would be guilty?'
> 'They've already told me.'
> 'And what do you intend to do? Don't you think that someday a few charitable people will care about what happens to you?'
> Looking at her poor clothing, she smiled."[288]

The "press conference" continued in similar fashion until the curate finally dismissed her. Only when the meeting stood in adjournment did Veuillot allow his emotion to become evident. "She is ignorant," Veuillot said, "but she's worth more than I am. I'm worthless."[289]

As difficult as the experience might have been for Bernadette, things were going to get worse. Other inquisitions were even more severe.

Tuesday, July 29, 1858
to Friday, August 27, 1858

Meanwhile, Mayor Lacadé was rethinking the recent actions he had taken to close the Grotto. At the very least, he was willing to take another look at the events there. Even the municipal council, at a recent meeting of the body, "decided that it ought to be competently informed about the principal constituents and properties of the Grotto water which had already become so famous."[290] The Council enlisted the help of Monsieur Filhol, Professor of Chemistry at the University of Toulouse, to re-analyze the water flowing from the spring at the Grotto that Monsieur Latour had analyzed back in early May.

Filhol's report concluded:

"It results from all this that the water of the Lourdes Grotto may be regarded as good drinking water, like most spring water to be found in mountainous districts where the soil is chalky. The water contains no active constituents which could give it therapeutic properties. It can be drunk without deleterious effects."[291]

A copy of the report was sent to Baron Massy with the following note:

"The extraordinary effects which I am assured have followed on the use of this water cannot be explained-at least they cannot be explained in the present state of science-by the nature of the salts shown by the analysis to be present in it."[292]

The report dashed Massy's hope of profiting from the therapeutic nature of the water and left the council in a position of having to address the subjects of the Apparitions and their aftermath. Yet, without therapeutic properties, science was hard pressed to provide any reasonable explanation for the cures that were associated with drinking or bathing in the spring water. Within the neighborhoods of Lourdes and in towns farther away, the range of miracles was spreading. Reports numbered in the hundreds and masses continued to flock to the Grotto in search of their own cures. Sores were healed, deformed limbs were restored, the blind could now see, the lame could walk, all because of the spring.

As much as the cures were a relief to the once afflicted, they were an embarrassment to the authorities or anyone not inclined to have faith. Regardless of the embarrassment of having no good scientific explanation, and despite the analytical reports verifying that the spring water posed no danger to the public health, the Prefect ruled that the barriers around the Grotto would remain in place.

Tossing the new scientific method to the wind, newspapers wrote editorials and articles in support of Massy's edict. Anti-cleric papers such as *Journal des Debats*, *Le Siecle*, and *La Presse* mocked the faithful who wasted their time at the Grotto. Monsieur Geurolt wrote in *La Presse*, "The miracle belongs to a phase of civilization which is fast disappearing."[293] Monsieur Bernard, likewise, wrote in *Le Siecle*, "It seems extraordinary to us that they can manufacture a miracle out of a hallucination, real or false, on the part of a child of fourteen and a trickling of water from the rocks of a grotto."[294] Another wrote, "Hydropaths also claim to obtain marvelous cures by the use of pure water, but they don't pretend they perform miracles."[295] Incredibly, the spring itself, despite not being there prior to the Visions, but now producing some 25,000 gallons of water each day, was disregarded as "a trickling of water from the rocks of a grotto."[296]

The reporters' positions are ironic when one considers that not one of the writers actually took the time to visit Lourdes, view the Grotto, or speak with eyewitnesses to the events that they were so quick to denounce in their papers. And these were not just any newspapers, but rather the most significant papers of the day. Regardless, the papers even sought to discredit the commission of inquiry established by Bishop Laurence even before it had met, implying that their conclusions had already been reached. In calling for the dissolution of the commission, and in presenting a long list of legal justifications for doing so, Prevost Paradol noted in the *Journal des Debats* that:

> "If the decision falls in favor of the miracle, it will tend to upset the equilibrium in that part of France between the civil and the religious powers. The ministers of a religion in whose favor such prodigies are claimed are quite different personages than those the provisions of the concordat had in mind. They would have a quite different influence on the population, and in the event of conflict they would dispose of a very different authority from that of the Prefect and the Council of State...."[297]

Yet, even while the debate raged over the impact a fourteen-year-old girl might have on the equilibrium between the civil and religious powers, the power of God was on full display at the Grotto.

Jeanne-Marie Massot-Bordenave couldn't walk. She had been crippled a long time ago and had to be carried by friends to the waters of the spring, whereupon she was immersed. She immediately recovered from her affliction. Marie Capdeveille was able to hear for the first time in years and prostrated herself in prayer when she heard the sweet sound of the bells of Lourdes. Despite the cures, the Grotto remained officially closed to the public.

For Bernadette, life continued pretty much as before. Though she could no longer go beyond the gate, she visited the Grotto every day to pray, and she attended school at the Hospice where, though many now believed in the truth of her Visions, she was still outcast. Even Mother Ursule Fardes, the school's Superior, failed to warm up to her.

Though trying hard, Bernadette struggled with school. She was understandably timid and had an inadequate knowledge of French. She at times even bordered on depression, sometimes describing herself as "stupid," expressing concern that she would forever remain "awkward and ignorant."

Lending to the problem at school was the fact that she was constantly badgered at home and at school by as many as twenty curious visitors each day that asked the same questions over and over again. Despite her lack of education and understanding, she had no trouble responding to the questions of those who interrogated her about her Visions; she just had no time to study or do homework that might have benefited her at school.

Yet she remained humble, ever so humble. When a priest knelt before her and asked for her blessing, she responded, "No, Father, it is you who should bless me."[298] Despite her abject poverty, she never accepted any gifts, though many were offered to her. Even when a bishop visiting Lourdes from another diocese stopped by to see her with an offering of a gold rosary, the child refused, instead giving him one of her own rosaries as a gift.

For many, Bernadette had become the object of veneration. For many others, the object of jealousy and hatred. People followed her all the time. Some jeered, "Look, there's the saint! Look, there's our saint!" It was even difficult to stop some of the curious from cutting snippets of her clothing to take home as a souvenir.

Bernadette was happiest at the Grotto. She longed to be there and to pray in silent reminiscence of her time with the Blessed Lady, but she couldn't. And now, as if striking the final blow to her desires, "Abbé Peyramale forbade her to go there anymore because growing crowds of people prone to excessive demonstrations invariably followed her around."[299] Bernadette recalled the words of Our Lady spoken on February 18th, *"I cannot make you happy in this world, but I promise to do so in the next."*

The upheaval in Bernadette's world continued. Père Hyacinth Loyson was a dynamic preacher with a large following. Though he would leave the Church on short order, at the moment he wanted to speak with the poor, ignorant, young girl that had, since mid-February, turned civic and religious affairs in Lourdes, and beyond, upside down. Loyson summoned Bernadette to his hotel room. The child, accompanied by Antoinette Tardhivail, complied. He was clearly unbelieving of any talk of heavenly visions and spoke to her gruffly in French. He distorted her responses and belittled the child for her inability to speak proper French. "The Lady would have done better to teach you to speak,"[300] he told her. Bernadette replied sardonically, "What she did not teach me was to make fun of people who didn't know any better."[301] The indignation and resentment of the response was not lost on Tardhivail.

Also around this time, Père Negré, a Jesuit priest who did not believe in the veracity of Bernadette's stories, was conducting his own inquiry. He had met the blind girl from Barèges that claimed she was cured and learned that she was never really blind, rendering her cure invalid. He had also investigated the spring at the Grotto and rather than finding the flowing spring of clear water that he heard about, he discovered a slow trickle of muddy water.[302] These discoveries prejudiced him against Bernadette's claims and now he wanted an opportunity to question Bernadette for himself. To accomplish that he asked to use the home of the pharmacist, Pailhasson.

Once again Tardhivail was asked by Bernadette to accompany her on the visit, if not for moral support, at least for company. "A priest wants to see me at Monsieur Pailhasson's," Bernadette told her, and "I don't want to go alone."[303]

Bernadette may have wished she had not gone at all! Père Negré wasted no time showing his contempt for the child. "My poor child," the priest said, "you saw a lady? You saw the devil!" He then tried to convince Bernadette that she didn't see the Lady's hands and feet, noting that the devil cleverly hides his hands and feet with shadows. The visionary-turned-accused remained peaceful and calm, noting to the contrary that she could absolutely see the Lady's hands and feet and they were beautiful.

Père Negré didn't think Bernadette was lying and "judged her entirely incapable of deception."[304] He honestly believed she may have seen something, but he was convinced that what she saw was the devil's deception. He also knew, from his years in the priesthood, that God does not "permit the devil to take a completely human form. He must betray himself by something belonging to the beast."[305] Thus, he believed that Bernadette must have been mistaken about seeing the Lady's hands and feet so clearly.

His altruistic reasons, however, were not shared with Bernadette and Antoinette. Consequently, Antoinette was shocked at the degree of vitriol in the priest's questioning, noting that "the tone of his voice showed his conviction that the vision was false."[306] She was indignant, but Bernadette was clearly hurt. Together, they left Pailhasson's house.

Within days, the "anti-Bernadette" sentiment spread like an airborne virus. Priests and bishops alike "threatened her with hell fire...and told her that if she said she saw the Blessed Virgin on earth, she would not see her in heaven."[307] Bernadette handled the threats admirably, often showing no emotion and generally doing so with a smile on her face. Perhaps she knew from the Blessed Virgin herself that such would never be the case, but whether or not Bernadette had any personal knowledge of her salvation, she never seemed to take any of the threats to heart and slowly, her sincerity and the integrity of her story won over hearts.

Friday, August 28, 1858

Following his interview with the visionary, Abbé Fonteneau, who would later become the Bishop of Agen, was added to the column of people who believed Bernadette had seen the Virgin Mary. He was both impressed with the clarity of the answers she provided to questions asked and was deeply struck by her approach to the interview. She never tried to convince him of her sincerity, she merely told her story and left it to his own discretion to believe her or not, hardly a sound strategy of someone making up the story.

And Fonteneau was not alone. Monseigneur Plantier, the Bishop of Nimes, was equally captivated. Abbé Peyramale arranged for him to interview Bernadette at the convent in Nevers. Though skeptical when he began, he left the meeting a believer. Even government royalty believed. The Count of Bruissard, who had referred to himself as "'a hardened sinner' in the article published by Guy de Pierrefeux,"[308] was convinced of her veracity after meeting with Bernadette. An avowed atheist, the Count was converted after visiting Bernadette following his reading of an article in the local newspaper on July 16 in which he learned that:

"Bernadette had had an apparition and that the Virgin had smiled at her, 'I resolved to go to Lourdes out of curiosity and catch the little one in a barefaced lie. So I went to the Soubirous home and found Bernadette on the doorstep, mending a black stocking. She seemed common to me; her sickly features, however, had a certain sweetness. At my request, Bernadette told me about the apparitions with a simplicity and self-confidence that struck me.

Well, now, I said, how did that beautiful lady smile? The little shepherd girl looked at me in surprise and after a moment of silence answered, Oh! Monsieur, one would have to be from heaven to make that smile again. Couldn't you make it for me? I'm an unbeliever and don't believe in the apparitions. Her face was clouded over and took on a severe expression. So Monsieur, you think that I'm a liar? I felt defenseless. No, Bernadette was not a liar, and I was on the verge of...asking for forgiveness. Since you are a sinner, she answered, I will make the Blessed Virgin's smile for you."

The Count found Bernadette so charming and her demeanor so unassuming that he was quickly taken by her. The enthusiasm of her testimony and her wide-eyed innocence left no doubt in his mind that Bernadette's story was legitimate.

Throughout the summer and into the fall, this was now the new normal for Bernadette. One interview after another driving the poor child to the point of exhaustion. Clergy and high-ranking government officials visited Bernadette by appointment made through the rectory, pilgrims and the curious stopped her on the street or went to the cachot, while others even met with her at the homes of her friends or at the hotel.

Abbé Peyramale grew concerned for the child's welfare. To protect Bernadette, he suggested that she move into the convent of the Sisters of Charity at the Hospice. He explained to the reluctant child that the sisters would take care of her and teach her to read, but Bernadette resisted. "I love my father and mother so much!" she said. "Besides, I need so little!"[309]

September 1858

Around mid-September, François Soubirous was finally able to move his family from the hole that was the cachot at 15 rue des Petits-Fosses and into slightly better accommodations near the church. He found his family a room to rent at the home of "Jean Deluc, the baker and cafe owner. Deluc was married to a daughter of Bibie Casterot, the sister of Bernadette's maternal grandmother."[310] All the while François continued looking for another opportunity to run a mill.

Friday, October 1, 1858
to Monday, October 4, 1858
Napoleon Bonaparte Takes Action
in Lourdes, France

Many of the good citizens of Lourdes had run out of patience with Prefect Massy. They wanted the Grotto reopened to the public and enlisted support in high places within the court system. It happened that Emperor Napoleon III was in Biarritz for the season. Originally settled by Vikings who invaded Gascony in 840, Biarritz lies within the Pyrenees-Atlantiques in the Nouvelle-Aquitaine region of France and is less than 100 miles from Lourdes. Its beautiful coastline and pristine beaches attracted many foreign leaders and dignitaries. Empress Eugenie, wife of Napoleon III, had a palace built for herself right on one of the beaches of Biarritz and it is from that palace that Napoleon Bonaparte governed for at least part of each year. He was there in early October when "high personages at the court" took an audience with him to convey the dissatisfaction of the people of Lourdes to their sovereign. Among them were

Msg. de Salinis, the Archbishop of Auch, and former Deputy de Res-segnier. The Emperor listened intently as they presented petitions "ur-gently demanding and claiming in virtue of the most sacred rights, the withdrawal of the arbitrary and violent measures of Baron Massy."[311] One petition read:

> "Sire, we do not pretend to decide in any way the ques-tion of the Apparitions of the Virgin, although, on the faith of astounding miracles, which they claim to have seen with their own eyes, almost all, in these districts believe implicitly in the reality of these supernatural manifestations. What is certain and beyond all dispute, is that this spring, which gushed forth all at once – and which has been closed to us in spite of the scientific analysis which proclaimed it to be entirely innocuous— has not done any harm to any one; what is certain is that, on the contrary, a great number of persons declare that they have recovered their health by its means. In the name of the rights of conscience, which are quite independent of all human power, allow those who be-lieve to go and pray there, if it suits them to do so. In the name of mere humanity allow the sick to go there to be cured, if such is their hope. In the name of intel-lectual liberty, allow those minds which seek for light from study and investigation to go there to discover their error or find the truth."[312]

The Emperor was not at all interested in the question of miracu-lous cures and Apparitions of Virgins. He did, however, take an extraor-dinary interest in justice, religious liberty, and intellectual freedom, and raised an eyebrow of concern at what he was told.

Incredibly, and seemingly against all odds and logic, the plead-ings of that meeting did not fall upon deaf ears. Almost immediately fol-lowing the meeting, Napoleon III ordered Prefect Massy to rescind the order of June 8, 1858, thereby removing the barriers from the Grotto and allowing public access to the spring once again.

Tuesday, October 5, 1858
9:00 AM

It was not what anyone expected, least of all Prefect Massy. After taking a hard stand to influence and manipulate what he considered an out-of-control affair at Massabielle, Massy had been rebuffed by the Emperor of France. He protested, but his protestations fell on deaf ears as Napoleon's judgment was "based on the evidence which had been laid before him and was irrevocable."[313] A second dispatch was immediately sent from Biarritz. This one left no doubt that the Emperor expected his order to be executed without any further delay. Massy would need to swallow his pride if he were to remain in office.

3:00 PM

Word of the Emperor's edict wound its way through the chain of local government. Now, the crier stood in the center of town. A drum began to roll, and the crier yelled the announcement from Mayor Lacadé. The barriers at the Grotto of Massabielle would be removed and the people would once again enjoy free access to the area.

The townspeople were overjoyed, though not really sure why their local officials had the sudden change of heart. Workmen dismantled both the barriers and the notices at the Grotto, and a crowd that numbered in the hundreds knelt and prayed in thanksgiving for the success of their pious revolt. They sang canticles and recited litanies to the Mother of God. They drank at the fountain and generally reveled in God's victory. Many could be seen kissing the ground of the newly reopened Grotto.

Sunday, November 17, 1858

Although Bishop Laurence had instituted the Commission of Inquiry at the end of July, it had been his desire that emotions cool before he permitted it to begin its work. Now, without fear that the members of his tribunal would face arrest by the police for entering the Grotto of Massabielle, he was ready.

11:00 AM

The hour was not yet noon when a group of four clergymen departed the rectory in Lourdes headed toward the rocks of Massabielle. They were members of the Commission and they took a circuitous route, hoping to avoid the attention of the crowds that might be going to the same place. It proved impossible, however, for four high-ranking priests to pass undetected along any route that led to the Grotto. By the time they arrived, over four hundred people were waiting to watch them conduct their investigation of the site. The clergymen took advantage of the opportunity to question the onlookers about the previous condition of the spring and other aspects of the area. Seeing the generous flow of water, they inquired of those present the condition that existed prior to Bernadette seeing her visions. They learned that no spring had existed until Bernadette, at the direction of the Virgin Mary, dug into the dirt. It was then, the people told them, that the enormous flow of the divine spring was established right before their own disbelieving eyes. The Commissioners could also see that the accounts of a slight trickling flow that they had read in the newspapers was clearly false.

12:00 Noon

To protect the privacy of their visit, the priests had asked Bernadette to join the Commission members at the Grotto at 11:30, but the child, unaware of time, arrived a half hour late. The members took turns questioning her "about the layout of the site: the niche on the cliff where the Virgin would appear and the interior cavity opening where 'she sometimes came down' to talk to her."[314]

With the crowd pressing in around them hoping to hear what was being said, they were beginning to interfere with the investigation of the Commissioners. The priests decided to adjourn for the moment. Before departing the Grotto, they knelt on the pebbled ground and prayed. Bernadette sat on a rock noting, "I'm really tired!"[315]

4:00 PM

The poor child would not have long to rest, however, as the Commission reconvened just a few hours later. This time they summoned Bernadette to testify in the sacristy of the parish church and the youthful seer subjected herself to yet one more round of interrogations. Before beginning the questioning, the Commission secretary summarized the earlier session at the Grotto, writing that Bernadette "presented herself before us with great modesty, but with remarkable self-composure. She displayed great calmness and absence of embarrassment, in the midst of so numerous an assembly, and in presence of distinguished ecclesiastics whom she had never seen before, but whose mission had been explained to her."[316]

Then the questions began. As she had so many times before, Bernadette recounted the Apparitions with remarkable accuracy. She lumped the words of Our Lady together as if they were spoken at one time. She paid no attention to months or dates as those things were of no meaning to her. It was the message on which she focused. She recounted the order to have a chapel built at the Grotto in commemoration of the Virgin Mother, the events leading to the sudden emergence of the fountain and the remarkable self-identification of the Lady as "the Immaculate Conception." She responded to every question but hesitated when asked about the order of Our Lady that a solemn procession be made to the Grotto. "Why did you not affirm that later?"[317] they wanted to know.

The confusion brought about by Abbé Peyramale's anger on March 2 had clouded her recollection before Police Commissioner Jacomet on March 18, and it was having the same impact today. "I'm not sure this order was given to me, but as for building the chapel, that I've always been sure of and I still am."[318]

The Commissioners also asked her about the blind girl of Luz, but as before, Bernadette could not explain why she was attracted to the girl or why the girl claimed to have been cured of something from which she was never really afflicted. "I didn't send for the girl from Luz. I didn't have the slightest inkling that she was in the crowd. But finding her on my way, I felt drawn to her, I don't know why, and I embraced her."[319]

The interrogation was over. Bernadette provided cohesive and consistent answers to all their questions, and they were satisfied that she was telling the truth.

Thursday, November 18, 1858
to Saturday, January 18, 1862

The beginning of 1859 brought with it the first sign of good fortune for François Soubirous and things began to look up for him and his family. The establishment of an official church inquiry into the events of the Grotto lent an air of legitimacy to the Apparitions and that lifted the social barriers that had destined the Soubirouses to the impoverished conditions under which they had lived. François was presented with yet another opportunity to rent a mill. This one, called the Gras Mill, was situated along the banks of the Lapaca River. "Now that people listened to him instead of turning their backs on him, he could take his chances like anyone else."[320] Time would prove the opportunity to be short-lived. For the time being, however, the family was able to relocate for the second time in just a few short months.

Meanwhile, the Commission members made visits to places near and far to investigate the extraordinary stories of cures which had been attributed to the waters of the spring at the Grotto of Lourdes. The Commissioners not only questioned the people who were cured, their family members and friends, but the medical personnel who had tended to their treatment and condition during the time of the affliction. Thus, "the method pursued by the tribunal of investigation was suggested by this double conception"[321] of human testimony and medical science.

Throughout the diocesan districts of Tarbes, Auch, and Bayonne, the Commissioners met with all those who had claimed to be cured by the waters of the Grotto, extracting from them the minutest of detail. The men of science on the Commission posed questions that were technical in nature while the others tended to more unscientific type queries. Once all the information had been gleaned by the priests and laymen of the Commission, the scientists such as Doctors Verges and Dozous issued a medical report stating their "opinion on the nature of the cure; sometimes rejecting the miracle to attribute the cessation of the malady in question to natural causes; sometimes declaring the fact to be utterly inexplicable, except by a supernatural action of divine power; and lastly, sometimes not arriving at any conclusion and remaining in doubt – a doubt, more or less, inclining to one or other of the above solutions."[322] The non-technical members of the Commission would likewise issue a separate report detailing their findings and conclusions.

Preconceived notions were left at the door as the Commissioners engaged in painstaking deliberations over the contents of the two separate reports issued for each of the many cases reviewed; "the entire knowledge of facts on the one hand and the conclusions arrived at by science on the other."[323] Even men of the cloth, those who may tend to be more apt to jump to an unscientific conclusion, realized "that nothing tends so much to discredit the miracles, proceeding from God, as false prodigies contrived by man."[324] Absolute truth was the sole objective of their research. They opened their deliberations to unbelievers as well as believers in an effort to promote the greatest transparency possible. They eliminated from their deliberations any vagaries and uncertainties, relying instead only on precise, well-founded, and irrefutable facts.

Every witness was sworn to tell the truth and they were asked to impart only that information that they had witnessed personally and had seen with their own eyes. As a result of this painstaking process, several alleged miracles were substantiated. Two, in fact, had only recently taken place shortly after the Prefect reopened the Grotto to the public. One of them occurred at Nay while the second took place at Tarbes.

In the town of Nay, a sixty-one-year-old widow by the name of Mme. Rizan was near death. She had been racked with perpetual pain for about 25 years. Cholera in 1832 had rendered her nearly completely paralyzed on the left side. Since then, she could move only a few steps at a time and only if supported by one of the interior walls of her house or an article of furniture.

She attended church only two or three times per year when others could carry her there. She could kneel only with the assistance of others and was able to rise from a kneeling position only in the same fashion. More recently, one of her hands became entirely atrophied. She vomited blood on a regular basis and could not eat solid food, surviving only on light soups and meat gravy. Perhaps owing to her lack of muscle tissue, she suffered always from fits of extreme cold, even in the summer months of July and August when her home still sported a blazing fire in the hearth.

The immediate past year had further exacerbated her condition, extending the paralysis on her left side from partial to total and now extended to her right leg. "Her atrophied limbs were tumefied beyond measure, as is sometimes the case with those of dropsical patients."[325] She was now bedridden and was unable to move of her own accord once placed into it. Though she had two children, her daughter Lubine was her only caregiver as her son Romain was unable to remain with her because of his job and his commercial house at Bordeaux.

Lubine needed to occasionally adjust Mme. Rizan's position from one side to the other to prevent the advent of bed sores, but those efforts fell short and she developed two very large and painful sores; one in the hollow of her chest and the other in her back. Even the skin on her sides was worn away from the constant contact with her bedclothes and her bloody flesh was exposed.

She was attended by two doctors. Dr. Talamon regarded her case as incurable. He stopped prescribing medication, thinking that even the slightest dosage might be injurious. Doctor Subervielle had prescribed some remedies, but those were essentially useless in providing relief to the poor woman. At times she couldn't determine if her limbs, her stomach, or her head caused her the most severe pain.

When Dr. Subervielle declared that the woman had but a few days to live, her son Romain was notified and arrived almost immediately. He and his mother hugged and said their heartfelt and final good-byes and then, being required to return to work, Romain "left his mother with the painful certainty of seeing her no more."[326]

Those final days found her in excruciating pain, causing her to yell out, "O God! Be pleased to put an end to this intolerable pain. Grant that I may either recover or die!"[327] Through the pain, however, the old woman made two requests. First, she sent word to her sister-in-law, who happened to be the Superior at the Sisters of the Cross at Izon, to make a Novena to the most Blessed Virgin requesting either recovery or death. The second request was to drink of the water from the Grotto of Massabielle. It was her neighbor, Mme. Nessans, who agreed to retrieve a bottle of the miraculous spring water as she was planning a trip to Lourdes.

On Saturday October 16, 1858, Mme. Rizan began to spit blood. It did not stop. "A livid tint spread over her emaciated countenance" and her eyes glossed over. All she could muster were pleas for God to take her and end her pain. As Dr. Subervielle left her, he assured Mme. Rizan's daughter, her neighbors, and the priests that watched her that her wish would be granted that night or early the following morning.

It was close to midnight when Abbé André Dupont began to cry freely, thinking that his friend had already passed, as he couldn't detect any sign of breathing. Others pointed out that she still exhibited signs of life.

Shortly after everyone had left, Mme. Rizan yelled to her daughter, "Lubine." The woman who had fallen to her knees in prayer rose quickly and approached the bed. "'My dear child,' said the dying mother to her in a strange tone of voice which seemed to proceed, as it were, from a heavy dream, 'go to the house of our friend Mme. Nessans, who was to have returned tonight from Lourdes. Beg her to give you a glass of the water from the Grotto. It is this water which is to cure me. The Blessed Virgin so wills it.'"[328]

Unwilling to leave her mother and go to the house of another at midnight, Lubine promised to do so in the morning. At daybreak on

Sunday, Lubine kept her promise, returning to her mother with a bottle of the water from the Grotto. Offering it to her mother she said, "And may the Blessed Virgin come to your assistance."[329]

Mme. Rizan drank and felt an immediate rush within her. She asked Lubine to wash her face and body with the water, a request Lubine obliged. As she washed the decrepit flesh of her mother, she could see it being restored to its former luster. Rizan herself could feel her strength being restored as she proclaimed herself cured.

After having been deprived for over twenty-four years, Rizan asked for some meat and bread, and even asked for help getting out of bed. Through her daughter's protestations, Rizan persisted until Lubine, in a state of shock and disbelief, helped her sit up. Rizan asked for her clothes, which had for many years been folded and stored in a wardrobe in another room. Lubine quickly went to retrieve them and when she returned, she gasped to see her mother had gotten out of bed and was now kneeling with clasped hands, praying before the mantle on which rested a statue of the Blessed Virgin Mary. Lubine was so terrified that she was unable to help her mother dress. It mattered not. Rizan needed no assistance. She rose from her knees, dressed herself, and returned immediately to her knees to give thanks.

It was now almost 7:00 AM and Lubine's cries could be heard by those returning from the first Mass of the day as they passed by the house. Thinking that Mme. Rizan had expired, several friends and neighbors entered the house and approached Lubine, "who was leaning against a half-opened door, with a countenance expressive of great consternation."[330] They expressed their words of consolation. "My mother has risen from the dead,"[331] is all Lubine could say in reply, with a voice laden with emotion. As the entourage brushed by her, they saw Rizan, dressed and lying prostrate in prayer before the image of Mary. "I am cured!" Rizan said. "Let us offer up a thanksgiving to the Blessed Virgin. Let all kneel down."[332] Not one among them could believe his eyes.

Word of the cure spread precipitously throughout the town of Nay so that by the next day, crowds of people filled the house. Each wished to touch the woman to whom life had been restored and each did so with the highest degree of emotion. Doctor Subervielle, who had also returned to the house, immediately acknowledged the supernatural character of the cure of his patient and friend.

It was not Lubine, but rather Abbé Dupont who penned a letter to Romain explaining that he was writing, not to bring news of his mother's death, but of her return to health. In a state of utter euphoria, Romain shared the letter with a friend who worked for the company that published the *Messager Catholique*. A few days later, the letter was published in its entirety in that paper.

Romain, meanwhile, had already departed for his trip back home. His mother waited patiently for the carriage to pull up to the house. When it did, and when Romain emerged from the carriage, she "rushed into his arms, weeping with tenderness and joy." The two lingered for an extended time, hugging and weeping with joyous emotion.

Another alleged miracle explored by the Commission involved a highly honorable family of Tartas in the Landes. A year following the April 1842 marriage of Adele de Chanton and Moreau de Sazenay, the two were in a state of apprehension as they awaited the birth of their first child. The doctors knew that childbirth would be difficult and shared their concern that it might present a certain danger. While Adele writhed in pain on her bed, Moreau's heart broke with empathy. Memories of his wedding, their young marriage, seemingly blessed by God with the promise of a child, and the hopes of the future that they planned together as a family, raced through his mind. The feelings of joy that had pervaded his being over the past several months were now replaced with irrepressible terror in the face of the doctors' concern over saving the lives of his young wife and their child.

Moreau immersed himself in prayer to the Blessed Virgin, the very Mother of Life, confident that She would hear his prayer. A short while later he heard the cry of his baby girl and announced that she would be named Maria. Despite protestations that the name was common and euphonious, Moreau was insistent that his daughter was to have the Blessed Virgin as her patroness and, owing to that persistence, the child not only bore the name of the Virgin, but, for the first three years of her life, donned only white, the color of the Virgin.

Over the course of the next sixteen years, Maria Moreau was blessed with a sister, Marthe, and was fortunate to receive her education at the Convent of the Sacred Heart at Bordeaux. In January 1858, Maria began to experience a problem with her sight, causing her to abandon her studies. There was nothing noticeable with the eye upon observance, but when the problem persisted, doctors "deemed it necessary to have a consultation with Monsieur Bermont, an eminent oculist at Bordeaux."[333]

Maria was brought there and left for examination. After many exams and consultations with experts, the doctors determined that Maria suffered from amaurosis, partial or total blindness without visible change in the eye, typically due to disease of the optic nerve, spinal cord, or brain. "'The case is a very serious one,' observed Monsieur Bermont. 'One of her eyes is gone and the other is in a most critical state.'"[334]

Her parents were immediately notified and returned to Bordeaux to pick up their daughter and take her home to begin the regimented treatment prescribed by the doctors. If the goal of the treatment wasn't to restore the blinded eye, it was certainly to save the remaining sight in the other. Though faithful to the application of all of the remedies prescribed throughout the winter, summer, and fall of the year, the treatments were ineffective and complete blindness seemed imminent. It was November and the Moreaus decided to take Maria to Paris in order to consult with the best doctors available to science and medicine. As they prepared to leave, they were met by the postman who delivered with their mail the weekly edition of *Messager Catholique* – the same edition that contained the letter of Abbé Dupont regarding the miraculous cure of Mme. Rizan of Nay.

Moreau opened the paper to that exact page and read the account of the miraculous cure. "He grew pale as he read it. Hope began to awake in the soul of the disconsolate father, and a ray of light penetrated his mind, or rather his heart."[335]He quickly knew that if the Blessed Virgin appeared in Lourdes, it was to perform miracles that would enable skeptics to believe. He immediately redirected his purpose to making a novena to the Blessed Virgin with a promise to dress Maria in white and blue, the colors of Mary, for a year following.

It happened that a local priest had in his possession a bottle of water from the spring at Lourdes enabling them to begin the novena immediately, on the eighth of November. They were supported in their prayer by family, friends, and neighbors who joined with them. Though

Moreau had immense faith, it was not shared by Maria. Adele refused to muster too much hope. They all prayed in front of a statue of the Blessed Virgin and though Maria and her sister wanted occasionally to rise from prayer, Monsieur Moreau never left his knees. He prayed so loudly that those hoping to take some rest immediately returned to their knees in prayer, until eventually, they slept.

The next morning, Maria awoke, immediately removing the bandage that covered her eyes. The eye which had only recently been attacked by the illness was restored to full strength as was the sight of the blinded eye. "'Marthe! Marthe!' she cried to her sister, 'I see! I see! I am cured!'"[336] Marthe, who shared a bedroom with Maria, jumped from her bed, ran toward her sister, and gazed on the eyes that, though once dead, could now see. Still in disbelief, Maria reached for a book to see if she was able to read.

Euphoric, she called out to their parents, crying, "Papa! Mamma! I can see, I can read, I am cured!"[337] Adele and Moreau ran to her room and they, along with Marthe, fell to their knees in prayers of thanksgiving. Though Maria was still in bed, she clasped her hands and joined her family in prayer.

A short time later, Maria Moreau and her parents visited the Grotto of the Apparition and deposited Maria's ordinary attire on the altar, returning wearing only the colors of the Queen of Virgins.

The Commissioners found the story of Maria's blindness and cure supported by one hundred and fifty of her student classmates as well as the Superior at the Convent of the Sacred Heart at Bordeaux, the medical men at that establishment supported the facts of her condition both before and after the cure. Bermont, the oculist who treated Maria, noted the cure was complete, adding that its instantaneous nature was "a fact, beyond comparison, which altogether exceeds the limits of medical knowledge...in which belief I have attached my signature."[338]

As for Maria, she wore the colors of the Virgin until the day of her marriage, which took place a couple of years later when she completed her education. On her wedding day, she returned to the Grotto to retire her maiden attire and assume her bridal robe. It was her desire to present her blue and white dress to another young girl beloved by the Blessed Virgin. A girl by the name of Bernadette. This was the only gift that Bernadette ever accepted, and she wore it for many years until it was no longer wearable. For Bernadette, the colors of the dress "always recalled to her mind the beneficent omnipotence of the divine apparition at the Grotto."

The girl that was once blind went on to have two children of her own. Though both were boys, each was given the baptismal name of Marie.

The miraculous cures attributed to the waters of the Grotto of Massabielle numbered in the hundreds, making any attempts to verify the facts of each an impossible task. Therefore, the Commissioners selected only thirty for examination, but those thirty were subjected to minute scrutiny. They rejected any case in which the cure was gradual and in concert with medical treatment as it could not be determined if the treatment or a miracle was responsible for the cure. Supernatural intervention was invoked, in fact, only when it was impossible to attribute the cure to any other cause, and any cure not effected instantaneously was rejected. Each cure was heavily documented and signed by the person cured as well as by numerous witnesses.

The final report submitted to Bishop Laurence divided into three categories the cures that the Commissioners investigated. The first category detailed the six cures that might be explained naturally. The second category was comprised of nine cures of which the Commissioners were inclined to admit some element of a supernatural agency. Of those in that category it might be said that the Commissioners exercised a high degree of caution following the dictates of prudence. Many of those cures might easily have been ascribed a supernatural causation but were not. The final category included fifteen cures that displayed the "most evident and undeniable manner of the supernatural character. All these cures were pronounced to have been incontestably miraculous."[339]

The conditions from which those fifteen were cured were very different, yet in each case the cure was sudden, striking, and total. All the cures were affected by the same element, Grotto water, which was administered either internally or externally or both. The Commissioners' report continued:

"Now, in the natural and scientific order, besides the fact of each remedy only being applied in a particular manner, it is clear that it only possesses one special virtue adapted to such or such a malady, but which is inefficacious, if not injurious, in all other cases. It is not, therefore, owing to any peculiar property inherent in its composition, that the water of Massabielle has succeeded in producing such numerous, extraordinary and different cures, and in suddenly putting to flight so many maladies of different and sometimes diametrically opposite nature.

And this is the more remarkable since science has authoritatively declared on the analysis furnished by the most eminent men, that this water does not in itself contain any mineral or therapeutic properties, and that, chemically speaking, it is nothing but pure water.

On glancing at these cures as a whole, one is struck at once with the facility, promptitude, and instantaneousness with which they issue from the bosom of their producing cause; with the violation and utter upsetting of all therapeutic methods which prevail in their accomplishment; with the contradictions which the precepts and provisions of science meet with; with that kind of disdain which makes sport of the long continuance, extent and resistance of the malady; with the hidden, but at the same time, real care with which the circumstances are arranged and combined, in order to show that in the cure which is being effected there is something going on quite out of the ordinary course of nature. Such phenomena are beyond the range of human intellect. How, in fact, can it comprehend the opposition which exists:

Between the simplicity of the means and the grandeur of the result? Between the unity of the remedy and the deliverance of the maladies? Between the short duration of the application of the curative agent and the slowness of the treatment prescribed by art or science? Between the sudden efficacy of the former and the tedious failure of the

latter? Between the chronic nature of the disease and the instantaneousness of the cure?
There is in all this a contingent Force superior to those which have been dispensed to nature and consequently foreign to the water which it employs for the manifestation of its power."[340]

The Bishop read the report with its striking facts. He discerned the investigatory skill and conscientious detail by which men deeply versed in both medical and chemical science declared their findings and found it to be convincing. His unbelief was allayed and his doubt clarified. Yet, he still wished for the report on these miraculous events to undergo the sanction of time. He would wait three years before taking any further steps.

During that time a second investigation was undertaken, allowing the passage of time to alter, perhaps even to contradict, the facts provided in the first investigation. No one advantaged themselves of the opportunity to alter the minutest detail of their testimony.

Friday, January 18, 1862

Bishop Laurence had deliberated long and hard. He had appointed a commission to investigate the events of Massabielle. The commission included clergy, medical professionals, and scientists. Interviews were conducted with the principals and tens of witnesses. Evidence was examined and reexamined. A report was submitted by the commission to the Bishop, suggesting that all the evidence pointed to the veracity of Bernadette's story and the authenticity of many of the cures. A long period of time was allowed to pass in order for witnesses and others to alter their story or change their testimony if they so desired. No one had and now, Bishop Laurence decided, was the time for him to pronounce judgement in the case of the Apparitions that took place in the Grotto of Lourdes.

Taking pen to paper the Bishop wrote a long synopsis of the events and the evidence declaring:

> "...We pronounce judgement that the Immaculate Mary, Mother of God, really appeared to Bernadette Soubirous on the eleventh of February 1858, and following days, to the number of eighteen, in the Grotto of Massabielle, near the town of Lourdes; that this Apparition is invested with every character of truth, and that the faithful have good ground for believing it to be certain."[341]

The Bishop further declared the appropriateness of worship to Our Lady of the Grotto of Lourdes and approved the construction of a sanctuary at the site in accordance with Our Lady's wishes. To initiate the construction, the Bishop purchased "from the Town of Lourdes the Grotto, the portion of land by which it is surrounded, and the entire group of the Rocks of Massabielle."[342]

Part V

Bernadette Joins
the Sisters of Charity
at Nevers

Since the events of the Grotto began to unfold in February 1858, Bernadette had no peace of which to speak. The number of pilgrims hoping for her time increased with each passing day. Inquiries, both of an official nature such as the one conducted under the auspices of the Bishop's order, and the impromptu, such as that arranged by Louis Veuillot, consumed a majority of her time.

By July 1860, Bernadette was being torn in many directions. She worked as a baby-sitter for Armantine Grenier; at the direction of her volunteer tutor, Antoinette Tardhivail, she tried to complete her missing schoolwork; she helped out at home performing the customary duties of the oldest daughter; and, she met visitors as required, sometimes traveling great distances to meet the demands. It all amounted to a crushing burden for which there was little relief. She had little occasion to rest or to sleep and her health suffered immensely as a result.

Monday, July 9, 1860
to Sunday, July 15, 1860

It was to this madness that Dominiquette Cazenave arrived at the Gras mill to visit Bernadette Soubirous at her parents' new abode. Louise was ecstatic to see her and took full advantage of the opportunity to ask her guest if she would teach Bernadette to sew. Dominiquette was happy to oblige but didn't want to do so under the constant interruptions that had become routine in the Soubirous household. "Let her come to the quiet of my house,"[343] she insisted. Louise knew that such a request would need the approval of Abbé Peyramale, who had limited the number of visits Bernadette could make into town. Seeking the pastor's approval was a task that Dominiquette was all too happy to undertake.

Upon her return home, Dominiquette took full advantage of the opportunity to describe to Abbé Peyramale the difficult conditions to which Bernadette was exposed, adding a plea to allow for a change of venue for the poor child. Peyramale was not ignorant of the difficult circumstances of Bernadette's life and harkened back to his plan of almost two years ago to place her with the sisters who ran the Hospice School. There she could live, continue her academic and domestic education, and eliminate a great deal of stress from her life. He made the proposal to the hospice anew.

His arrangement met with the approval of Mother Superior, Mere Ursule Fardes, who willingly accepted Abbé Peyramale's offer despite her reluctance to believe Bernadette's story of the Apparitions. Both Peyramale and Fardes established rigorous rules for the child's protection and her care was entrusted to Sister Victorine Poux.

One such rule to which Bernadette was subjected was a denial of any visitor without explicit permission from the rectory. François and Louise opposed the Abbé's plan, wishing not to be separated from their daughter for the second time in her short life. It wasn't until Peyramale agreed to allow for a permanent exception that would allow them to visit Bernadette anytime that they softened their position.

With that understanding, François and Louise reluctantly consented to allow Bernadette to once again depart her loving home and the care and protection of her parents, to begin a new life with the Sisters of Charity at Nevers. Dr. Dozous joined the Soubirouses in questioning the wisdom of such a move. He had been fired from the Hospice and did not approve of Bernadette being entrusted to the care of one who did not believe in the veracity of her claims. Neither were the Tardhivail sisters pleased. Perhaps most importantly, Bernadette opposed the move. She loved her family very much and cherished the responsibilities of being the oldest daughter. Moving would cut her off from the kind of human relationships so essential to the life of any child. Despite the many protestations, the die had been cast. On Sunday July 15, 1860, Bernadette left the loving confines of her parents' home and care to begin a new chapter in her life. At the tender age of sixteen and a half years, Bernadette hugged her parents and departed the home in which she would never live again.

Monday, July 16, 1860
to Monday, December 31, 1860
Bernadette's Life at Nevers

There were many students and nuns within the Hospice who were happy about Bernadette's stay at the school. Bernadette, however, was not one of them. The Hospice was both a hospital and a school and boarders were separated into two distinct classes: the demoiselles of the bourgeoisie, and the charity cases, comprised of girls of more modest means albeit of good character. Because of her class schedule, Bernadette was required to live with the demoiselles, who were considered among the privileged, something anathema to Bernadette, who instinctively felt more comfortable living with and among the poor.

Though Bernadette struggled with the sacrifice required in leaving her family and rooming with those who took her outside of her comfort zone, life at the Hospice did have an upside. The absence of outside distractions and the convenience of on-site medical attention would allow Bernadette to complete a school year with somewhat regular attendance.

Even with this advantage, the child found educational progress to be slow. By New Year's Eve, she still found it difficult to write a short note to her parents. When it was pointed out to Bernadette that her inability to write well was of little consequence since neither François nor Louise knew how to read, Bernadette noted that her concern was in disappointing the nuns at Nevers, the thought of which caused her great angst.

Tuesday, January 1, 1861
to Monday, March 24, 1862

Just a few months into the new year, Bernadette's academic development showed a marked improvement. Perhaps it was her persistence and the dedication to her work that was responsible for a vast progress in both her reading and her writing skills. Regardless the cause,

Bernadette was now able to use those skills as a means of self-expression and this made her very happy. For the first time she was able to write her own account of the Apparitions of 1858 that had come to define her young life.

On the domestic front, too, the child was coming into her own. She had become a rather gifted amateur seamstress with a mastery of stitches and materials. She was likewise quite adept at embroidery. Bernadette also knew how to have fun, earning her a reputation as "the life of the party."[344] One companion noted that "she was always happy."[345] Though hindered by asthma, Bernadette often played with the younger children, resorting to less strenuous activity. Many times she could be found swinging the rope as others jumped over it. "Knucklebones, hide and seek, and blindman's bluff"[346] were other games that seemed to bring sweet moments of joy to Bernadette.

Bernadette could be mischievous, though she refused to participate in pranks, no matter how innocent. And she could be stubborn, though generally exhibiting that behavior privately rather than in front of other children.

Time is never static, and its passage had transformed Bernadette and her classmates from girls to young women. At seventeen, they were becoming more conscious of their appearance and their dress, and this awareness was not without its complications. One day at church, some of her friends "apparently absorbed in their prayer books, were secretly reading cheap romantic novels, about which they later sentimentally spoke among themselves. Bernadette was scandalized to the point of turning her natural repugnance to such reading into a matter of principle. 'Don't learn how to read,' she told her younger sibling Marie one day. [Sister] Victorine caught her giving this bad advice by the Hospice's hall window. 'Bernard!' (that is how she sometimes called Bernadette.) 'Why are you saying that to Marie?' 'Ah! We come from a family where it's better.' 'But why?' insisted the nun. Even in her anger, Bernadette wouldn't betray her companions for all the world. 'That's the way it is. It's better that way,'"[347] she said.

Sister Victorine admired Bernadette. Her ordinariness was something to be emulated. But there was one issue that she and the other nuns at Nevers would not emulate – the child's repulsion to money. They found it excessive, especially when the gift was intended for the Church. Initially Bernadette would simply refuse any amount offered her, a practice for which the nuns would scold her. Later, she would simply say, "There's a poor-box..."[348] Even when circumstance required her to accept money, she would immediately hand it to Mother Superior. It was simply Bernadette's nature to attach to nothing and to give away whatever she had.

Her propensity to give of what she had and to protect others tended toward the extreme though, and was sometimes problematic. Such was the case one day during class. Bernadette decided to share with classmates the snuff that had been prescribed as treatment for her asthma. A commotion arose as each girl shared a snort. When the nun scowled, Bernadette rose immediately to confess, "I'm the one, Sister! I offered a pinch of snuff to my neighbors."[349]

Life at Nevers was not all study and play however, and there were times when her classmates shared the curiosity of so many others from in and around Lourdes regarding her visions. Bernadette shied from the spotlight and seldom spoke of the Apparitions with her classmates. She changed the subject whenever it was raised and rarely discussed it except when so ordered by a superior. What she did do was receive Communion at every opportunity offered her which was, at the least, every Sunday and occasionally on weekdays.

If Bernadette enjoyed playing with her friends and receiving Communion, she had an equally intense dislike for the spotlight. She certainly had had enough of that during her many interrogations regarding the Apparitions and certainly had no desire to be the subject of a photo shoot.

It might be argued that French inventor Joseph Nicephore Niepce was the father of photography, having used a homemade camera in 1816 to produce a partially successful photograph on paper coated with silver chloride. It was his partner, Louis Daguerre, however, who continued Niepce's experiments and unveiled the first publicly used camera in 1839. It was the daguerreotype on which Abbé Bernadou, a chemistry teacher at the minor seminary, captured the first images of Bernadette sometime between October 1861 and March 1862. Bernadou had purchased his camera for purposes of recording art and history.

Certainly, Bernadette's celebrity presented appropriate cause in that regard, thereby justifying Bernadou's use of the equipment to photograph the visionary.

Nothing during those early years at Nevers, however, was cause of greater concern than the issue of Bernadette's health. The bulk of responsibility for her healthcare fell to Sister Victorine, who from November 1861 was assigned the task of watching out for her. She was clearly kept busy with Bernadette's chronic asthma, but in addition noted that the poor child suffered from "toothaches, frequent rheumatism in her leg; a painful shoulder, almost causing her to faint...; a chronic cough, vomiting or coughing up blood (frequently), [and] occasional palpitations."[350] It was the violent asthma attacks, however, that caused the most stress. Frequently confining Bernadette to bed, the attacks were the source of much of the child's suffering, causing her to cry out on more than one occasion, "Open my chest!"[351]

Some of the attacks were so severe that, several times, the nuns thought sure Bernadette would not survive and sent for her parents. Bernadette's brother Jean-Marie recounted that many times, his parents François and Louise, as well as other members of the family, would all get up and go to the Hospice. "We would kneel beside my sister's bed, as if we were witnessing her final moments,"[352] he said.

Despite her constant pain, Bernadette never let on. Sister Victorine noted that without knowing her well, one might not even realize she suffered. The nun attributed much of her problem to the relentless badgering that Bernadette had to endure for so long. For a while, the visits were minimal, but before long, they were constant. The nuns would protect her from interruption during class time but encouraged visitors during recreation and ordered Bernadette to greet them. Bernadette despised having to leave her friends at play just to go answer the same questions over and over again, but the nuns frequently reminded her that "the apparitions did not take place for your amusement but for the people."[353] The persuasiveness of their position scarcely diminished her repulsion.

Sometimes Bernadette would simply cry at the door as she observed upwards of forty people waiting for her at one time. The nuns would offer words of encouragement as she wiped the tears away before entering the sitting room. The people would ask for prayers, touch her rosary, make her touch theirs, and ask a multitude of questions, none of which was original. After obliging their requests and answering their questions, Bernadette would rejoin her friends at play as though never interrupted.

Abbé Pomian eventually prohibited her from touching rosaries or allowing people to take snippets of her hair or other relics. More often than not she could be overheard saying, "I am forbidden from doing so."[354] During Bernadette's entire stay at the Hospice, "the sisters feared she would grow spoiled, so they made it their duty to humiliate her in public,"[355] saying that she was nothing and had accomplished nothing. Some said things even worse, implying that Bernadette was nothing but a charity case and, if the Virgin did appear to her, it was not because she deserved it. Though the words hurt Bernadette, she had no ill will toward those who made the comments. Rather, she held the hurt in secret, generally exuding joy.

Tuesday, March 25, 1862

It had been a long time since Bernadette had been allowed to return to the Grotto, but Antoinette Tardhivail had petitioned for permission to bring her there, and Mother Superior, against all odds, granted the request. Antoinette and Bernadette knelt and prayed before the hollow in which the Mother of God had appeared to Bernadette many times just two years prior. They prayed the Rosary and Bernadette basked in the figurative warmth, comfort, and joy of recalling those wonderful moments when she conversed with the Blessed Virgin Mary.

Wednesday, March 26, 1862
to Sunday, April 20, 1862

Bernadette awoke from the night's sleep unable to breathe. While some attributed her painful attempts to breathe to the chronic asthma, doctors soon discovered that the child suffered from an inflammation of one of her lungs, which prompted a very serious condition.

Her friends were greatly concerned as was her doctor. Antoinette was particularly worried, and to add to her anxiety, public rumor suggested that it was she who was responsible for Bernadette's condition by exposing her to the currents at the Grotto. Antoinette wept at the accusation but continued to pray ardently for her friend's recovery.

On about April 20, Antoinette's prayers, and those of many others, were answered. Bernadette's infection cleared, and she was able to once again move about, though she was left with a persistent pain in one of her legs. At the insistence of the Tardhivail sisters, Mother Superior allowed them to take Bernadette to the Grotto one more time, this time so they could all give thanks to God and his Blessed Mother for restoring Bernadette to good health. The very next day, however, Bernadette suffered a relapse, and this time the condition affected both lungs.

Monday, April 28, 1862

Bernadette's face was flushed as she coughed and choked on the fluid that filled her lungs, but when she opened her eyes she beheld the sight of two strangers standing over her bed. "Don't talk," said Elfrida, one of the strangers, "just touch these objects." Elfrida Lacrampe, whose father owned the Pyrenees Hotel, had forced her way into the Hospice. Back on February 25, 1858, she had accompanied Jean-Baptiste Estrade to the Grotto and witnessed the emergence of the spring that Bernadette had unearthed at the direction of the Virgin Mary. Since that day, the one-time denier who called Bernadette a liar, was, in fact, a believer. Elfrida was with Lina, a servant to an English family living in Pau. Lina, a Protestant unbeliever who wanted nothing to do with Bernadette, was joined at the Hospice by her husband Joseph, who worked as a servant in Lourdes for a different family. It was Joseph, a Catholic, who sought the favor of having Bernadette touch the objects in the hope that his prayer for his wife's conversion to Catholicism might become a reality.

Disappointed at Bernadette's unwillingness to touch the things she had taken, Elfrida kissed the sick child and turned to leave. It was then that Lina fell to her knees and began to sob. Though panting for breath, Bernadette looked at Lina, saying, "Madame, get up, I beg of you, it makes me feel sad." Lina remained still. Bernadette repeated her request, adding "Stay here if you wish, but please sit down."[356]

Lina sat by the bed and continued to sob into her hands. Bernadette was so moved by the woman's anguish that she felt compelled to offer her something, but had only the cross and medal that she wore on her neck. "No, no, nothing. I'm unworthy," Lina responded. Elfrida cut the rope that held the cross and medal around Bernadette's neck. Bernadette then handed them to Lina saying, "Here, Madame, the cross is for you and the medal is to remind you of me." Sensing the conversion, Elfrida instructed her friends that it was time to leave and together they departed the room*.

That afternoon, Bernadette's condition worsened. With death an imminent possibility, the nuns sent for her mother Louise and Dr. Balencie called for a consulting doctor. He hoped that a different doctor might offer a varying opinion, but that doctor's examination confirmed Balencie's suspicions, and it was suggested that Bernadette receive the final sacraments. Abbé Pomian arrived to administer the last rites of the Catholic Church as the two doctors departed the room "shaking their heads pessimistically."[357] Bernadette made her confession with great difficulty as she was virtually unable to speak, prompting Abbé Pomian to ask that she respond with gestures rather than with voice. The Abbé also wanted to offer Bernadette Communion, but knew that she could not swallow. He decided, therefore, to break off just a small particle from the consecrated host and give it to her with water from the Grotto. "That was when the dying girl's expression changed. The obstruction had suddenly disappeared. She began breathing freely. Bernadette felt like laughing and crying but held back in order to make a prayerful thanksgiving. Finally, she said, 'I'm cured. It's as if a mountain has been lifted from my chest.' There was no longer anything that impeded her speech. She added, 'Monsieur L'Abbé, you brought me a good doctor.'"

*Two years later, Joseph returned to Lourdes with the cross and medal that Bernadette had given his wife. Lina had indeed converted from Protestantism to Catholicism a few months after visiting Bernadette and then died just two years after her conversion.

Bernadette ate and drank and wanted to get out of bed, but seeing that it was already nighttime, the Superior suggested that the recovered patient postpone that effort until morning. Bernadette slept through the balance of the night without even a hint of a cough.

Tuesday, April 29, 1862

Bernadette was up early, dressed, and waited the arrival of her doctor whom she greeted in the visitors room. Doctor Balencie was surprised when he saw the child standing, but didn't let it affect his professional demeanor, commenting instead that the medications he prescribed apparently worked exceedingly well. When informed that she hadn't taken any of the medicine, he noted that she must not have been as sick as he previously thought.

Bernadette didn't give much attention to the cause of her cure, she was just happy to feel better and quickly resumed her studies and her daily chores of sewing, cooking, cleaning, and caring for the sick.

Wednesday, April 30, 1862
to Sunday, April 3, 1864
Cures

That is how life went for Bernadette over the course of the next couple of years. Daily visitors and sporadic illness punctuated her days. She was consumed with her chores when she wasn't doing schoolwork or bedridden with asthma or some other chronic illness, and many people continued to experience cures from the miraculous waters of the spring at the Grotto.

Cures such as the one experienced by the girl from Marciac, a commune in the Gers department in the southwest of France. She arrived in Lourdes at about four o'clock in the afternoon of Saturday July

25, 1863 and went immediately to the Hospice to see Bernadette. Her arm had been in a sling since suffering a fall while helping her mother. She lost the use of the entire arm after the accident and had not used it for so long that the fingers of her hand were contracted and thin. Though unable to use her arm, she still experienced tremendous pain from it and was not able to have it touched without crying out. After seeing Bernadette, she went to the Grotto to pray. When her prayers were complete, she bathed her arm in the spring water. At that very moment, the arm sprang to life. Her fingers straightened, and the pain vanished. The coachman who had taken her to the Grotto was in disbelief. "He was frozen on seeing the girl all of a sudden raise and stretch out her arm, then open and close her hand which had been completely useless only a few moments before."[358]

Or like that of the twenty-three-year-old Catherine Duros who had arrived on Wednesday August 5, 1863 in such bad condition that Bernadette was asked to visit her at the Hotel Maumus where she lay in bed. "Bernadette sent her to the spring where she was cured on the spot."[359]

The Statue

On Friday September 17, 1863, Bernadette was called from the schoolyard, where she was enjoying recreation with her classmates. Joseph Fabisch, a renowned sculptor of the time, had been asked to sculpt a statue of the Virgin Mary as She appeared to Bernadette in 1858. He paced nervously while awaiting Bernadette's arrival. He wondered if he would be able to extract from the memory of the child enough detail to fulfill the terms of his contract which specified that the apparition needed to be "depicted as accurately as possible."[360]

The sculptor's worry was for naught, however, as the child's memory of the most beautiful vision of the Blessed Mother was as fresh that day as on the days of Her appearance. Bernadette was able to provide extraordinary detail about the Virgin: Her features, Her clothing, and Her surroundings. No question was unanswered, and no detail left to chance. The two would meet several times over the ensuing months.

While the sculptor progressed in his work to bring Bernadette's apparitions to life, there were many attempts by the Sisters and others to preserve Bernadette's humility and those were sometimes the cause of her great sorrow. The visionary, for example, was not allowed to visit her family on February 4, 1864 when they welcomed into the world Bernadette's little brother Jean. Nor was she allowed to attend the services for her godfather Jean-Marie Vedere, who died on February 20, and, in March of 1864, Bernadette was assigned the task of writing letters to pilgrims who requested prayers. Certainly not her first choice of assignment.

By November 1863, Joseph Fabisch had produced a plaster model, and subsequently a clay statue of the Lady as She had appeared at Lourdes. Though he worked feverishly, he failed to produce something fitting the most accurate description provided him by the child. Regardless, on Wednesday March 30, 1864, he carried his masterpiece to the Hospice, where it was displayed for Abbé Peyramale, the Mother Superior, and Bernadette, the latter of which was surprisingly unimpressed. "No, that's not it,"[361] was all she would say.

Monday, April 4, 1864

Bernadette's dissatisfaction was obvious to all in the room, but her frustration was officially suppressed, and on April 4, 1864 the statue was unveiled triumphantly. While Bernadette seldom revealed her own emotional disappointment at the artist's result, she did confide her true feelings to Elfrida Lacrampe and again two years later when Père Cros asked her if the statue in the Grotto looked like the Blessed Virgin. Bernadette answered with a look that Cros couldn't describe, "Not a bit."[362]

Bernadette was not allowed to attend the dedication, as Abbé Peyramale thought her insufficiently recovered from her recent bout with asthma. He also wanted to preserve her humility. Bernadette, though disappointed, obeyed without reservation. To her surprise, however, cousin

Jeanne Vedere arrived at the Hospice for a visit to Bernadette's bedside after attending the ceremony at the Grotto. Bernadette asked Jeanne if she was able to procure a piece of the blue cloth that had covered the statue prior to the unveiling. Jeanne had not. Though she acknowledged seeing the blue cloth at the ceremony, she knew not of its current whereabouts. Bernadette then asked Sister Marie Geraud to "'get what I asked you to put in the closet.' The sister brought back a pretty blue box with a big piece of material used to wrap up the statue." Bernadette gave Jeanne a rather large swatch which she later cut "into pieces to share with more than twenty people."[363]

Jeanne's visit, and Bernadette's gift of the cloth were not the only surprises that Bernadette would be part of on that day. The visionary chose the backdrop of the festivities of the dedication of the statue to Our Lady of Lourdes to announce to Mother Superior that she had decided to join the Sisters of Charity at Nevers as a nun. In actuality she had decided it a long time ago, prior to April 8, 1858 during the time of the Apparitions, and reported it to Adelaide Monlaur who wrote about it in a letter bearing that date.

For some time, Bernadette had a strong desire to serve God as a nun. Initially she was drawn to that vocation by her Aunt Bernarde Casterot, who had suggested that Bernadette might enjoy a contemplative life. The child mentioned to Aunt Basile in early 1858 that she might want to enter the Carmelite Order. She also shared her sentiments with Marthe du Rais at the time of her First Communion on June 3, 1858. It was Abbé Peyramale, however, who first suggested that the Sisters of Charity might be a more suitable order for someone suffering from the type of health issues with which Bernadette was afflicted.

Bernadette was not convinced, but after residing with the Sisters for two years, her heart was moved from a life of contemplation to one of serving the sick and the poor, and so that day she made a formal request of Mother Superior to join her Order. Mother seemed pleased, noting that she would take the request to the Bishop. When word of Bernadette's decision became public, many speculated that this, in fact, may have been one of the three secrets imparted to Bernadette by the Virgin Mary. Brother Leobard confronted Bernadette directly with the inquiry, noting, "I know at least one [secret], it's that you must become a nun."

Bernadette bowed her head and said nothing, causing many to believe that her silence implied that Brother Leobard hit the nail on the head. Still, there is no evidence that the decision was made by anyone other than Bernadette after prayerful reflection.

Tuesday, April 5, 1864
to Tuesday, February 7, 1865

Bernadette continued to receive visitors. Far more than she or her fragile health could take. On October 3, 1865, she received another surprise visit from her cousin Jeanne Vedere. That time, Jeanne, who was also awaiting the consent of her parents to enter the convent, had requested permission from the Superior to take Bernadette to Momeres for the day. Because she was enjoying relatively good health on that day, permission was granted. In fact, Bernadette would be allowed to spend an extraordinary amount of time with her cousin in Momeres that fall. She also spent an inordinate amount of time with photographers, who clearly wanted to memorialize the visionary in photographs for all generations to enjoy. Jeanne and Bernadette returned to Lourdes on November 19 when they visited with, among other people, Abbé Peyramale. It was while she was back in Lourdes that Bernadette received the good news that her request to join the Sisters of Charity at Nevers had been granted. She was very excited and went promptly to tell her parents.

By December 1864, Bernadette was academically and mentally ready to begin her religious formation. Unfortunately, her health would not cooperate, as she fell into relapse at just about that time. It wasn't until February 7, 1865 that the child was able to get out of bed.

Sunday, July 29, 1866

Forty-four postulants took the habit on the feast day honoring Saint Martha, while an additional nineteen novices, including

Bernadette, made their profession. It was only Bernadette's height, or lack of it, that enabled the curious to pick her from the group of religious that day. Bishop Forcade presided over the clothing ceremony and gave each novitiate a veil and a new name by which they would forever be known. Looking to Bernadette in turn, Bishop Forcade said, "Sister Marie-Bernard, may the Lord clothe you with the new self, created according to the likeness of God in true righteousness and holiness. Amen."[364]

Bernadette was grateful for the habit that made it difficult for others to identify her as the visionary at Lourdes. She liked to bring the veil forward, providing her even more privacy from the curious. Within the novitiate, however, she was often mocked by those who just couldn't understand the constant flow of visitors that fawned over the child, but it mattered little to Bernadette, who often said that she came to the motherhouse to hide.

The official photograph of Sister Marie-Bernard.
That was the name assigned Bernadette after entering the convent.

During the several months that followed, the novitiates were trained by working at various houses of the congregation. It became a problem for Sister Marie-Bernard, at least in the mind of her Superior, who thought it better to keep her out of the community and in the motherhouse. Being an exception weighed heavily on the novice, however, as she longed to be able to go out and work in the community. Above all else, she missed being able to pray at the Grotto and spent many nights crying over the depravation.

Wednesday, August 15, 1866
to Wednesday, October 24, 1866

Despite her assignment in the motherhouse, Sister Marie-Bernard worked very hard as a nurse's aide, perhaps as a means of compensating for being left behind while the others were establishing ties and caring for those in the community. There were still those within the convent who didn't believe that the Blessed Virgin had appeared to Bernadette and there were others who resented the fact that She did.

By mid-August, Sister Marie-Bernard was exhausted and reported to the infirmary. By mid-September, her asthma grew worse, restricting her to bed. She suffered a great deal during that time and on many occasions the other nuns thought her very near to death. Throughout the ordeal, however, Marie-Bernard never complained about her illness. "It is necessary," she said. "It's nothing."[365] In fact, she often showed more concern over the health of those entrusted to watch her. "Rest in that armchair," she would frequently say to her caretakers. "I'll call you when I have to."[366]

Thursday, October 25, 1865

Sister Marie-Bernard's health had deteriorated beyond the point of hope for recovery. The other nuns prayed and burned candles before the statue of the Blessed Virgin, but it all seemed in vain. Doctor Robert Saint-Cyr proclaimed that she would not last the night and her infirmary-mate was transferred to another room. She was prepared for death and given the Catholic Rite of Extreme Unction, later known as the Last Rites. The Council was called into emergency session and tried to secure the Bishop's dispensation necessary to quickly admit her to religious profession prior to her impending death.

7:00 PM

Unfortunately, the Bishop had not yet returned from his Confirmation tour. When he did, at about 7:00 PM, he was immediately apprised of the urgency by two of the Sisters. Upon being told that Sister Marie-Bernard would not last the night, he immediately agreed to go personally to the motherhouse to receive her profession. Arriving at Sister Marie-Bernard's bedside just a short time later, he found the patient panting. His eyes immediately focused on the basin of blood that Sister Marie-Bernard had just vomited. Leaning over the bed he said softly, "'You're going to die, my dear child, and I'm told that you wish to make your profession. Here I am to receive it.' In a faint, choppy voice, Sister Marie-Bernard responded, 'I won't be able to say the formula...no strength.' 'That's no trouble,' Bishop Forcade said, 'I will say it for you. All you'll have to do is say: Amen...So be it.' And so it was."[367] The Bishop spoke a few words of encouragement to her and begged her not to forget him in heaven. Then, without saying another word, he left.

Sister Marie-Bernard would not die that night and her vows, as with any taken at the point of death, were invalidated upon her recovery, in accordance with canonical law. Though not officially a Sister of Charity, Bernadette had, however, been professed, was in fact a member of the congregation, and therefore could not be sent away. That made her very happy.

Saturday, December 8, 1865

Sister Victorine Poux from the Hospice in Lourdes was on her way to Vespers when she decided to stop and visit Louise Soubirous, who had been ill. Sister Victorine spoke to Louise about Bernadette and promised that she would write a letter to her visionary daughter. Louise liked that idea and nodded her approval. Sister Victorine said her good-byes and before leaving, promised to return after Vespers. It was the feast of the Immaculate Conception and it was a very special day, as it marked the first time that Vespers would be celebrated at the crypt in the Grotto. Sister Victorine arrived back to the Soubirous home a little more than an hour later only to learn that Louise had died while she prayed at Vespers.

Monday, December 10 or Tuesday, December 11, 1865

A few days later, Bernadette received the devastating news that her mother had passed away at the age of only forty-one. She had been worn down by the type of toil that poverty brings. Bernadette was overcome with sorrow, having received word of her mother's death even before hearing of the illness that caused it. She was comforted, however, in learning that her mother died on the Feast of the Immaculate Conception, knowing that it was a sign from God signifying that her beloved mother was now in heaven.

Saturday, February 2, 1867 to Tuesday, October 29, 1867

Bernadette remained in the infirmary for over a year, but on February 2, the day had arrived when she would finally leave and return to the novitiate to live as a novice. Her greeting was less than desirable, however, as Mother Marie-Therese wasted no time in letting Bernadette know that she was entering into the time of testing. Mother even went so far as to say, presumably in a joking fashion, that they were now going to beat her. Mother Marie-Therese didn't cater to anyone and was said to have despised privileged souls. She did whatever she needed to do in order to humble them. Bernadette was squarely in her cross-hairs.

Despite the admonitions, Sister Marie-Bernard remained the center of attention of the other novices, something that upset Mother Superior, who treated Bernadette harshly. Other novitiates noted how Mother Marie-Therese corrected Bernadette curtly and without feeling, hurting Bernadette with words so harsh that they at times caused the novice to turn pale. Mother Marie-Therese even mocked Bernadette's lowly background. Yet, Bernadette always expressed her joy at being at the novitiate and always spoke to and about her Superior with the most gracious words of love and respect.

In addition to the harsh treatment, Bernadette was continuously hounded by the visits of strangers wanting to meet her and talk about the visions, something the novice had hoped would have ended. Despite her inner feelings of regret, she cheerfully dealt with all of the challenges presented to her, but she despised those visits. She did, on the other hand, greatly anticipate taking her final vows.

Wednesday, October 30, 1867
Afternoon

Bernadette had waited a very long time for the moment. She and forty-three fellow novices would make their profession for the vows of poverty, chastity, obedience, and charity, at a Mass celebrated at Saint-Gildard's. Despite her weakened physical condition, Bernadette's voice was steady and her movements reverent, throughout.

The ceremony, presided over by Bishop Forcade, took place in the conference hall of the novitiate. Each nun was called individually to receive her crucifix, book of Constitutions, letter of obedience, and her assignment to one of the many houses of the congregation that were scattered all over France. Forty-three in all were called, but not Bernadette.

Confused, the Bishop leaned toward Superior General, Mother Joséphine Imbert, who was sitting next to him, to inquire as to why Bernadette's name had not been called. "'Monseigneur, she is good for nothing,' Mother Joséphine said softly and with a smile that was meant to conceal her apparent contempt. The Bishop motioned for Bernadette to approach. As she did so Bishop Forcade said, 'Sister Marie-Bernard! Nowhere!' Then, as Bernadette knelt before him, expecting to receive her book and crucifix, he softly said, 'Is it true, Sister Marie-Bernard, that you are good for nothing?' 'It is true,' she replied. 'Well then, my poor child, what are we going to do with you?' the Bishop asked. Bernadette looked down. 'I told you in Lourdes when you wanted me to join the community; and you answered that it would make no difference...'"[368] Her answer took the Bishop by surprise and he said nothing for a moment. The Superior General broke the awkward silence suggesting that, out of charity, Sister Marie-Bernard might remain at the motherhouse to clean up the infirmary and make teas for the patients. "'Since she's nearly always sick, it would suit her just fine,' Mother Joséphine continued. 'She's only good for blowing embers into flame.'"[369] The Bishop agreed, and Sister Marie-Bernard promised to try. She then received her book, a crucifix, a rosary, and a blessing from the Bishop who announced, "I assign you to the post of praying."[370]

Most would have been humiliated by the indignation with which Bernadette was approached on what many might consider the most important day of her life. Bishop Forcade, however, held Bernadette with no contempt, but rather used the humiliating banter to justify assigning Sister Marie-Bernard to the motherhouse, a highly-sought after assignment never given to a newly professed sister. It was a way to protect Bernadette from the prying public without causing a sensation within the convent. No doubt the unsuspecting Bernadette was deeply hurt by the treatment. Still, she never betrayed her feelings, instead remaining humble and offering all her sacrifice to Jesus, who himself was mocked and ridiculed to his last breath.

Sister Marie-Bernard began her work in the infirmary as the assistant infirmarian that very day. Hers were all the menial chores – everything from filling flower vases to cleaning toilets. She would deliver medications with a kind word and remind those in the infirmary to be silent during quiet time. She soon earned a reputation for dexterity, firm-ness, and precision, often saying to others, "See God in your superiors" and "When you obey, you can't go wrong."[371]

Thursday, October 31, 1867
to Tuesday, October 30, 1873

On April 6, 1869, the assistant infirmarian joined the ranks of the infirmed, having suffered a severe asthma attack that kept her bed-ridden through Easter. Bernadette coughed up blood by the half-basinful. Sister Cecile Pages, for three weeks, tended to Bernadette and applied blistering agents. Despite her pain, Bernadette joked with her caretakers who, after consultation with the doctors, thought she might die that very night by coughing up blood. Once again, after battling all the way to the threshold of death's door, Bernadette recovered, and from May 15, 1870 to the beginning of 1872 remained in relatively good health.

Sister Marie-Bernard worked diligently in the service of God, never questioning authority, always displaying profound humility, and forever accepting of the duties assigned. She worked for and with Sister Marthe, who, as the official infirmarian, was responsible for taking com-plex pharmaceutical measurements. Marie-Bernard worked closely with Marthe and was naturally tapped to fill in for her when Marthe took sick and was sent home to rest on April 12, 1870. Marthe returned to the motherhouse on June 9 but was still too ill to return to work. Her condi-tion only worsened and on November 8, 1872, she died, leaving Berna-dette to officially perform her duties. Despite the precise and complex nature of the position, Sister Marie-Bernard held the post until October 30, 1873. It was not only the medication she prepared and administered that made her so successful in the work she performed, but the generous spirit with which she performed it, often times offering advice covering both the medical and spiritual realms. Yet, her maternal demeanor did not adversely impact her ability as a strict disciplinarian when the situa-tion required, such as the day when Sister Julienne Capmartin, one of the infirmed, disobeyed the order of strict bedrest. After being told several times to keep well covered in bed in order to perspire, Sister Marie-Bernard found Sister Julienne reading from her Children of Mary manual. Marie-Bernard snatched the book away from her saying, "Now, here's a bit of zeal sewn up with disobedience...."[372] Despite all her efforts to retrieve it, Sister Julienne never saw her book again.

Though Bernadette loved being of service to God through her service of others, she unquestionably still despised the visits that interrupted the performance of those duties. And, if she thought that she might escape the insanity of multitudes who sought those visits simply by living and working in the motherhouse, she was sadly mistaken. The visits continued in relentless pursuit of all things Bernadette. They were from the high-ranking and the well-connected. They included those who wanted to hear the story of the Apparitions from Bernadette's own lips; to those who wanted to pray with her; to those who sought cures for themselves or for their loved ones; and to those who sought to record, for historical purposes, every minute detail of what she had witnessed at the Grotto and at Lourdes.

In fact, she became an unwitting pawn in a dispute between several local historians, each writing varying accounts of the Apparitions, and each seeking to make their version the official account of the Catholic Church. The dispute reached all the way to the Vatican and ensnared a reaction from the Pope who, also unwittingly, took sides in the dispute. The effort of each one to twist the words of Bernadette for his own purposes reduced the visionary to tears on more than one occasion. The ordeal also aided in the diminution of her already fragile health.

The Franco-Prussian War

International events were also impacting life at the motherhouse at Nevers and, indeed, throughout the whole of France. Prussian ambitions that sought to extend German unification created in the French an intense fear that the European balance of power might shift. Consequently, on July 16, 1870, the French Parliament voted to declare war on

Prussia. Just three days later, the French army prepared to invade German territory. The German forces, who were able to mobilize much faster than their French counterparts, invaded northern France, and the war was on.

Mother General, who had returned from Rome on July 7, 1870, wasted no time putting the sisters at the disposition of the Ministry of War. A field hospital was established at Saint-Gildard and military personnel were brought into the motherhouse. The efforts, however, were in vain.

While the war wouldn't officially end for another five months, the outcome was, for all intents and purposes, decided in the Battle of Sedan on September 1, 1870, just forty-five days after it started. On that day, over 17,000 Frenchmen were killed or wounded and 21,000 were captured. Before nightfall, Napoleon III called off the attacks and within twenty-four hours he surrendered and was taken prisoner, along with 104,000 of his soldiers. The battle resulted in a total Prussian victory as Prussia captured not only the entire French army but their leader as well.

The result was equally disastrous for the motherhouse. "On September 6, twenty-five novices were sent to communities in the south [and] the postulants were sent home to their families. The Prussians were coming. About a hundred militiamen came to replace the sick and wounded in the convent."[373] Cannons were installed on the inner terrace of the motherhouse and in the gardens of the novitiate.

Chaos reigned in the motherhouse, in the novitiate, and throughout all of France. If the people were ever in need of a sign it was at that moment. Perhaps that sign came on the evening of October 24, 1870. As Mother Eleonore Cassagnes, the secretary general of the congregation peered out her window, she noticed the horizon ablaze with a strange light that made it appear as though the sky was a sea of blood. The strange phenomenon lasted from seven to nine o'clock and was seen by many. Without a scientific explanation for the strange lightshow on display that night, Sister Marie-Bernard murmured, "And still, they will not be converted."[374]

By December 9, 1870, the Prussians were indeed at the borders of the department and Bernadette was interrogated yet again, this time by the Chevalier Gougenot des Mousseaux. His concern was whether

Bernadette had received any revelations from the Blessed Virgin regarding the fate of France. Bernadette had nothing to offer him and told him so. Asked if there should be anything to fear, Bernadette replied, "I only fear bad Catholics."[375]

It was also about that time that the miraculous power of the Blessed Virgin was on full display once again. A fire in the pharmacy of the motherhouse severely burned a novice. Without any tranquilizing medication, the novice screamed in agony for 24 hours straight. Sister Marie Bernard suggested giving her water from Lourdes and praying to the Blessed Mother. They did so, and "just a few minutes later, the poor sister's pains subsided, and she stopped screaming."[376]

Death Haunts Bernadette

Bernadette's challenges continued into 1871 when the death of those she loved the most seemed to follow in rapid succession. Her sister Toinette's daughter Bernadette died on February 12, followed quickly by the passing of her beloved aunt Lucile on March 16. The deepest cut of all, however, came between those two deaths with the passing of her father. François, whom Bernadette loved more than any other, died suddenly on the evening of March 4, 1871 after vomiting blood. Finally, on August 23, another of Toinette's children died, this time it was her son Bernard.

Though grief-stricken, Bernadette remained upbeat, relishing the many visitors she had from Lourdes, sharing memories, stories, and photographs of the Grotto and other events taking place in the town. These visits brought her joy despite the hardship of loss and the pain of illness.

The relative stretch of good health enjoyed by Bernadette for the past several months ended in January 1872. That is when she suffered another typical winter setback. A year later, in mid-January 1873, she suffered a much more severe attack that lasted almost four months. She recovered only briefly before being stricken again on June 3, 1873 with a relapse that caused her to receive the Extreme Unction for at least the third time. She eventually recovered, causing her to remark to one of the other nuns, "They didn't want me up there," but her recovery was not complete, and she was officially relieved of her duties as the infirmarian on October 30, 1873.

Wednesday, October 31, 1873
to Wednesday, July 5, 1876

For a time, Sister Marie-Bernard resumed the function of the assistant infirmarian, but the diminution of responsibility bothered her. She longed for more work and was eventually given the added duty of assistant sacristan where she vested the altar boys. Despite being elated with the extra duties, her health continued to decline and by late 1874 she was no longer able to perform any regular duties. Her condition deteriorated further and from April to mid-June 1875, Bernadette was confined to her bed. Though she suffered greatly, she was never heard to complain. Sister Joséphine, the novitiate responsible for cleaning Bernadette's room, reported that she would find her smiling despite spending sleepless nights in pain. The summer brought about some relief, but Bernadette relapsed in October.

In November, she began coughing up so much blood that concern for her life was renewed and she was again confined to her bed until May 1876. She was able in June to attend Mass for the first time in six months, but that is not to imply that she had returned to health. Unable to tolerate much food, Bernadette had become very thin and weak. Regardless, in August, she resumed some very light work such as sweeping. During that time, she also wrote to her godchild, Bernadette Nicolau, noting in the letter that she suffered very little. Despite the admirable attitude with which Bernadette approached her work and her illness, she had become frail to the point of being unable to even write.

Bernadette was no longer an active participant in the events taking place in Lourdes. She hadn't been since the time that the Blessed Mother had instructed her to inform the priests that a church was to be built in the Grotto. Yet, the fruits of her efforts in convincing church leaders to do so had been slowly realized. Now, some eighteen years later, the inhabitants of the town of Lourdes and those from beyond its borders were enthusiastic in their observance of the consecration of the new basilica built just as the Lady had instructed. The day would also mark the coronation of the statue of Our Lady of Lourdes.

From July 1 through July 3, 1876, the town celebrated. Unable to attend, Bernadette received the pilgrims from Nevers and entrusted them to deliver to Lourdes letters that she had written: letters for her family, for Abbé Peyramale, and even one meant for the Virgin Mary herself.

The consecration and coronation ceremonies were attended by over three thousand priests and a crowd of pilgrims exceeding one hundred thousand. Abbé Perreau received permission from the Mother General to report to Bernadette all the news of the ceremonies and of the people of Lourdes, particularly of those in her family. Bernadette listened as he enthusiastically described the dedication and coronation and told her about the exuberant crowd. Then she asked Abbé Perreau if he would deliver her best wishes to Abbé Peyramale, the priest she once feared. "Tell him I think of him every day," she said, "that I pray for him and I ask for his blessing..."[377]

Saturday, December 15, 1877
to Wednesday, April 16, 1879

The winter of 1877-78, as with all winters, hastened the decline of Bernadette's health. In fact, the weakened health condition with which she began the winter was simply too much from which to recover. Despite a slight remission at the start of summer 1878, Bernadette remained confined to her bed almost exclusively, able to navigate to the first floor of the motherhouse only a few times for the purpose of attending prayer in the chapel. She suffered from exhaustion and excruciating pain caused by bone decay in her knee. By October of that year, however, Bernadette could not leave her room at all. She had one of the sisters pin holy pictures to the curtains of her room, which she now referred to as her white chapel.

On December 8, 1878, and continuing until December 12, Bernadette was subjected to her final live deposition, this one from Fr. Emmanuél de Montagnac, who was preaching a retreat at the Nevers hospital. Unbeknownst to Bernadette, the questions asked and answered during this interview were actually fodder for a new project commissioned by Bishop Jourdan of Tarbes and Lourdes to satisfy his sense that the historical documentation that existed to date was inadequate. To remedy that concern, Fr. Cros had actually been working for the past couple of years toward the compilation of a new historical record. He had interviewed over two hundred witnesses, receiving written accounts from many of them. He collected the plethora of diocesan papers thought to be lost, and he gathered official papers that had been collected by civil authorities in 1858. He essentially assembled every bit of evidence that existed relating to matters of Bernadette and her visions.

Cros had everything he needed except Bernadette's own version of the story. He tried to meet with her on August 24, 1878 but was rebuffed. Now, essentially unable to return to Nevers, the task of interviewing Bernadette fell to Father Sempe and others. They asked questions provided them by Fr. Cros and written on a piece of paper with two columns. The column to the left were his numbered questions while the column to the right was left blank, providing a space for the recording of Bernadette's answers. The questions asked were answered to the satisfaction of the interviewers, but not to the complete contentment of Cros. Three final attempts were made to follow up the deposition with written questions. Some of those queries were raised because of answers provided by Bernadette during the first interview. Others resulted from either sloppy note-taking or a failure of the interviewers to deliver the questions in a way that Bernadette could understand. The first follow-up was on January 12, the second on January 30, and the last on March 3 of 1879. Despite lingering questions, no other attempts to reach out to Bernadette proved fruitful as her failing health prevented her from responding further.

A tumor had produced rigidity in her knee, causing it to swell to the point that it caused excruciating pain. In addition, her leg below the knee atrophied from non-use. Her pain was unspeakable and movement impossible, even when attempted by others. Any movement of her leg at all, even while asleep, caused her to scream out in pain. Despite the agony caused by the swollen knee and withered leg, Bernadette remained gracious, letting nothing of her torment show.

Bernadette dictated letters to her family, trying to reassure them that she was doing better, but they were not fooled. On March 18, 1879, Bernadette's sister Toinette, and her husband Joseph Sabathe, arrived for a visit, only to find Bernadette very sick. Abbé Febvre, a frequent visitor over the past few months, prepared a list of Bernadette's ailments. It read "Chronic asthma, chest pains accompanied by the spitting-up of blood, that lasted for two years; an aneurysm, stomach pains, a tumor on the knee, which, during a sizable length of time, forced the servant of God to remain motionless...finally, over the last two years, decay of the bones to such an extent that her poor body was subjected to all kinds of pains. Meanwhile, abscesses formed in her ears and caused partial deafness which was very painful for her..."[378] It was later discovered that the tumor in her knee stemmed from tuberculosis.

At 2:00 in the afternoon of Friday, March 28, 1879, a chaplain arrived at Nevers. He gave Bernadette Holy Communion as Viaticum, then administered the sacrament of Extreme Unction. After the brief words of the chaplain, Bernadette said in a clear voice and in the presence of many Sisters, "My dear Mother, I ask your forgiveness for all the trouble I have caused you by my failures in religious life and I also ask forgiveness of my companions for the bad example I have given them...especially my pride." In amazement, the Sisters gathered around their dying friend. They knew firsthand just how humble Bernadette was, and they couldn't believe that she might possibly think that vanity was to be listed among her sins, let alone the prime sin.

It marked the fourth time that Bernadette received Extreme Unction (the Anointing of the Sick) and still she would linger in agony for several additional days. Holy Week ended on Easter Sunday April 13, 1879 just as it had arrived on April 6, with Sister Marie-Bernard writhing with excruciating pain. The nun could sense that she was in her final days. She asked for the removal of all the holy pictures she had pinned to her curtains. Pointing to the crucifix that hung on her wall she said, "This is enough for me."[379]

Tuesday, April 15, 1879
to Wednesday, April 16, 1879
Bernadette's Final Hours

The pain Bernadette felt during Holy Week piqued over the early days of the ensuing week. Following evening prayers at around 9:00 on the night of April 15, Sister Alphonse Guerre, a novice, visited Bernadette's room. Noticing that her patient appeared worn and weak, she decided to stay by her beside for the night. So weakened was her condition that, despite the intense pain, Bernadette could manage only an occasional, mostly inaudible moan. Her body was riddled with bed sores and several times Bernadette asked Sister Guerre if she could turn her over in hope of finding a more comfortable position in which to lay. Several sisters assisted with this task so as to cause the least amount of trauma to her body, but that challenge proved too great a task.

And so it went throughout the night and into the following morning. By 11:30 AM on Tuesday April 16, 1879, Bernadette sought to leave her bed for the presupposed comfort of the cushioned armchair. She hoped to take some of the pressure off the raw flesh that constituted her many bed sores. The Sisters obliged and carefully moved her into the chair, completing the task just in time for the ringing of the bells signaling the start of lunch. As many of the Sisters retreated to the lunchroom, Bernadette also tried to take a bit of food but met with no success. Her breathing was more labored and the intensity of the pain was increased. Abbé Febvre was called to hear her confession and the others recited the prayers of the dying.

Between 1:30 PM and 2:00 PM

Throughout the ordeal, Bernadette fixed her gaze on the crucifix which hung on the wall of her room and firmly clutched her own crucifix, squeezing it tightly and holding it to her heart. "She longed to have it remain there forever, and [the Sisters] even fastened it on with a cord, for fear it would be dislodged by involuntary movements brought on by the pain."[380] Somewhere between 1:30 and 2:00 PM, Mother Eleanor Cassagnes turned to Bernadette saying, "you are...on the cross." Bernadette collected all her strength and stretched out both arms toward the crucifix mounted on the wall. "My Jesus," she said, "Oh, how I love him!"[381]

2:00 PM

At 2:00 PM, one of Bernadette's companions entered the room. Looking at the pathetic form of their friend's curled body, only one dared speak, but that one asked the question they were all thinking. "'Do you suffer a lot?' 'This is all good for heaven,'"[382] Bernadette responded. The companion offered to ask the Immaculate Mother to provide some comfort, but Bernadette protested, "No, not comfort, but strength and patience."[383] Shortly thereafter, she adjusted herself as if trying to sit up. With her eyes raised up and fixed on a single point, and her entire body trembling, she cried out, "'Oh! Oh! Oh!' It didn't appear to be a cry of pain, but rather one of surprise. Those present thought that she had had another vision, but before they could speak, Bernadette raised her trembling hand and placed it gently on her heart. Releasing her eyes from the gaze she said, 'My God, I love you with all my heart, all my soul, all my strength.'"[384]

3:00 PM

Suddenly the bell rang out, signaling the impending start of litanies. Some left the room, retreating to chapel to join the community in prayer as Bernadette expressed a desire to rest. Shortly after three o'clock, however, Sister Nathalie arrived and observed Bernadette completely absorbed in contemplation, clutching her crucifix. At once, Bernadette extended her arms toward the nun and with an expression foreign to Nathalie, said, "'My dear Sister, forgive me...Pray for me...Pray for me.' Sister Nathalie and two infirmarians fell to their knees to pray. The patient joined in their invocations, which she repeated in a barely audible whisper."[385] Bernadette looked toward the Sister on her left and then, with an expression that could be interpreted only as intense pain and total surrender, she looked toward heaven, "stretched her arms out in the form of a cross and cried out loudly: 'My God.'"[386] The sisters reacted with a shiver and they continued to pray. The dying child of God joined them with the words, "Holy Mary, Mother of God, pray for me, a poor sinner."[387]

Speaking was becoming near impossible for Bernadette now. She held out her arms toward Sister Nathalie and looked directly into her eyes, her own eyes pleading for help. Sister Nathalie remembered her vow to Bernadette from the night prior, promising to help Bernadette thank the Virgin to the very end. She offered the Blessed Mother words of thanks as Bernadette repeated them softly in her mind. As she did, Bernadette gestured for something to drink and, making a large sign of the cross, took the vial of medicine that they handed her and swallowed a few drops. Bernadette, still clutching her crucifix to her heart, exhaled her final breath as the Mother of God came to deliver Bernadette's soul to Jesus.

The visionary child arrived in heaven, leaving behind a body that just moments before was wracked with pain. It now looked peaceful and rested. The other nuns even described her as beautiful. Sister Marie-Bernard had been tormented in her final years with spiritual terrors which for her were more painful than her inability to draw breath. She had described them as far more terrifying than the physical pain she endured.

As a humble child of innocence, Bernadette had spoken "of the apparitions only to say that she 'had been unworthy' and that 'through her lack of gratitude' she deserved to be condemned.... God put an end to this anguish only at the moment when He was preparing to crown His beloved daughter."[388]

During the next days, Bernadette's body lay in state in a white-draped coffin at the convent of Saint-Gildard in Nevers. She was later buried at that same location. In 1890, the liturgical feast of Our Lady of Lourdes was established by Pope Leo XIII for celebration in the Diocese of Tarbes on February 11. On November 13, 1907, Pope Pius X proclaimed that the feast day would be observed throughout the universal church.

Destined for sainthood, Sister Marie-Bernard was beatified on Sunday, June 14, 1925. Her body was exhumed and though entombed for over 45 years, was found to be incorrupt. Eight years later, on December 8, 1933, the Feast of the Immaculate Conception, Pope Pius XI declared the suffering servant of Mary a saint. To this day, one hundred and forty years after her death, the incorrupt body of Saint Bernadette rests for all to see in a glass encasement in the reliquary at Saint-Gildard's convent. Remarkably, Saint Bernadette looks exactly as she did at the time of her death.

The body of Saint Bernadette now lies in a glass enclosure at the Chapel of Saint Gildard Convent in Nevers, France. She was canonized a saint by Pope Pius XI on December 8, 1933, the feast of the Immaculate Conception. Though initially specified as February 18th, the day Our Lady promised to make her happy, not in this life, but in the next, the Feast of Saint Bernadette is celebrated in some places on April 16th, the anniversary of her death.

Part VI

Miracles and Cures

Since February 1858, pilgrims from every corner of the earth have traveled to France to visit the small town of Lourdes. Of those who make the pilgrimage, millions from all over the world have experienced a spiritual healing, while hundreds of thousands have been cured of physical ailments, all owing to the waters flowing from the miraculous spring of Lourdes. Some visit Lourdes for the expressed purpose of seeking a cure. Others simply want to pay homage to God and thank his Blessed Mother for always pointing us in the direction of Her Son and for giving us additional signs of his glory. Regardless of the reason for the daily processions, the conversions and other miracles attributable to Lourdes that began in 1858 continue to this very day.

One such celebrated case is that of Gabriel Gargam, a Catholic born in 1870. While in his mid-twenties, Gargam took a job as a traveling mail sorter for the Orleans Railway Company. In December of 1899, while sorting mail on a trip from Bordeaux to Paris, the train on which he was working collided with another. Each train was traveling at a high speed and the damage was extensive to both property and life. Gargam was thrown over fifty feet from the train and lay in the snow unconscious for over seven hours before being discovered. He was very close to death and later found to be paralyzed from the waist down.

In the first eight months following the horrific accident, Gargam, once a burly man, had wasted away to a mere seventy-eight pounds. He was unable to digest solid food and could eat only with the aid of a tube, a medical procedure that could be done only once each day. His condition required the assistance of two trained nurses that needed to be with him day and night.

This was Gabriel Gargam's new life and his doctors said he would remain in that condition until his death. He filed a lawsuit against the railroad and was awarded 6,000 francs each year plus an indemnity of 60,000 francs by the Appellate Court which upheld the lower court rulings. As a result of the judicial proceedings, his medical condition as documented by many doctors who testified at the trial, and the facts of the accident, are fully detailed and are all a matter of court record.

Gargam had lost his faith at the age of fifteen and by the time of his accident, he had not been to church in fifteen years. "His aunt, who was a Catholic nun of the Order of the Sacred Heart, begged him to go to Lourdes,"[389] but he refused. It was only the relentless pleading of his mother that convinced him to go, albeit grudgingly, some two years after the accident. During those years he had never been able to leave his bed, making the transport a very difficult one. Despite the use of a stretcher, the exertion caused him to faint and remain unconscious for a full hour. Attendants feared he would die on the journey and asked him to abandon the pilgrimage, but his mother insisted they continue.

Once at Lourdes, Gargam confessed and received Holy Communion. Then he was carried to the spring where he was gently placed in its waters, but rather than experiencing a cure, his condition worsened, and it appeared to all that he had died. After a time, seeing that he was neither breathing nor moving, they began to wheel his carriage back to the hotel and sorrowfully discussed his death.

It was at that moment that a priest passed by the carriage. He carried a Sacred Host and "pronounced Benediction over the sorrowful group around the covered body."[390] Suddenly, the blanket covering Gargam's body started to move and then he sat up. Bystanders were astonished, and his family flabbergasted, as his body lifted to a sitting posture. Then "Gargam said in a full, strong voice that he wanted to get up."[391] Thinking him delirious before death, his family tried to comfort him, but they could not restrain him. He stood, walked a few paces, and pronounced himself cured. The many observers that stood witness to the strange event fell to their knees to thank God and His Blessed Mother for yet another display of God's power at the shrine at Lourdes.

Gargam had on only the garments of an invalid and therefore had to be carried to the hotel in the carriage in which he had arrived. There he dressed and walked about as if he had never been injured. Then he sat at the table and ate his first meal in two years.

On August 20, 1901, no less than sixty doctors, many of whom were prominent in their profession, examined the former invalid and "without stating the nature of the cure, they pronounced him entirely cured. Gargam, out of gratitude to God in the Holy Eucharist and His Blessed Mother, consecrated himself to the service of invalids at

Lourdes."[392] For over fifty years, Gargam and the woman he married following his cure, returned to Lourdes each year and worked as a *brancardier,* one who helped the sick at Lourdes. He continued the practice until just seven months prior to his death in March 1953 at the age of eighty-three.

John Traynor was a soldier from Liverpool, England, who, at the age of thirty-five, enlisted as a soldier in the Naval Brigade of the Royal British Marines in 1914. His is "One of the most amazing and most inexplicable"[393] stories arising out of World War I.

In October 1914, while participating in the unsuccessful Antwerp expedition, he was hit in the head with shrapnel from an attack and remained unconscious for five weeks. Once recovered sufficiently to return to battle, he was assigned to Egypt, where he was shot in the leg. He again recovered and was in action during the disastrous Anglo-French assault on the Dardenelles where allied forces hoped to reach Constantinople (present-day Turkey) and interrupt the Turkish alliance with Germany. The troops, however, were massacred by Turkish machine gunners as they disembarked from the steamship *River Clyde.* Traynor successfully reached shore, but "was sprayed with bullets and was wounded in the chest and head"[394] during a bayonet charge on May 8. A bullet also penetrated his right arm, lodging just under his collar bone.

Traynor had a laundry list of injuries. His right arm was paralyzed, and the muscle atrophied. He was paralyzed from the waist down and suffered epileptic seizures, as many as three times a day. Over the next six years he underwent four surgeries on his arm, but none was successful. To reduce the impact of the epileptic seizures, doctors operated on his brain. Not only was the surgery unsuccessful, but the resulting one-inch hole in his skull required a silver plate to protect the brain, which could be seen pulsating through his skin.

After spending months in the hospital, Traynor was provided discharge from the army with a total disability for which he was awarded a full pension. His new life required that he be lifted from his bed to his wheelchair each morning and from his wheelchair to his bed each evening. The total care required between those two events was too much for his wife and children to provide, and arrangements were made for admittance to the Mosley Hill Hospital for Incurables.

Traynor learned in July 1923 that his diocese was organizing a pilgrimage to the shrine at Lourdes. A devout Catholic, he enjoyed a special devotion to the Blessed Virgin Mary and decided to sign up for the pilgrimage. He cashed in a gold sovereign that he was saving for an emergency to put a down payment on the ticket. The doctors joined his wife in objecting to the trip, saying that it might kill him. Even the government ministry of pensions objected, but Traynor would not be deterred. He and his wife sold furniture and jewelry to finance the balance of the excursion.

News of his trip made him somewhat of a local legend. Newspapers carried the story and there were many people there to greet him at the train station. During the train ride, Traynor became so ill that three times the priests accompanying the pilgrimage tried to have him taken off the train and sent to a hospital, but there were no hospitals near any of the three scheduled stops. By the time he reached Lourdes on July 22, his companions noted that he was "more dead than alive."[395] He was immediately taken to Asile, where two Protestant girls from Liverpool who heard about his trip volunteered to serve as his nurses.

During his first six days he had several hemorrhages and a number of epileptic seizures. His health was so bad that one woman wrote to his wife saying that "there was no hope for him and that he would be buried in Lourdes."[396]

Despite his condition, Traynor bathed in the water from the Grotto on nine different occasions. On the afternoon of July 25, while in the water, his legs suddenly became agitated. He tried to stand, but his aides prevented him from doing so. They instead dressed him and wheeled him to Rosary Square for the Blessing of the Sick. As the Bishop of Rheims made the sign of the cross over him with the Monstrance, Traynor's arm was fiercely restless. He burst the bandages and blessed himself for the first time in eight years, using his dead arm. There was no pain, no vision, according to Traynor, simply a realization that "something momentous had happened."[397]

He tried to stand, but thinking he was having an epileptic seizure, the caretakers gave him a shot to quiet him and took him back to the Asile. They gave him several shots each time he tried to stand until he quieted for the night. In the morning, he got out of bed, quietly dressed, knelt to say the Rosary, then ran outside past the *brancardiers* and toward the Grotto. Despite not having walked since 1915, and weighing only 112 pounds, he easily out-ran the pursuing *brancardiers*. When they reached him, he was on his knees, praying to the Blessed Mother at the Grotto.

Traynor "did not completely realize what had happened to him. He knew that a great favor had been bestowed upon him and that he should be thankful, but he had no idea of the magnitude of the favor. He was completely dazed. It did not seem strange to him that he was walking, and he could not figure out why everyone was staring at him. He did not remember how gravely ill he had been for many years."[398]

That changed during the return train ride home. Archbishop Keating of Liverpool came to his compartment and said, "John, do you realize how ill you have been and that you have been miraculously cured by the Blessed Virgin."[399] It was at that moment that the full memory of his injuries was restored, and he began to cry. Archbishop Keating also shed tears and the two wept for a very long time.

Traynor did not tell his wife of the cure until she met him on the platform of the train station where she could see with her own eyes the power of God. Hundreds of others were also on hand for his return. Though they had read in the Liverpool papers of the miracle that had taken place at Lourdes, they kept the news from John's wife so as not to spoil the surprise.

The miracle associated with John Traynor did not stop at his cure, however. The two Protestant girls who had agreed to serve as Traynor's nurses during his stay at Lourdes converted to Catholicism, as did their families and the Anglican minister from their church.

In 1926, three years after his cure, the Medical Bureau issued its report. "Traynor was examined again, and it was found that his cure was permanent. 'His right arm which was like a skeleton,' the report read, 'has recovered all its muscles. The hole near his temple has completely disappeared. He had a certificate from Dr. McConnell of Liverpool attesting that he had not had an epileptic attack since 1923. It is known that when the important nerves have been severed, if their regeneration has not been effected (after the most successful operations this would take at least a year) they contract rapidly and become dried up as it were, and certain parts mortify and disappear. In Mr. Traynor's case, for the cure of his paralyzed arm, new parts had to be created and seamed together. All these things were done simultaneously and instantaneously. At the same time occurred the instant repair of the brain injuries as is proved by the sudden and definite disappearance of the paralysis of both legs and of the epileptic attacks. Finally, a third work was effected which closed the orifice in the brain box. It is a real resurrection which the beneficiary attributes to the power of God and the merciful intercession of Our Lady of Lourdes. The mode of production of this prodigious cure is absolutely outside and beyond the forces of nature.'"[400]

John Traynor returned to Lourdes each year to assist the sick as a *brancardier*. He did so until his death, which occurred on the Feast of the Immaculate Conception twenty years later on December 8, 1943.

The Lessons from Lourdes

The events that took place in the Grotto of Massabielle outside of the little town of Lourdes, France, were nothing short of extraordinary. Our Lady appeared to Bernadette eighteen times, not only changing the life of a young peasant girl, but impacting the entire world, particularly those willing to accept what could not be seen. There is no need to offer further proof of the Apparitions. There will always be deniers who, despite being exposed to events that cannot be explained by all of our known science and medicine, will still refuse to believe in the miraculous. To everyone else, no further evidence or explanation is required to understand that something miraculous took place in that Grotto of Massabielle some 161 years ago, and that the miracles of Lourdes continue unabated to this very day.

Yet, even the faithful look to the events as more than just the production of a miraculous spring responsible for so many cures. Lessons emanate from the Apparitions at Massabielle and those lessons continue to have a dramatic impact on the lives of millions of people throughout the world. Gabriel, the author and producer of True Faith TV, in his video entitled "Lessons from Lourdes: Our Lady of Lourdes and St. Bernadette," discusses five lessons that can be gleaned from the appearances of Our Virgin Mother at Lourdes. The spiritual significance of these lessons has been repeated many times by Our Lady in various apparitions.

God's Divine Providence

The very fact that Bernadette was at the Grotto of Massabielle on February 11, 1858 was in and of itself miraculous. It was certainly God's Providence that brought her together with the Blessed Lady that day and the events leading up to the meeting are a testament to the absolute Providence of God. A re-examination of the facts bears this out.

Bernadette was raised in abject poverty. Her family lived in a single room that had been declared unfit to house prisoners. It was the impoverished condition that provided the need to scavenge for branches to stoke the fire for warmth and for bones for the soup. It was Bernadette's mother Louise who was going to go out scavenging that day, but Providence intervened through the innocence of a child who asked Louise if she, Bernadette, and Toinette could go scavenging instead.

Despite Bernadette's poor health and the extreme cold and dampness of the overcast and foggy day, Louise consented, against all odds, to allow Bernadette to accompany Jeanne and Toinette. A woman, encountered through a chance meeting as she hung laundry on her clothesline, directed the girls to the Grotto where, she told them, they would find twigs and bones.

They did indeed find a treasure trove of wood, but it lay on the opposite shore of a flowing river of ice-cold water. The River Gave, because of repair work being done to a mill dam, just happened to be shallow enough to allow the girls safe passage across on foot. Bernadette, however, was unable to enter the ice-cold water because of her frail health. Unable to cross with the others, Bernadette was left alone long enough to share the recitation of a Rosary with the mysterious Lady of the Grotto.

After that meeting, and others like it, Bernadette delivered a message to the priest, a message from the Mother of God insisting that a church be built on the site of the Apparitions. Unlikely though it may be, the priests obliged, and that Grotto is today the most popular and visited pilgrimage in the Catholic Church. It is a place of spiritual conversion and physical healing and Our Lady knew from the beginning that it would be, referencing the processions of today in her message to Bernadette in 1858.

Some might chalk these events up to fate or coincidence. Others, however, can see the powerful and absolute Providence of God at work in bringing Bernadette together with Jesus' Blessed Mother. So too, can we find God's Divine Providence in our lives by embracing our own suffering and poverty for the greater good.

The Importance of the Rosary

Bernadette did not know many prayers. She didn't even know her Catechism. She was, however, "pious, virtuous and obtained a high degree of holiness, and she was faithful to the rosary."[401] She carried her beads everywhere. When she first encountered the vision of the Lady, Bernadette was understandably frightened. She was young, alone, and seeing a woman, glowing brilliantly, and standing in the hollow of a rock wall some fourteen feet off the ground. Yet, she did not run. Rather, she took the rosary from her pocket, knelt on a rock, and began to pray. Our Lady also carried her rosary, draped on her right arm. She too joined in a silent rosary, moving Her lips and keeping count on Her own beads. Throughout Her eighteen appearances, Our Lady didn't always speak, but She always had the rosary draped over Her right arm.

The message is clear to those who want to receive it. The rosary is powerful, and we should always carry it with us and recite it. Our Lady hears those prayers even if we can't hear Her say it with us. The crowds gathered in the Grotto in the winter of 1858 couldn't hear Her either, but they prayed the Rosary with assurance that Our Lady was listening and had heard them.

The Diabolical

During the fourth appearance of Our Lady to Bernadette, the child was distracted by a crash and voices arguing. One voice, louder than the rest, several times yelled, "Save yourself." Bernadette knew not who they were but sensed that they were diabolical. Without a word, Our Lady simply looked in their direction and they were driven off. So great is the power of Mary "that a single glance can drive off a legion of angry devils."[402]

During the course of the Apparitions, Mary revealed to Bernadette three secrets that concerned only her. Our Lady also taught Bernadette a prayer, word for word, and asked that it be recited every day. Neither the prayer nor the secrets were ever revealed by Bernadette, but the lesson has not been lost. Prayer is powerful whether recited by everyone or by a single person. That prayer is always heard, and its power should not be underestimated. If we live in a state of grace and pray the Rosary daily, even if we pray it alone, the devil cannot harm us.

We Must Do Penance, Make Reparation for Sins, and Pray for the Conversion of Sinners

Several times, "Our Lady encouraged Bernadette to do penance, to pray for sinners and to sacrifice for their conversion."[403] Though no one could hear the private conversation being spoken between Bernadette and the Blessed Mother, the crowd of people in attendance could see tears roll down the cheeks of the child as she "gasped, 'Penance, Penance, Penance.'"[404] Many times Our Lady instructed Bernadette to walk on her knees, to kiss the ground and to eat bitter plants. Always Bernadette complied and said she did it for sinners and for their salvation. Even after her Apparitions ended, Bernadette remained mindful of the need to pray and to sacrifice for sinners, selecting to join a religious order based on their practice of prayer, penance, and mortification.

Praying for sinners and their salvation is important because the human race is at risk of losing its salvation. Hell is a real place, it is not simply a concept that we can define as we wish. It is real, and the main goal of the Church is for the salvation of souls. The salvation of souls is the reason that Jesus was born as man, and it is the very reason that he died.

Our prayers, penance, and sacrifice work toward the salvation of souls and that is the very reason Mary has asked us to say, do, and make them. "That should give us confidence that souls will be converted and saved through these things."[405] Mary's primary goal is to keep us close to Her Son, and prayer, penance, and sacrifice will accomplish this.

Suffering

We will never know the three secrets imparted to Bernadette by Our Lady, "but some speculate that they had to do with Bernadette's own suffering and death at the young age of thirty-five."[406] For her entire life Bernadette suffered physical pain, excruciating pain that brought her to the brink of death many times. At the convent, however, she also "suffered a terrible mystical anguish, a desolation, a darkness in her soul where she felt completely abandoned by God. She felt completely alone [and] sadness overtook her heart."[407]

Despite the pain, Bernadette prayed to suffer well. She didn't look toward a cure or remediation of her suffering, she knew that wasn't God's plan for her. She was told by Our Lady that she would not have happiness in this life, but in the next. Like Bernadette, we are all going to experience pain. We will all suffer and eventually we will all die. This, after all, is the valley of tears. We, however, are called to embrace our cross, to accept our suffering and to offer it for the conversion of sinners and for the salvation of souls.

Mary's promise to Bernadette is the same promise that she gives each of us. If we pray the Rosary daily, if we offer our lives to Jesus through Mary, we too will have happiness in the next life. And isn't that exactly what we all live for?

End Notes

[1] Lasserre, Henri, Our Lady of Lourdes, (Translated from the French) D. & J. Sadler, 1870. Page 191.

[2] Ibid.

[3] Ibid. Page 193.

[4] Ibid. Page 194.

[5] Ibid.

[6] Ibid.

[7] Ibid. Page 196.

[8] Ibid.

[9] Ibid. Pages 196-197.

[10] Ibid. Page 198.

[11] Deery, Joseph Monsignor, Our Lady of Lourdes, The Newman Press, 1958. Page 3.

[12] Ibid

[13] Deery, Joseph Monsignor, Our Lady of Lourdes, The Newman Press, 1958. Page 5

[14] Lasserre, Henri, Our Lady of Lourdes, (Translated from the French) D. & J. Sadler, 1870. Pages 16 – 17.

[15] Ibid. Pages 18-19.

[16] Harris, Ruth, Lourdes: Body and Spirit in the Secular Age, Penguin Books, 1999.

[17] Laurentin, Rene', Bernadette: A Life of Saint Bernadette Soubirous in Her Own Words, English Edition Copyright, 2000, Daughters of St. Paul. Page 3.

[18] Deery, Joseph Monsignor, Our Lady of Lourdes, The Newman Press, 1958. Page 11

[19] Sandhurst, B.G., We Saw Her, Longman's Green and Co.1953. Page 7.

[20] Deery, Joseph Monsignor, Our Lady of Lourdes, The Newman Press, 1958. Page 12

[21] Deery, Joseph Monsignor, Our Lady of Lourdes, The Newman Press, 1958. Page 12

[22] Harris, Ruth, Lourdes: Body and Spirit in the Secular Age, Penguin Books, 1999.

[23] Laurentin, Rene', Bernadette: A Life of Saint Bernadette Soubirous in Her Own Words, English Edition Copyright, 2000, Daughters of St. Paul. Page 7.

[24] Ibid.

[25] Ibid.

[26] Ibid. Page 13.

[27] Deery, Joseph Monsignor, Our Lady of Lourdes, The Newman Press, 1958. Page 15

[28] [28] Laurentin, Rene', Bernadette: A Life of Saint Bernadette Soubirous in Her Own Words, English Edition Copyright, 2000, Daughters of St. Paul. Page 12.

[29] Ibid.

[30] Sandhurst, B.G., We Saw Her, Longman's Green and Co.1953. Page 14.

[31] Sandhurst, B.G., We Saw Her, Longman's Green and Co.1953. Page 7.

[32] Laurentin, Rene', Bernadette: A Life of Saint Bernadette Soubirous in Her Own Words, English Edition Copyright, 2000, Daughters of St. Paul. Page 7.

[33] Ibid.

[34] Ibid. Page 9.

[35] Ibid. Page 15.

[36] Ibid. Page 16

[37] Lasserre, Henri, Our Lady of Lourdes, (Translated from the French) D. & J. Sadler, 1870. Page 22.

[38] Deery, Joseph Monsignor, Our Lady of Lourdes, The Newman Press, 1958. Page 17.

[39] Lasserre, Henri, Our Lady of Lourdes, (Translated from the French) D. & J. Sadler, 1870. Page 34.

[40] Deery, Joseph Monsignor, Our Lady of Lourdes, The Newman Press, 1958. Page 28

[41] Ibid. Page 18.

[42] Ibid.

[43] Ibid.

[44] Husenbeth, F. C., Our Blessed Lady of Lourdes: A Faithful Narrative of the Apparitions of the Blessed Virgin Mary at the Rocks of Massabielle, Near Lourdes, in the Year 1858., Robert Washbourne, London, 1870. Page 3.

[45] Sandhurst, B. G., We Saw Her, Longmans, Green and Co. 1953. Page 54.

[46] Laurentin, Rene', Bernadette: A Life of Saint Bernadette Soubirous in Her Own Words, English Edition Copyright, 2000, Daughters of St. Paul. Page 23.

[47] Deery, Joseph Monsignor, Our Lady of Lourdes, The Newman Press, 1958. Page 21.

[48] Laurentin, Rene', Bernadette: A Life of Saint Bernadette Soubirous in Her Own Words, English Edition Copyright, 2000, Daughters of St. Paul. Page 25.

[49] Ibid.

[50] Ibid.

[51] Ibid.

[52] Ibid.

[53] Sandhurst, B. G., We Saw Her, Longmans, Green and Co. 1953. Page 58.

[54] Ibid. Page 59.

[55] Ibid. Page 60.

[56] Laurentin, Rene', Bernadette: Bernadette Speaks: A Life of Saint Bernadette Soubirous in Her Own Words, English Edition Copyright, 2000, Daughters of St. Paul. Page 27.

[57] Husenbeth, F. C., Our Blessed Lady of Lourdes: A Faithful Narrative of the Apparitions of the Blessed Virgin Mary at the Rocks of Massabielle, Near Lourdes, in the Year 1858., Robert Washbourne, London, 1870. Page 10.

[58] Deery, Joseph Monsignor, Our Lady of Lourdes, The Newman Press, 1958. Page 22.

[59] Sandhurst, B. G., We Saw Her, Longmans, Green and Co. 1953. Page 61.

[60] Ibid. Pages 61 and 62.

[61] De Saint-Pierre, Michael, Bernadette and Lourdes, (Translated from the French by Edward Fitzgerald) Farrar, Straus and Young, 1954. Page 29.

[62] Ibid.

[63] Ibid.

[64] Lasserre, Henri, Our Lady of Lourdes, (Translated from the French) D. & J. Sadler, 1870. Page 50.

[65] Laurentin, Rene', Bernadette Speaks: A Life of Saint Bernadette Soubirous in Her Own Words, English Edition Copyright, 2000, Daughters of St. Paul. Page 30.

[66] Ibid.

[67] Ibid.

[68] Ibid.

[69] Ibid. Page 31

[70] De Saint-Pierre, Michael, Bernadette and Lourdes, (Translated from the French by Edward Fitzgerald) Farrar, Straus and Young, 1954. Page 30.

[71] Laurentin, Rene', Bernadette Speaks: A Life of Saint Bernadette Soubirous in Her Own Words, English Edition Copyright, 2000, Daughters of St. Paul. Page 33.

[72] Husenbeth, F. C., Our Blessed Lady of Lourdes: A Faithful Narrative of the Apparitions of the Blessed Virgin Mary at the Rocks of Massabielle, Near Lourdes, in the Year 1858., Robert Washbourne, London, 1870. Page 13.

[73] Laurentin, Rene', Bernadette Speaks: A Life of Saint Bernadette Soubirous in Her Own Words, English Edition Copyright, 2000, Daughters of St. Paul. Page 33.

[74] Husenbeth, F. C., Our Blessed Lady of Lourdes: A Faithful Narrative of the Apparitions of the Blessed Virgin Mary at the Rocks of Massabielle, Near Lourdes, in the Year 1858., Robert Washbourne, London, 1870. Page 14.

[75] Deery, Joseph Monsignor, Our Lady of Lourdes, The Newman Press, 1958. Page 23.

[76] De Saint-Pierre, Michael, Bernadette and Lourdes, (Translated from the French by Edward Fitzgerald) Farrar, Straus and Young, 1954. Page 32.

[77] Ibid.

[78] Ibid.

[79] Husenbeth, F. C., Our Blessed Lady of Lourdes: A Faithful Narrative of the Apparitions of the Blessed Virgin Mary at the Rocks of Massabielle, Near Lourdes, in the Year 1858., Robert Washbourne, London, 1870. Page 15.

[80] Ibid. Page 16.

[81] Lasserre, Henri, Our Lady of Lourdes, (Translated from the French) D. & J. Sadler, 1870. Page 60.

[82] Husenbeth, F. C., Our Blessed Lady of Lourdes: A Faithful Narrative of the Apparitions of the Blessed Virgin Mary at the Rocks of Massabielle, Near Lourdes, in the Year 1858., Robert Washbourne, London, 1870. Page 17.

[83] De Saint-Pierre, Michael, Bernadette and Lourdes, (Translated from the French by Edward Fitzgerald) Farrar, Straus and Young, 1954. Page 34.

[84] Ibid.

[85] Husenbeth, F. C., Our Blessed Lady of Lourdes: A Faithful Narrative of the Apparitions of the Blessed Virgin Mary at the Rocks of Massabielle, Near Lourdes, in the Year 1858., Robert Washbourne, London, 1870. Page 19.

[86] De Saint-Pierre, Michael, Bernadette and Lourdes, (Translated from the French by Edward Fitzgerald) Farrar, Straus and Young, 1954. Pages 34 and 35.

[87] The New American Bible, The Book of Genesis, Chapter 3, Verse 15. Oxford University Press, Oxford, New York.

[88] The Catholic Gentleman Website - https://www.catholicgentle-man.net/2015/01/devil-hates-blessed-virgin-much-love/

[89] De Saint-Pierre, Michael, Bernadette and Lourdes, (Translated from the French by Edward Fitzgerald) Farrar, Straus and Young, 1954. Page 34.

[90] Ibid.

[91] Ibid. Page 37.

[92] Ibid.

[93] Ibid. Page 39.

[94] Ibid. Page 38.

[95] Ibid. Page 42.

[96] Ibid.

[97] Ibid.

[98] Laurentin, Rene', Bernadette: Bernadette Speaks: A Life of Saint Bernadette Soubirous in Her Own Words, English Edition Copyright, 2000, Daughters of St. Paul. Page 35 & 37.

[99] Husenbeth, F. C., Our Blessed Lady of Lourdes: A Faithful Narrative of the Apparitions of the Blessed Virgin Mary at the Rocks of Massabielle, Near Lourdes, in the Year 1858., Robert Washbourne, London, 1870. Page 21.

[100] De Saint-Pierre, Michael, Bernadette and Lourdes, (Translated from the French by Edward Fitzgerald) Farrar, Straus and Young, 1954. Page 46.

[101] Ibid. Page 44.

[102] Ibid. Pages 44-45.

[103] Husenbeth, F. C., Our Blessed Lady of Lourdes: A Faithful Narrative of the Apparitions of the Blessed Virgin Mary at the Rocks of Massabielle, Near Lourdes, in the Year 1858., Robert Washbourne, London, 1870. Page 22.

[104] De Saint-Pierre, Michael, Bernadette and Lourdes, (Translated from the French by Edward Fitzgerald) Farrar, Straus and Young, 1954. Page 46.

[105] Laurentin, Rene', Bernadette: Bernadette Speaks: A Life of Saint Bernadette Soubirous in Her Own Words, English Edition Copyright, 2000, Daughters of St. Paul. Page 37.

[106] Ibid. Page 37.

[107] De Saint-Pierre, Michael, Bernadette and Lourdes, (Translated from the French by Edward Fitzgerald) Farrar, Straus and Young, 1954. Page 47

[108] Laurentin, Rene', Bernadette: Bernadette Speaks: A Life of Saint Bernadette Soubirous in Her Own Words, English Edition Copyright, 2000, Daughters of St. Paul. Page 47.

[109] Husenbeth, F. C., Our Blessed Lady of Lourdes: A Faithful Narrative of the Apparitions of the Blessed Virgin Mary at the Rocks of Massabielle, Near Lourdes, in the Year 1858., Robert Washbourne, London, 1870. Page 25.

[110] De Saint-Pierre, Michael, Bernadette and Lourdes, (Translated from the French by Edward Fitzgerald) Farrar, Straus and Young, 1954. Pages 48-49.

[111] Ibid. Page 49.

[112] Ibid.

[113] Ibid.

[114] Ibid.

[115] Ibid.

[116] Laurentin, Rene', Bernadette: Bernadette Speaks: A Life of Saint Bernadette Soubirous in Her Own Words, English Edition Copyright, 2000, Daughters of St. Paul. Page 48.

[117] The evidence of Jean-Baptiste Estrade.

[118] Husenbeth, F. C., Our Blessed Lady of Lourdes: A Faithful Narrative of the Apparitions of the Blessed Virgin Mary at the Rocks of Massabielle, Near Lourdes, in the Year 1858., Robert Washbourne, London, 1870. Page 27.

[119] De Saint-Pierre, Michael, Bernadette and Lourdes, (Translated from the French by Edward Fitzgerald) Farrar, Straus and Young, 1954. Page 51.

[120] Ibid.

[121] Husenbeth, F. C., Our Blessed Lady of Lourdes: A Faithful Narrative of the Apparitions of the Blessed Virgin Mary at the Rocks of Massabielle, Near Lourdes, in the Year 1858., Robert Washbourne, London, 1870. Page 28.

[122] De Saint-Pierre, Michael, Bernadette and Lourdes, (Translated from the French by Edward Fitzgerald) Farrar, Straus and Young, 1954. Page 52.

[123] Ibid. Page 53.

[124] Laurentin, Rene', Bernadette: Bernadette Speaks: A Life of Saint Bernadette Soubirous in Her Own Words, English Edition Copyright, 2000, Daughters of St. Paul. Page 50.

[125] Husenbeth, F. C., Our Blessed Lady of Lourdes: A Faithful Narrative of the Apparitions of the Blessed Virgin Mary at the Rocks of Massabielle, Near Lourdes, in the Year 1858., Robert Washbourne, London, 1870. Pages 29 & 30.

[126] Ibid. Page 30.

[127] Laurentin, Rene', Bernadette: Bernadette Speaks: A Life of Saint Bernadette Soubirous in Her Own Words, English Edition Copyright, 2000, Daughters of St. Paul. Page 50.

[128] Ibid. Page 58.

[129] Ibid. Page 59.

[130] Ibid. Page 53-54.

[131] Ibid. Page 60.

[132] Ibid. Page 63.

[133] Ibid.

[134] Ibid. Page 64.

[135] Ibid. Page 57.

[136] Husenbeth, F. C., Our Blessed Lady of Lourdes: A Faithful Narrative of the Apparitions of the Blessed Virgin Mary at the Rocks of Massabielle, Near Lourdes, in the Year 1858., Robert Washbourne, London, 1870. Page 31.

[137] Ibid. Page 32.

[138] Ibid.

[139] Ibid. Page 31.

[140] Ibid. Page 33.

[141] Ibid. Page 34

[142] Ibid. Pages 34-35.

[143] Husenbeth, F. C., Our Blessed Lady of Lourdes: A Faithful Narrative of the Apparitions of the Blessed Virgin Mary at the Rocks of Massabielle, Near Lourdes, in the Year 1858., Robert Washbourne, London, 1870. Page 37-38.

[144] Ibid. Page 38.

[145] Ibid.

[146] Ibid.

[147] Ibid.

[148] Ibid. Page 39.

[149] Laurentin, Rene', Bernadette: Bernadette Speaks: A Life of Saint Bernadette Soubirous in Her Own Words, English Edition Copyright, 2000, Daughters of St. Paul. Page 54.

[150] Ibid. Page 53.

[151] Ibid.

[152] De Saint-Pierre, Michael, Bernadette and Lourdes, (Translated from the French by Edward Fitzgerald) Farrar, Straus and Young, 1954. Page 58

[153] Ibid. Page 59

[154] Husenbeth, F. C., Our Blessed Lady of Lourdes: A Faithful Narrative of the Apparitions of the Blessed Virgin Mary at the Rocks of Massabielle, Near Lourdes, in the Year 1858., Robert Washbourne, London, 1870. Page 41.

[155] Ibid.

[156] Ibid.

[157] Husenbeth, F. C., Our Blessed Lady of Lourdes: A Faithful Narrative of the Apparitions of the Blessed Virgin Mary at the Rocks of Massabielle, Near Lourdes, in the Year 1858., Robert Washbourne, London, 1870. Page 41-42. Psalm lxxxvi. 15-17

[158] Ibid. Page 42.

[159] De Saint-Pierre, Michael, Bernadette and Lourdes, (Translated from the French by Edward Fitzgerald) Farrar, Straus and Young, 1954. Page 60.

[160] Husenbeth, F. C., Our Blessed Lady of Lourdes: A Faithful Narrative of the Apparitions of the Blessed Virgin Mary at the Rocks of Massabielle, Near Lourdes, in the Year 1858., Robert Washbourne, London, 1870. Page 43.

[161] De Saint-Pierre, Michael, Bernadette and Lourdes, (Translated from the French by Edward Fitzgerald) Farrar, Straus and Young, 1954. Page 60.

[162] Laurentin, Rene', Bernadette: Bernadette Speaks: A Life of Saint Bernadette Soubirous in Her Own Words, English Edition Copyright, 2000, Daughters of St. Paul. Page 57.

[163] The New American Bible, Zechariah Chapter 13:1. Oracles Concerning the End of False Prophesy. Oxford University Press, Oxford, NY. Page 1575.

[164] Husenbeth, F. C., Our Blessed Lady of Lourdes: A Faithful Narrative of the Apparitions of the Blessed Virgin Mary at the Rocks of Massabielle, Near Lourdes, in the Year 1858., Robert Washbourne, London, 1870. Page 45.

[165] Laurentin, Rene', Bernadette: Bernadette Speaks: A Life of Saint Bernadette Soubirous in Her Own Words, English Edition Copyright, 2000, Daughters of St. Paul. Page 64.

[166] Husenbeth, F. C., Our Blessed Lady of Lourdes: A Faithful Narrative of the Apparitions of the Blessed Virgin Mary at the Rocks of Massabielle, Near Lourdes, in the Year 1858., Robert Washbourne, London, 1870. Page 45.

[167] De Saint-Pierre, Michael, Bernadette and Lourdes, (Translated from the French by Edward Fitzgerald) Farrar, Straus and Young, 1954. Pages 60-61.

[168] Ibid. Page 61.

[169] Ibid. Pages 62-63.

[170] O'Neill, Michael, The Miracle Hunter Website, June, 2018. http://miracle-hunter.com/marian_apparitions/approved_apparitions/lourdes/miracles1.html#bouriette.

171 De Saint-Pierre, Michael, Bernadette and Lourdes, (Translated from the French by Edward Fitzgerald) Farrar, Straus and Young, 1954. Page 63.

172 Ibid.

173 Ibid.

174 Ibid. Page 64.

175 Husenbeth, F. C., Our Blessed Lady of Lourdes: A Faithful Narrative of the Apparitions of the Blessed Virgin Mary at the Rocks of Massabielle, Near Lourdes, in the Year 1858., Robert Washbourne, London, 1870. Page 49.

176 De Saint-Pierre, Michael, Bernadette and Lourdes, (Translated from the French by Edward Fitzgerald) Farrar, Straus and Young, 1954. Page 65. (an eyewitness account of the spectacle.)

177 Laurentin, Rene', Bernadette: Bernadette Speaks: A Life of Saint Bernadette Soubirous in Her Own Words, English Edition Copyright, 2000, Daughters of St. Paul. Page 67.

178 Ibid.

179 Ibid.

180 De Saint-Pierre, Michael, Bernadette and Lourdes, (Translated from the French by Edward Fitzgerald) Farrar, Straus and Young, 1954. Page 69.

181 Laurentin, Rene', Bernadette: Bernadette Speaks: A Life of Saint Bernadette Soubirous in Her Own Words, English Edition Copyright, 2000, Daughters of St. Paul. Page 69.

182 Lasserre, Henri, Our Lady of Lourdes, (Translated from the French) D. & J. Sadler, 1870. Page 180.

183 Laurentin, Rene', Bernadette: Bernadette Speaks: A Life of Saint Bernadette Soubirous in Her Own Words, English Edition Copyright, 2000, Daughters of St. Paul. Page 80.

184 Ibid. Page 79.

185 De Saint-Pierre, Michael, Bernadette and Lourdes, (Translated from the French by Edward Fitzgerald) Farrar, Straus and Young, 1954. Page 68.

186 Ibid.

187 Ibid. Page 69.

188 Lasserre, Henri, Our Lady of Lourdes, (Translated from the French) D. & J. Sadler, 1870. Page 181.

189 De Saint-Pierre, Michael, Bernadette and Lourdes, (Translated from the French by Edward Fitzgerald) Farrar, Straus and Young, 1954. Page 72.

190 Laurentin, Rene', Bernadette: Bernadette Speaks: A Life of Saint Bernadette Soubirous in Her Own Words, English Edition Copyright, 2000, Daughters of St. Paul. Page 79.

191 Ibid.

192 Lasserre, Henri, Our Lady of Lourdes, (Translated from the French) D. & J. Sadler, 1870. Page 186.

[193] Laurentin, Rene', Bernadette: Bernadette Speaks: A Life of Saint Bernadette Soubirous in Her Own Words, English Edition Copyright, 2000, Daughters of St. Paul. Page 81.

[194] Ibid. Page 82.

[195] Ibid. Page 83 & 84.

[196] Ibid. Page 84

[197] Ibid.

[198] Ibid. Pages 84 & 85.

[199] De Saint-Pierre, Michael, Bernadette and Lourdes, (Translated from the French by Edward Fitzgerald) Farrar, Straus and Young, 1954. Page 68.

[200] Laurentin, Rene', Bernadette: Bernadette Speaks: A Life of Saint Bernadette Soubirous in Her Own Words, English Edition Copyright, 2000, Daughters of St. Paul. Page 88.

[201] Ibid.

[202] Ibid.

[203] Ibid. Page 90

[204] Ibid. [From the journal of Jean-Marie Doucet.]

[205] Ibid. Page 92

[206] Ibid. Page 93.

[207] Ibid. Page 94.

[208] Ibid.

[209] Ibid. Page 95

[210] Ibid.

[211] Ibid.

[212] Ibid.

[213] Ibid. Page 96.

[214] Ibid.

[215] Ibid. Page 97.

[216] Ibid. Page 98.

[217] Ibid.

[218] Ibid. Page 99.

[219] Ibid. Page 100.

[220] Ibid.

[221] De Saint-Pierre, Michael, Bernadette and Lourdes, (Translated from the French by Edward Fitzgerald) Farrar, Straus and Young, 1954. Page 79.

[222] Laurentin, Rene', Bernadette: Bernadette Speaks: A Life of Saint Bernadette Soubirous in Her Own Words, English Edition Copyright, 2000, Daughters of St. Paul. Page 101.

[223] Ibid. Page 103

[224] Ibid. Page 102 and 103.

[225] Ibid.

[226] Ibid.

[227] Ibid. Pages 102 – 103.

[228] Several years later, when Doctor Balencie was no longer under the thumb of Prefect Massy, he repudiated the report of 1858.

[229] Ibid. Page 105

[230] Page De Saint-Pierre, Michael, Bernadette and Lourdes, (Translated from the French by Edward Fitzgerald) Farrar, Straus and Young, 1954. Page 80.

[231] Ibid. Page 106.

[232] Ibid.

[233] De Saint-Pierre, Michael, Bernadette and Lourdes, (Translated from the French by Edward Fitzgerald) Farrar, Straus and Young, 1954. Page 81.

[234] Laurentin, Rene', Bernadette: Bernadette Speaks: A Life of Saint Bernadette Soubirous in Her Own Words, English Edition Copyright, 2000, Daughters of St. Paul. Page 101.

[235] De Saint-Pierre, Michael, Bernadette and Lourdes, (Translated from the French by Edward Fitzgerald) Farrar, Straus and Young, 1954. Page 81.

[236] Ibid. Page 82.

[237] Ibid.

[238] Laurentin, Rene', Bernadette: Bernadette Speaks: A Life of Saint Bernadette Soubirous in Her Own Words, English Edition Copyright, 2000, Daughters of St. Paul. Page 109.

[239] De Saint-Pierre, Michael, Bernadette and Lourdes, (Translated from the French by Edward Fitzgerald) Farrar, Straus and Young, 1954. Page 87.

[240] Ibid. Page 85.

[241] Ibid. Page 86

[242] Ibid.

[243] Ibid.

[244] Ibid.

[245] Ibid.

[246] Ibid.

[247] Laurentin, Rene', Bernadette: Bernadette Speaks: A Life of Saint Bernadette Soubirous in Her Own Words, English Edition Copyright, 2000, Daughters of St. Paul. Page 110.

[248] Ibid.

[249] Lasserre, Henri, Our Lady of Lourdes, (Translated from the French) D. & J. Sadler, 1870. Page 240.

[250] Ibid. Page 242.

[251] Laurentin, Rene', Bernadette: Bernadette Speaks: A Life of Saint Bernadette Soubirous in Her Own Words, English Edition Copyright, 2000, Daughters of St. Paul. Page 91 (as reported in the *Ere Imperiale* on May 8, 1858.)

[252] Ibid. Page 92.

[253] Laurentin, Rene', Bernadette: Bernadette Speaks: A Life of Saint Bernadette Soubirous in Her Own Words, English Edition Copyright, 2000, Daughters of St. Paul. Page 113

[254] Ibid. Page 114.

[255] De Saint-Pierre, Michael, Bernadette and Lourdes, (Translated from the French by Edward Fitzgerald) Farrar, Straus and Young, 1954. Page 94

[256] The Miracle Hunter – List of Approved Miracles. http://miracle-hunter.com/marian_apparitions/approved_apparitions/lourdes/miracles1.html1

[257] Ibid.

[258] It is the birth of that child, who was ordained a priest in 1882, that so precisely dates the miracle.

[259] Ibid.

[260] De Saint-Pierre, Michael, Bernadette and Lourdes, (Translated from the French by Edward Fitzgerald) Farrar, Straus and Young, 1954. Page 95.

[261] Ibid.

[262] Ibid. Page 96.

[263] Ibid. Page 97

[264] Laurentin, Rene', Bernadette: Bernadette Speaks: A Life of Saint Bernadette Soubirous in Her Own Words, English Edition Copyright, 2000, Daughters of St. Paul. Page 114.

[265] Ibid.

[266] Ibid. [The language of the report is a bit disjointed which may have reflected the excitement with which the report was written.]

[267] Ibid. Page 115.

[268] Ibid. Page 116.

[269] Letter written by Abbé Peyramale to Monseigneur Laurence, Bishop of Tarbes, June 4, 1858. De Saint-Pierre, Michael, Bernadette and Lourdes, (Translated from the French by Edward Fitzgerald) Farrar, Straus and Young, 1954. Page 101

[270] De Saint-Pierre, Michael, Bernadette and Lourdes, (Translated from the French by Edward Fitzgerald) Farrar, Straus and Young, 1954. Page 101.

[271] Ibid. Page 103.

[272] Ibid. Page 107.

[273] Ibid. Page 107-108.

[274] Ibid. Page 108.

[275] Ibid. Page 110.

[276] Ibid. Page 123.

[277] Ibid. Page 124.

[278] NOTE: Wikipedia notes that in colloquial usage of the term, especially in France, class distinctions are implied by the very meaning of the term Patois, since in French, *patois* refers to any sociolect associated with uneducated

rural classes, in contrast with the dominant prestige language (Standard French)) spoken by the middle and high classes of cities, or as used in literature and formal settings. Bernadette had little understanding of the French language and generally spoke Patois.

[279] Ibid. Page 126.

[280] Ibid.

[281] Ibid. Page 127.

[282] Ibid. Page 128.

[283] Lasserre, Henri, Our Lady of Lourdes, (Translated from the French) D. & J. Sadler, 1870. Page 339

[284] Ibid.

[285] De Saint-Pierre, Michael, Bernadette and Lourdes, (Translated from the French by Edward Fitzgerald) Farrar, Straus and Young, 1954. Pages 111-112.

[286] Ibid. Pages 112-113.

[287] Ibid. Page 113.

[288] Laurentin, Rene', Bernadette: Bernadette Speaks: A Life of Saint Bernadette Soubirous in Her Own Words, English Edition Copyright, 2000, Daughters of St. Paul. Page 129.

[289] Ibid.

[290] Ibid. Page 114. (From the Minutes of the Meeting of the Municipal Council of Lourdes.)

[291] Ibid.

[292] Ibid.

[293] Ibid. Page 116.

[294] Ibid.

[295] Ibid.

[296] Ibid.

[297] Ibid. Page 117.

[298] Ibid. Page 127.

[299] Ibid. Page 133.

[300] Ibid. Page 130.

[301] Ibid.

[302] NOTE: Père Negré viewed the spring at the Grotto following the destruction of the pipe that collected the water and the Casterot's basin by the police.

[303] Ibid. Page 130.

[304] Ibid. Page 132.

[305] Ibid.

[306] Ibid. Page 131.

[307] Ibid. Page 132-133.

[308] Ibid. Page 133.

[309] Ibid. Page 139.

[310] Laurentin, Rene', Bernadette: Bernadette Speaks: A Life of Saint Bernadette Soubirous in Her Own Words, English Edition Copyright, 2000, Daughters of St. Paul. Page 120.

[311] Lasserre, Henri, Our Lady of Lourdes, (Translated from the French) D. & J. Sadler, 1870. Page 379.

[312] Ibid. Page 379-380.

[313] Ibid. Page 382-383.

[314] Ibid. Page 140.

[315] Ibid.

[316] Ibid. Page 390-391.

[317] Ibid. Page 141.

[318] Ibid.

[319] Ibid.

[320] Laurentin, Rene', Bernadette: Bernadette Speaks: A Life of Saint Bernadette Soubirous in Her Own Words, English Edition Copyright, 2000, Daughters of St. Paul. Pages 142-143.

[321] Ibid. Page 392.

[322] Ibid. Page 393.

[323] Ibid.

[324] Ibid.

[325] Ibid. Page 396.

[326] Ibid. Page 398.

[327] Ibid.

[328] Ibid. Page 400.

[329] Ibid.

[330] Ibid. Page 403.

[331] Ibid.

[332] Ibid.

[333] Ibid. Page 413.

[334] Ibid.

[335] Ibid. Page 414.

[336] Ibid. Page 417.

[337] Ibid. Page 418.

[338] Ibid. Page 420.

[339] Ibid. Page 423 & 424.

[340] Ibid. Pages 424-426.

[341] Ibid. Page 438-439.

[342] Ibid. Page 440.

[343] Laurentin, Rene', Bernadette: Bernadette Speaks: A Life of Saint Bernadette Soubirous in Her Own Words, English Edition Copyright, 2000, Daughters of St. Paul. Page 167.

[344] Ibid. Page 173.

[345] Ibid.
[346] Ibid. Pages 173-174.
[347] Ibid. Page 175.
[348] Ibid. Page 176.
[349] Ibid.
[350] Ibid. Page 181.
[351] Ibid.
[352] Ibid.
[353] Ibid. Page 183.
[354] Ibid.
[355] Ibid. Pages 183-184.
[356] Ibid.
[357] Ibid. Page 195.
[358] Ibid. Page 202.
[359] Ibid.
[360] Ibid. Page 216.
[361] Ibid. Page 228.
[362] Ibid.
[363] Ibid. Page 230.
[364] Ibid. Page 337.
[365] Ibid. Page 341.
[366] Ibid.
[367] Ibid. Page 345.
[368] Ibid. Page 369.
[369] Ibid.
[370] Ibid. Page 370.
[371] Ibid. Page 400.
[372] Ibid. Page 405.
[373] Ibid. Page 415.
[374] Ibid.
[375] Ibid. Page 416.
[376] Ibid.
[377] Ibid. Page 462.
[378] Ibid. Page 518.
[379] Ibid. Page 523.
[380] Ibid. Page 529.
[381] Ibid.
[382] Ibid.
[383] Ibid.
[384] Ibid. Page 530.
[385] Ibid. Page 531.
[386] Ibid.

387 Ibid.

388 Ibid. Page 617

389 www.olrl.org/stories/, Miracles of Lourdes, Our Lady of the Rosary Library, Prospect, KY

390 Ibid.

391 Ibid.

392 Ibid.

393 https://www.timesofmalta.com/articles/view/20111110/life-features/The-miracle-of-WWI.393186, Mizzi, John A. The Miracle of WWI, November 10, 2011 and www.olrl.org/stories/, Miracles of Lourdes, Our Lady of the Rosary Library, Prospect, KY.

394 https://www.timesofmalta.com/articles/view/20111110/life-features/The-miracle-of-WWI.393186, Mizzi, John A. The Miracle of WWI, November 10, 2011.

395 Ibid.

396 Ibid.

397 Ibid.

398 Ibid.

399 Ibid.

400 Ibid.

401 Gabiafterhours, YouTube Channel. Lessons from Lourdes: Our Lady of Lourdes and St. Bernadette. February 10, 2017.

402 Ibid.

403 Ibid.

404 Ibid.

405 Ibid.

406 Ibid.

407 Ibid.

Bibliography

Books

Bible, The New American, Oxford University Press

Clarke, Richard F. S.J., Lourdes: Its Inhabitants, Its Pilgrims, and Its Miracles. Benzinger Brothers, 1888.

Deery, Joseph Monsignor, Our Lady of Lourdes, The Newman Press, 1958.

De Saint-Pierre, Michel, Bernadette and Lourdes. Farrar, Straus and Young, 1954.

Harris, Ruth, Lourdes: Body and Spirit in the Secular Age. Viking, 1999.

Hussenbeth, F. C., D.D., V.G., Our Blessed Lady of Lourdes: A Faithful Narrative of the Apparitions of the Blessed Virgin Mary at the Rocks of Massabielle, Near Lourdes, in the Year 1858. Robert Washburn, 1870.

Lasserre, Henri, Our Lady of Lourdes. D. & J. Sadlier, Translated from French, 1870.

Laurentin, Rene', Bernadette: A Life of Saint Bernadette Soubirous in Her Own Words. English Edition, Daughters of St. Paul, 2000.

Marnham, Patrick, Lourdes: A Modern Pilgrimage. Coward, McCann & Geoghegan, Inc., First American Edition, 1981.

Sandhurst, B.G., We Saw Her. Longman's Green and Co.1953.

Internet Sources

Biography Online, "Biography of Bernadette Soubirous." https://www.biographyonline.net/spiritual/bernadette-soubirious.html.

Britannica Encyclopedia, "Second Empire: French History." https://www.britannica.com/topic/Second-Empire.

Catholic Gentleman, The, "Why the Devil Hates the Blessed Virgin So Much (And Why You Should Love Her). https://www.catholicgentleman.net/2015/01/devil-hates-blessed-virgin-much-love/.

Catholic News Agency, "Our Lady of Lourdes." https://www.catholicnewsagency.com/resources/mary/popular-marian-devotions/our-lady-of-lourdes.

Center for Disease Control and Prevention, "Cholera – Vibrio Cholerae Infection." https://www.cdc.gov/cholera/general/index.html

Cor Jesu Sacratissimum, "The Story of St. Bernadette and Lourdes, Parts I – X, by Bernard St. John." https://www.google.com/search?ei=LLLYW6CONsnj_Aa4o4WgBA&q=cor+

jesu+sacratissimum%2C+the+story+of+st.+berna-
dette+and+lourdes%2C+by+bernard+st.+john&oq=cor+jesu+sacratissi-
mum%2C+the+story+of+st.+bernadette+and+lourdes%2C+by+ber-
nard+st.+john&gs_l=psy-
ab.12...6651.27195..29021...3.0..0.199.5524.57j8......0....1..gws-
wiz.......0j0i71j0i20i263j0i22i30j33i299j33i160j33i22i29i30.QVcs1-5tW5U.

Encyclopedia.com, "1850-1877: World Events: Selected Occurrences Outside
the United States." https://www.encyclopedia.com/history/news-wires-white-
papers-and-books/1850-1877-world-events-selected-occurrences-outside-
united-states.

French Economic Situation, "French Economic Situation 1847 – 1852."
https://www.ohio.edu/chastain/dh/feco.htm.

Lourdes Sanctuaire, "The Message." https://www.lourdes-france.org/en/.

Macrohistory and World Timeline, "Timeline: 1841 to 1850."
http://www.fsmitha.com/time/ce19-5.htm.

MedjugorjeUSA, "The Apparitions of Our Lady of Lourdes, France."
http://www.medjugorjeusa.org/lourdes.htm.

Miracle Hunter, The, "List of Approved Lourdes Miracles." http://www.mira-
clehunter.com/marian_apparitions/approved_apparitions/lourdes/mira-
cles1.html.

Miracle Hunter, The, "Lourdes, France." http://www.miraclehunter.com/mar-
ian_apparitions/approved_apparitions/lourdes/index.html.

Miracle Hunter, The "The Messages." http://www.miraclehunter.com/mar-
ian_apparitions/messages/lourdes_messages.html.

Miracle Hunter, The, "Official Church Statements." http://www.miracle-
hunter.com/marian_apparitions/statements/index.html#lourdes%5C.

Miracle Hunter, The, "Report of the Episcopal Commission." http://www.mira-
clehunter.com/marian_apparitions/statements/lourdes_comm_report.html.

Miracles of Lourdes, "Introduction to Lourdes, The Story of Gabriel Gargam
and the Story of John Traynor." https://olrl.org/stories/lourdes.shtml.

National Catholic Register, "Is This Marian Apparition a Bridge Between
Lourdes and Fatima?" http://www.ncregister.com/blog/joseph-pronechen/is-
this-approved-marian-apparition-a-bridge-between-lourdes-and-fatima.

Spirit of Notre Dame, The, by Dorothy V. Corson, "A Cave of Candles: The
Story Behind the Notre Dame Grotto." https://www3.nd.edu/~wcaw-
ley/corson/corson1.htm.

ThoughtCo, "The Rulers of France: From 840 Until 2017."
https://www.thoughtco.com/rulers-of-france-840-until-2015-3861418.

Times Malta, "The Miracle of WWI. By John Mizzi, November 10, 2011" https://www.timesofmalta.com/articles/view/20111110/life-features/The-miracle-of-WWI.393186.

Tradition in Action, Inc. "The Lourdes' Miracle of Gabriel Gargam." https://www.traditioninaction.org/religious/h106_Lourdes.htm.

Wikipedia, "Second French Empire." https://en.wikipedia.org/wiki/Second_French_Empire.

Wikipedia, "List of French Monarchs." https://en.wikipedia.org/wiki/List_of_French_monarchs.

World Health Organization, "Cholera Fact Sheets." http://www.who.int/newsroom/fact-sheets/detail/cholera.

Periodicals

National Geographic Magazine, The Story of Mary: From Biblical World to Today. May 2018.

About the Author

Historian Paul F. Caranci is Rhode Island's former Deputy Secretary of State. He dedicated his life to public service, history and writing. The author of seven published books, Caranci's articles have appeared in a plethora of magazines and online news services. He has written two award-winning books; Scoundrels: Defining Corruption Through Tales of Political Intrigue in Rhode Island (Dorry Award for Non-Fiction Book of the Year, 2016), and The Hanging and Redemption of John Gordon: The True Story of Rhode Island's Last Execution (Selected by the Providence Journal as one of the top five non-fiction books of the 2013). His most recent book, The Promise of Fatima: One Hundred Years of History, Mystery, and Faith was named a finalist in the International Book Awards.

Paul serves on the Board of Directors of the Association of Rhode Island Authors (ARIA) and the Rhode Island Publications Society. He is a co-founder of The Municipal Heritage Group. He is also a former member of the Heritage Harbor Museum Board of Directors, the RI Heritage Hall of Fame Board of Directors, and the Board of Directors of the American Diabetes Association – Rhode Island Affiliate. He served on the Board of Directors of the Diabetes Foundation of Rhode Island for sixteen years serving as its Chairman for two of those years.

Paul is married to his childhood sweetheart, Margie. The couple has two adult children, Heather and Matthew, and four grandsons, Matthew Jr., Jacob, Vincent and Casey. They reside in Rhode Island.

This is his ninth book.

Also by the Author...

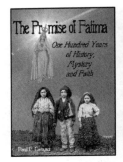 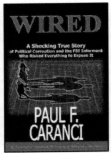 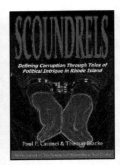 

  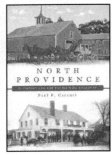

*Available at online retailers, bookstores
and www.StillwaterPress.com*

*Paul Caranci is available to speak at your conference or function,
or to your civic, church, political, or ethnic group or club.
You may contact him at*

municipalheritage@gmail.com

www.PaulCaranci.com

ORDER FORM

Please use the following to order additional copies of:

1. I Am the Immaculate Conception: The Story of St. Bernadette and Her Apparitions at Lourdes ($20.00)
2. The Promise of Fatima: One Hundred Years of History, Mystery & Faith ($20.00)
3. Wired: A Shocking True Story of Political Corruption and the FBI Informant Who Risked Everything to Expose It ($23.00)
4. Scoundrels: Defining Political Corruption Through Tales of Political Intrigue in Rhode Island ($20.00)
5. Monumental Providence: Legends of History in Sculpture, Statuary, Monuments and Memorials ($20.00)
6. The Essential Guide to Running for Local Office ($15.00)
7. The Hanging & Redemption of John Gordon: The True Story of Rhode Island's Last Execution ($20.00)
8. North Providence: A History & The People Who Shaped It ($20.00)
9. Award Winning Real Estate in a Depressed or Declining Market ($10.00)

_____ (QTY) _____(Title) X _____ (Price) = $ _____

_____ (QTY) _____(Title) X _____ (Price) = $ _____

_____ (QTY) _____(Title) X _____ (Price) = $ _____

_____ (QTY) _____(Title) X _____ (Price) = $ _____

_____ (QTY) _____(Title) X _____ (Price) = $ _____

Total for books $_____ + Postage** $_____ = TOTAL COST $_____

**Postage: Please add $3.00 for the first book and $1.50 for each additional book ordered.

Payment Method:

____ Personal Check Enclosed (Payable to **M. Caranci Books**)

____ Charge my Credit Card

    Name:_____ BILLING ZIP CODE:_____

    Visa_____ Master Card_____

    Card Number:_____ EXP:_____/_____CSC (3 digit code) _____

    Signature:_____

Ship My Book To:

Name _____

Street _____

City _____State:_____Zip:_____

Phone _____Email:_____

MAIL YOUR COMPLETED FORM TO:
Paul F. Caranci
26 East Avenue
North Providence, RI 02911
You may also order using my Email address at municipalheritage@gmail.com or by calling me at 401-639-4502
Please visit my Website at www.paulcaranci.com

243

39907669R00146

Made in the USA
Middletown, DE
22 March 2019